ISBN 978-0-364-59860-3
PIBN 11041057

This book is a reproduction of an important historical work. Forgotten Books uses state-of-the-art technology to digitally reconstruct the work, preserving the original format whilst repairing imperfections present in the aged copy. In rare cases, an imperfection in the original, such as a blemish or missing page, may be replicated in our edition. We do, however, repair the vast majority of imperfections successfully; any imperfections that remain are intentionally left to preserve the state of such historical works.

... 30

... 30

... 16 ...?
... Parallelen mit Theil .. (..30.) 36/37

C. v. Orelli (Realenzyklop. f. protestant.
Theologie 3 Bd. 23 S. 653 ... über Jacobi
Arbeit ... ; ... die ...
Deutung, die das Lied ... ."
Vgl. auch Theolog. Literaturzeitung 1963 Nr. 4
... Freiburg 1917

Das Hohelied,

auf Grund arabischer und anderer Parallelen

von neuem untersucht

von

Dr. Georg Jacob, ✗

ao. Professor an der Universität Erlangen.

Berlin,

Mayer & Müller.

1902.

Dem Andenken seines hochverehrten Lehrers

Eduard Reuß,

weiland Professor der Theologie an der Kaiser-Wilhelms-Universität

zu Straßburg,

widmet diese Studie

der Verfasser.

I.

Die kritische Theologie gehört zu unsern jüngsten Wissen=
schaften; für das Alte Testament beginnt sie eigentlich erst
mit Reuß und Wellhausen [1]). Wir dürfen uns daher nicht
verhehlen, daß wir noch bei den ersten Anfängen stehn. Das
gilt namentlich auch vom Hohen Liede; hat doch gerade die=
ses bis in die jüngste Zeit hinein vielleicht von allen Erzeug=
nissen der Weltlitteratur am schwersten unter exegetischer
Mishandlung zu leiden gehabt.

Die allegorische Deutung

lag ja dem mittelalterlichen Orient nahe, dessen Mystik reli=
giöse Probleme in erotischen Bildern zu behandeln liebt, und
Budde hätte bei genauerer Kenntnis dieser Litteratur die Be=
hauptung schwerlich gewagt, daß diese Erklärungsweise nur
bei dem Hereinbrechen „halber Barbarei" wieder auf den Schau=
platz treten könnte [2]). Im Gegenteil ist es bedauerlich, daß

---

1) Eduard Reuß zeichnete ein unter den Theologen seltenes Fein=
gefühl für das Natürliche, Ungezwungene, Poetische aus; Wellhausen
hat die philologische (Lachmann'sche) Methode eigentlich zum ersten
Mal auf den alttestamentlichen Kanon angewendet. Während er
durch kritische Quellenscheidung einen historischen Rahmen zu gewin=
nen suchte, beginnt ein Eindringen in das Verständnis des wirklichen
Textinhalts erst mit Gunkel's Genesis; vorher war man über Aus=
legungen nach verschiedenen Tendenzen, zu denen auch die Entwicke=
lungstheorie gerechnet werden muß, niemals weit hinausgekommen.

2) Preußische Jahrbücher 78. Band 1894 S. 92.

ihre wissenschaftliche Durchführung, welche natürlich von einem eingehenden Studium der Parallelen ausgehen müßte, in den von Rosenmüller angebahnten Anfängen stecken blieb [1]).

Der Sprache der Propheten ist die Auffassung des Verhältnisses Jahve's zu seinem Volk unter dem Bild der Ehe geläufig [2]). Naturgemäß suchten die alten jüdischen Allegoristen diesen Vorwurf im Hohen Liede. Für die Christen wandelte sich das auserwählte Volk in die Kirche, der göttliche Bräutigam in Christus. Die Durchführung dieser und mobifizirter heilsgeschichtlicher Allegorien zwang zu den unnatürlichsten Geschmacklosigkeiten [3]). Dennoch war damit noch nicht die Allegorie überhaupt abgethan.

Den richtigen Weg würden leicht Analogien aus der islâmischen Litteratur gewiesen haben. So schildert Imruulqais in seiner Muʻallaqa, wie er sich in ʻOnaiza's Sänfte drängt und zu ihr spricht (ed. Lyall Vers 15[b]):

„wa-lâ tubʻidînî min ganâki ʼl-muʻallili“
(entferne mich nicht von deiner durststillenden frischgepflückten Frucht.)

„Ihre frischgepflückte Frucht“, so erklärt Tebrîzî's Kommentar, „ist das, was er sich von ihr an Küssen pflückt.“ Auch das Verbalsubstantiv der 5ten Form desselben Stamms, at-taġannî (das Fruchtpflücken) steht in der erotischen Poesie häufig für

---

1) Das alte und neue Morgenland, 4. Band, Leipzig 1819 S. 179 ff.

2) Vrgl. z. B. Jesaia 62, 4, 5, Ezechiel 16.

3) Vrgl. Ed. Cunitz, Histoire critique de l'interprétation du cantique des cantiques: Thèse présentée à la faculté de théologie de Strasbourg ... pour obtenir le grade de bachelier en théologie, Strasbourg 1834; S. Salfeld, Das Hohelied bei den jüdischen Erklärern des Mittelalters: Magazin für die Wissenschaft des Judentums, 5. Jahrg. 1878; Wilhelm Riedel, Die Auslegung des Hohenliedes in der jüdischen Gemeinde und der griechischen Kirche, Leipzig 1898; Sebastian Euringer, Die Auffassung des Hohenliedes bei den Abessiniern, Leipzig 1900.

ben Liebesgenuß, vrgl. z. B. 1001 Nacht ed. Habicht III S. 188 Z. 8, S. 190 Z. 3 und die Erzählung von Mesrûr (1001 Nacht ed. 1311 h IV S. 70) enthält den Vers:

„wa-kul min thimâri 'l-wasli fî γaibati 'l-ba'li.“
(und iß von den Früchten der Liebesvereinigung in Ab=
wesenheit des Gatten.)

Türkisch scheftali bedeutet sogar in Prosa: Pfirsich, Kuß, Umarmung, vrgl. z. B. Kúnos, Oszmán=török népköltési gyüjteményi I S. 144 [1]), und der Perser sagt bûse tschîden Kuß pflücken: Hâfiz ed. Brockhaus Nr. 295, 2. Sa'dî läßt in seinem Bustân (ed. Graf S. 354) einen Greis einem jun= gen Manne, der über die Bösartigkeit seiner Gattin klagt, erwidern:

Tschu ez gulbunî dîde bâschî γweschî [2])
Rewâ bâsched, er bâri γâresch keschî;
Diraγtî ke pêweste bâresch γwerî,
Teḥammul kun ângah ke γâresch γwerî
(Wenn du vom Rosenstrauch Freude erfahren,
Magst du auch die Last seines Dorns tragen;
Ein Baum, dessen Frucht du immer issest,
Ertrage, wenn du auch seinen Dorn issest.)

Ich könnte die Belege natürlich noch reichlich mehren. Man vergleiche mit ihnen Stellen des Hohen Liedes wie 2, 3: „Wie ein Apfelbaum unter den fruchtlosen [3]) Bäumen,

---

1) Natürlich gehört in diesen Zusammenhang die verbotene Frucht Genesis 3 und der Apfel, mit welchem im Eingange so vieler türkischer Märchen z. B. des Billur köschk der Derwisch dem un= fruchtbaren König zu Nachkommenschaft verhilft, indem er eine Hälfte von ihm, die andere von der Königin essen läßt, ferner der Apfel der Venus und Anderes, wenn auch der ursprüngliche Sinn in diesen Fällen verdunkelt ist.

2) In Poesie schreibe ich so für γôschî des folgenden Reims wegen.

5) Das Targûm giebt 'ês hai-ja'ar dem Sinne nach gewiß rich=

so ist mein Geliebter unter den Jünglingen; in seinem Schatten weil' ich gerne, während seine Frucht meinem Gaumen mundet."

oder den Schluß des 4. und Anfang des 5. Kapitels, welche die Geliebte einem Düfte ausströmenden Garten vergleichen, dessen köstliche Frucht der Geliebte kostet, ferner 7, 14, wo das Bild besonders kraß durchgeführt wird. Das Einathmen der Düfte, das Pflücken der Blumen, das Essen der Früchte, das Trinken des Weins müssen nach orientalischen Analogien Tropen für den Liebesgenuß sein. In der That sind neuere Ausleger auch ohne Kenntnis islâmischer Parallelen zu dieser Auffassung vorgeschritten, im Einzelnen aber kämpft sie noch immer mit Schwierigkeiten.

Durch Verfolgung des eben angedeuteten Gedankengangs ist es erst neuerdings Paul Haupt [1]) gelungen, für eine bisher unklare Stelle die befriedigende Erklärung zu finden; 1, 12 nämlich übersetzte noch Siegfried:

„So lange der König auf seinem Festumzuge (mêsab) war, Gab meine Narde ihren Duft von sich."

Die herrschende Auffassung stellt sich den Bräutigam bei seinem mêsab von der Braut getrennt vor, woraus die Schwierigkeit erwächst, daß man im Nachsatz eher den entgegengesetzten Sinn erwartet, denn die Narde für etwas Übelriechendes zu erklären, ist ein Ausweg, den wir dem Targûm überlassen wollen s. Hagiographa Chaldaice S. 148 oben. Mêsab hat bereits Franz Delitzsch als „Tafelrunde" gedeutet, ohne jedoch den natürlichen Sinn zu verstehn. Erst Haupt erkannte, daß hier „bei seinem Mahl" soviel wie „beim Liebesgenuß" bedeute und glaubte ferner aus mêsab Schmaus für

_____ ____

tig durch îlân serâq wieder s. Hagiographa Chaldaice, Paulus de Lagarde edidit, Leipzig 1873 S. 149 Z. 4.

1) Difficult Passages in the Song of Songs: Sonder=Abzug aus dem Journal of Biblical Literature ohne genauere Angabe des Bandes, Ortes und Jahres.

sôb **2**, 17 die entsprechende Bedeutung „schmause, genieße" folgern zu können [1]), wodurch auch dieser Vers einen ansprechenden Sinn erhielte:

„Bis die Morgenluft weht und die Schatten schwinden, genieße und werde doch gleich, mein Geliebter, der Gazelle oder dem Jungen der Mähnenschafe in den Felsklüften."

Für die Übersetzung beter Kluft [2]) spricht bitrôn: II Sam. **2**, 29; aijâl bezeichnet hier wie Hiob **39** Anfang höchstwahrscheinlich das Mähnenschaf Ovis tragelaphus [3]), dessen Jungen gut zu den Gazellen (nicht aber Antilopen) passen [4]). Taleinschnitte bilden nun in der Wüste Rendezvousorte für Liebespärchen vrgl. Imruulqais Muʻallaqa ed. Lyall Vers 29 und Burckhardt's Bemerkungen über die Beduinen und Wahaby, Weimar 1831 S. 67. So soll der Geliebte hier mit der Geliebten im zerklüfteten Gebirge den Blicken entzogen, „würzige Bergkräuter weiden", eine vollständige Parallele zu dem „in Lilien Weiden", s. unten. Auch die altarabische Poesie schildert die Gazelle fast immer weidend, vrgl. z. B. das Nasîb der Muʻallaqa *Tarafa's* [5]), und Psalm **42**, 2 den aijâl, wie er sich nach den Wasserbächen sehnt.

---

1) Für Hifʻil und Puʻal von sâbab giebt Dalman die Bedeutung „zu Tische liegen" an.

2) Haupt's Deutung der hârê beter (a. a. O. S. 69/70) als mons Veneris kann höchstens als Nebenanspielung in Betracht kommen, das Bild der Gazelle aber verlangt zunächst eine andere Ausführung. In der 8, 14 anhangsweise gegebenen Gestalt des Verses würden die Varianten berach und besâmim auf Misverständnis beruhende Verdeutlichungsversuche darstellen.

3) Vrgl. mein Beduinenleben² S. 21.

4) **4**, 5 enthält wol nur einen zufälligen Anklang; die beiden letzten Worte des Verses gehören bereits zum folgenden Einschub, wie der Vergleich der Varianten 4, 5 u. 6 mit 2, 16 u. 17 lehrt.

5) Vrgl. mein Beduinenleben² S. 119.

In ähnlichem Sinne wird „essen" 5, 1 gebraucht:
„Ich komme in meinen Garten, meine Schwester Braut,
ich sammle meine Myrrhe sammt meinem Balsam, ich esse
meine Wabe sammt meinem Honig, ich trinke meinen Wein
sammt meiner Milch. Eßt, Genossen, trinkt und zecht,
Geliebte!"

Der Sinn der Bilder ergiebt sich aus dem Vorangeschick=
ten; persische Dichter gebrauchen den Ersatz des Honigs scheker
(Zucker) für Lippe und Kuß des Geliebten; Schwierigkeiten
bereitet lediglich die Deutung der Schlußaufforderung. Bei
den Arabern gehört die walima (der Hochzeitsschmaus) aller=
dings zu den wichtigsten Hochzeitszeremonien[1]); denkt man
jedoch beim Schluß an diese, so wären die Begriffe „essen"
und „trinken" zuerst bildlich, dann eigentlich zu fassen. Frei=
lich findet sich ein ähnlicher Wechsel bei kerem (Weinberg)
1, 6, aber in wirkungsvoller Steigerung, während 5, 1 ein
unerträgliches Herabsinken zur Prosa vorläge. Wir werden
demnach auch für die Schlußworte an der einmal gegebenen
Allegorie festhalten müssen, sollten aber nicht immer wie Budde
und Siegfried gleich ans „Heiraten"[2]) denken. Der Jüngling,
welcher den ganzen Vers sprechend gedacht ist, fordert seine
Genossen auf das Leben gleichfalls zu genießen und Liebes=
tändelei zu treiben.

Wie wir bereits (bei 2, 17) gesehn haben, modifizirt sich
das Bild des Essens bisweilen in das des Weidens (pasci),
so 6, 2:

„Mein Geliebter ist in seinen Garten hinabgestiegen zu den
Balsambeeten, um in den Gärten zu weiden und Lilien zu
rupfen."

---

1) Ich wähle diesen Ausdruck absichtlich, vrgl. Goldziher, über
Geheimehen bei den Arabern: SA. aus dem 68. Bande des Globus.

2) Über diesen prinzipiellen Fehler der beiden neuesten Kom=
mentare s. unten.

„Lilien rupfen" steht an dieser Stelle, wie Budde treffend bemerkt, nur, weil der Ausdruck „weiden" bereits vergeben ist, sonst heißt die Phrase „in Lilien weiden" (2, 16, 4, 5, 6, 3) und bedeutet nach obigen Parallelen, wie Haupt a. a. O. S. 69 hervorhebt, nichts anders als „ζώνην λύειν". Man dachte bei dem Bilde, da Schwertlilien nur an feuchten Stellen wachsen, wol zunächst an saftige Weide, dann aber auch an die Augenweide, die eine mit Lilien bestandene Wiese in Palästina darbietet, denn „auch Salomo in aller seiner Herrlichkeit war nicht angethan wie eine von ihnen." Ähnlich ist auch 7, 3ᵇ zu fassen. Daß man aus 5, 13 schließen kann, daß unter „Lilien" zunächst die Lippen zu verstehn sind, glaube ich nicht; Lisân al-'Arab sagt unter „sausan", daß es viele Arten gäbe und die weiße die beste sei.

Wie das Essen beziehungsweise Weiden ist auch das Trinken zu deuten; das Bild des Weinbergs mit seinen Früchten vermittelt den Übergang. Gleich im Eingange des Hohen Liedes 1, 2 und 4, ferner 4, 10 werden wir auf die Bedeutung des Weins durch die vergleichende Parallele hingewiesen, in welche er mit den Liebkosungen gestellt wird. Ebenso ist 7, 3ᵃ zu verstehn. Betrachten wir unter diesem Gesichtspunkt, indem wir uns noch den oben übersetzten Vers 5, 1 vergegenwärtigen, 2, 4, 5:

„Er hat mich ins Weinhaus gebracht, und sein Panier über mir war Liebe. Stärkt mich mit Traubenkuchen, erquickt mich mit Äpfeln, denn liebeskrank bin ich."

Über die γâja der Weinschenken, das Abzeichen, daß in ihnen noch Wein zu haben ist, s. meine Studien in arabischen Dichtern; sie wird beispielsweise in der Mu'allaqa des Lebîd und des 'Antara erwähnt und entspricht dem degel. Zum Verständnis des Schlusses verweise ich auf W. Max Müller, Die Liebespoesie der alten Ägypter (Leipzig 1899) Lied 12 Strophe 2, woselbst die von ihrem Geliebten Getrennte klagt, daß ihr Kuchen wie Salz, süßer Most wie Vogelgalle schmecke.

Es scheint also, daß man die Liebeskranke durch Kuchen und Wein zu kuriren suchte; so erklärt sich das kî unseres Textes. Schwer wird allerdings auszumachen sein, ob sich die Liebende nur geistig in ein Weinhaus versetzt träumt oder letzterem nach der Absicht des Dichters Realität zukommen soll; auch die wandernde Weinschenke des alten Arabiens bot Gelegenheit zum Liebesverkehr; vrgl. ferner das altägyptische Lied 5 Vers 6, 7 bei W. Max Müller a. a. O.:

„Gieb mir meine Schwester heute Nacht [in] die Laube. Voll ist sie von (allerlei) Wein.“

Die Allegorie des HL. variirt stets den einen Vorwurf: „Liebesgenuß“. In Übereinstimmung mit dieser Vorstellungsreihe erklärte Eduard Reuß in seinen Vorlesungen die kleinen schu'âlîm (2, 15) weit ansprechender als Budde und Siegfried für Nebenbuhler. Schon wiederholt wurde darauf hingewiesen, daß Stellen wie Psalm 63, 11 für schû'âl die Bedeutung „Schakal“ näher legen als „Fuchs“. In meinem Beduinenleben[2] S. 18 ff. glaube ich gezeigt zu haben, daß auch arab. dhi'b nicht Wolf, sondern „Schakal“ bedeutet. Die altarabischen Dichter schildern dieses Tier häufig, wie es hungernd umherschleicht um Beute zu suchen und dreist sich dem Feuer, an dem gebraten wird, bald von dieser, bald von jener Seite nähert, in der Hoffnung ein Stück Fleisch zu erhaschen, ja bisweilen ein Kind raubt. So liefern auch hier die arabischen Dichter einen trefflichen Kommentar zu den obigen Verse (2, 15):

„Fangt uns die Schakale, die kleinen Schakale, welche die Weinberge schädigen, während unsere Weinberge in Blüte stehn.“

Wenn die doppelte Allegorie der Schakale und der Weinblüte, wie so oft, nur notdürftig zusammenpaßt, so braucht man deshalb nicht etwa Siegfried's Erklärung, daß die Füchse durch Benagen der Wurzeln 2c. den Weinberg schädigen, heranzuziehen. Vielleicht schwebte Klagelieder 5, 18 vor.

Wahrscheinlicher stellt sich jedoch die Verschiebung als ein Resultat der Beeinflussung durch den blühenden Weinberg in Vers 13 dar. Auch das derbere Bild des Früchtenaschens, das man erwartet, würde nach der Sprache unseres Buchs wieder den Liebesgenuß bedeuten und unsere Auffassung der Schakale bestätigen.

Der Apfelbaum 8, 5 hat noch unlängst Budde Schwierigkeiten bereitet; „aber", bemerkt er, „daß sie (oder er) unter dem Apfelbaum, unter freiem Himmel geboren sein soll, das ist wiederum so abenteuerlich, so zufällig, daß man nicht weiß, was man damit machen soll." Schon Hugo Grotius hat, wie Paul Haupt a. a. O. S. 65 mitteilt, diesen Apfelbaum mit dem 2, 3, 5 in Parallele gestellt und in dem von uns ausgeführten Sinne gedeutet. Obschon dieser Gedankengang durch das Buch nahe gelegt ist, scheint er mir 8, 5 wider das unmittelbare Empfinden zu verstoßen und ich möchte hier die wörtliche Auffassung vorziehn. Ist doch die Situation gar nicht so „abenteuerlich" und „zufällig", wie Budde meint, wenn man nur die wirklichen Verhältnisse berücksichtigt. Schon Franz Delitzsch bemerkt: „Hoelemann erinnert an Sûre 19, 23 [1]), wonach 'Isâ der Sohn Marjam's unter einer Palme geboren worden ist." Es handelt sich um eine weitverbreitete Sitte. Vrgl. z. B. Heinrich Schurtz, Urgeschichte der Kultur S. 189: „„Infolge abergläubischer Vorstellungen, schreibt v. Schrenck, „die sich bei den Giljaken wie bei allen Völkern hauptsächlich an die Geburt und den Tod des Menschen knüpfen, wird bei ihnen das Weib in der Zeit, da es am meisten der Schonung und Pflege bedarf, während der Niederkunft und in den auf dieselbe folgenden Tagen, troß Wind und Wetter unbarmherzig aus dem Haufe gewiesen." Dieser Unsitte schreibt v. Schrenck wol mit Recht einen Teil der Schuld an der langsamen Vermehrung der Giljaken zu. Bei zahlreichen Völkern gemäßigter und tropischer Landstriche, wo der Geburts=

---

1) Bei Delitzsch steht fälschlich 32 ff.

akt fern von den Wohnungen im Wald oder am Meeres=
strande vollzogen wird, sind die Folgen weniger bedenklich.“

Mit den besprochenen Versen glaube ich die Grenzen der
allegorischen Deutung festgelegt zu haben. Es handelt sich
um keine neue Erkenntnis. Doch findet man auch bei neue=
ren Theologen noch zahlreiche Rückfälle in die Künstelei der
alten Allegoristen, so sieht Siegfried in den Füchsen „die
Lasten und Beschwerden der Ehe“ [1]), in dem Pannier (2, 4)
„lockendes Liebeswerben des Bräutigams“ 2c.

Die dramatische Deutung,

welche die allegorische ablöst, hat diese jedoch an Willkürlich=
keiten womöglich noch übertroffen.

Gegen die dramatische Auffassung an sich sind allgemeine
Bedenken mit Unrecht, noch neuerdings wieder von Dvořák [2])
ins Feld geführt worden. Ernst Groffe hat in seinen An=
fängen der Kunst (1894) gezeigt, daß sich der dramatische
Trieb schon bei den Naturvölkern primitivster Stufe regt und
man diese Dichtungsgattung geradezu als die älteste bezeichnen
kann [3]). Burckhardt schildert die mit Einzel= und Chorgesängen
verbundenen Tanzspiele der Sinai=Beduinen in seinen Be=
merkungen über die Beduinen und Wahaby S. 204 ff.
Wahrscheinlich bezieht sich auch Deut. 22, 5 auf Gebräuche,
welche in die Sphäre der Anfänge des Schauspiels gehören.
Daß auch der islâmische Orient des Mittelalters neben
Schattenspielen von wirklichen Komödianten dargestellte Possen
kannte, habe ich in meiner Abhandlung: Türkische Volks=

---

1) Vrgl. S. 10 Anm. 2.

2) Exegetisches zum Hohenliede: Sitzungsberichte der böhmischen
Gesellschaft der Wissenschaften, Prag 1901.

3) Der Klassizismus hat auch hier durch Dekretirung einer, wie
es scheint, unnatürlichen Volksentwickelung zur Norm unheilvolle
Vorurteile erzeugt.

litteratur (Berlin 1901) S. 37 ff. gezeigt. Ist es nach alle-
dem durchaus nicht ungereimt im HL. dramatische Elemente
auch über die unverkennbaren Dialoge hinaus zu suchen, so
zeugen doch die von den Anhängern der dramatischen Theorie
bisher zu Tage geförderten Resultate von gänzlicher Ver-
ständnislosigkeit für die Sachlage; es sei nur an die Ent-
deckung des 5aktigen Schema's, welche dem Scharfsinn
Stickel's glückte, des Ballets, getanzt von den Töchtern Jeru-
salems, und schließlich der großartigen Dekorationen erinnert,
über welche die königl. Hofbühne zu Jerusalem verfügte [1]).
Immer neue auftretende Personen wurden erkannt, sogar
Stimmen aus dem Volk [2]) und der Kutscher Salomo's ein
gewisser 'Ammi-nâdîb. Gelang es dem etwaigen Zuschauer
noch sich unter ihnen zurechtzufinden, so war doch ein Verständnis für die in ihren Reden kaum angedeutete Handlung
von ihm um so weniger zu verlangen, als die Personen des
Stücks offenbar selbst aus einander nicht klug wurden und
die Erklärer in ihrer Auffassung des Inhalts nach allen entgegengesetzten Richtungen auseinandergehn [3]), sogar in der
Hauptfrage, ob die Schûlammitin den Salomo eigentlich liebt
oder verabscheut. Noch immer gehen neue dramatische Konstruktionen aus der Werkstatt der Theologen hervor. Ich be-
kenne sie nicht alle gelesen zu haben. Von den zahlreichen
mir bekannten Erzeugnissen dieser Richtung habe ich wirklich
philologische Arbeit nur im Kommentar von Franz Delitzsch
gespürt, den seine gründliche Kenntnis des Späthebräischen
vor manchen Sprachvergewaltigungen bewahrte, aber auch er
war mehr gelehrt als kritisch, mehr poetisch als geschmackvoll.

1) Vrgl. Paul Baarts, Das Hohelied Salomonis, Nürnberg
o. J. S. 9.

2) Ebendaselbst S. 16.

3) Vrgl. die Zusammenstellung der Meinungsverschiedenheiten
bei Eduard Reuß, Geschichte der heiligen Schriften alten Testaments,
Braunschweig 1881 S. 221 ff.

Trotz der Begeisterung einzelner dramatischer Exegeten für den ästhetischen Wert ihrer Fabrikate scheint man einen Aufführungsversuch, der die krankhaften Illusionen vielleicht am schnellsten zerstört hätte, niemals gewagt zu haben.

Lieder-Hypothese.

So blieb es Eduard Reuß vorbehalten diesem Hexen= sabbat ein Ende zu bereiten. Von Straßburg ging auch die zweite Entwickelungsphase des Verständnisses unseres Buches aus, die sich an den Namen Budde's knüpft. Reuß vertrat mit Nachdruck die Auffassung Herder's, der im Schîr hasch= schîrîm weder einen tieferen Sinn noch eine durchdachte Kom= position suchte, sondern darin lediglich eine Sammlung ero= tischer Lieder erblickte; auch Herder hatte Vorgänger, er selbst weist namentlich auf Opitz hin: „Der erste deutsche Dichter ward auch Übersetzer des Hohenliedes, Opitz. Und zwar über= setzte er seiner würdig, in Liedern, nicht als Drama, nicht als mystische Hypothese"[1]). Die Brücke von Herder zu Reuß bildete des letzteren Lehrer, Johann Gottfried Eichhorn.

Nur eine Modifikation der Lieder-Hypothese ist die Auf= fassung unseres Buchs als Sammlung von Hochzeitsgesängen, zu der Konsul Wetzstein's Mitteilungen über die Hochzeits= gebräuche der syrischen Fellâhen den Anstoß gaben[2]), indem

---

1) J. G. von Herder, Sämmtliche Werke, Zur Religion und Theologie, 4. Theil, Stuttgart und Tübingen 1827 S. 140.

2) Wetzstein, Die syrische Dreschtafel: Zeitschrift für Ethno= logie V 1873 S. 270 ff. Aus dieser Arbeit und brieflichen Mit= teilungen stellte Franz Delitzsch die Bemerkungen zu seinem Kom= mentar über das HL. (Ausgabe: Leipzig 1875) zusammen, die aber von wirklich brauchbarem Material nur sehr wenig enthalten, was nicht in der „Syrischen Dreschtafel" zu finden wäre. Die Etymo= logien sind teilweise bedenklich; zu den Namen der Tänze vergl. Dalman, Palästinischer Diwan S. XXXIII.

er unter anderm berichtete, daß Bräutigam und Braut wäh=
rend der Hochzeitswoche als melik (König) und melika (Königin)
von ihren Freunden, die den Hofstaat vorstellen, bedient
werden[1]). Zusammenhängen mag damit ein arabisches Sprich=
wort, das sich schon bei Meidânî († 1124 D) findet[2]): kâda
'l-'arûsu an jakûna malikan (der Bräutigam ist beinahe ein
König). Nachdem dann zuerst Hitzig[3]), wie man übersehen
hat, und nach ihm Bernhard Stade[4]) in der Schûlammitin
des HL. die Schûnammitin Abîschag (I. Kön. 1 u. 2) er=
kannt hatte, lag es nahe den König Salomo des HL. als
Hochzeitsmaske des Bräutigams und die Schûlammitin als
solche der Braut zu fassen. Unwahrscheinlich ist die Identi=
fikation Salomo's mit dem Bräutigam nur 8, 11 u. 12, viel=
mehr scheinen hier beide im Gegensatz zu einander zu stehn;
vermutlich haben wir jedoch in dieser Stelle bereits eine spä=
tere Anfügung. 1, 5 hat schon Wellhausen die falsche Punk=
tation (Salomo für Salma) richtig gestellt[5]). Daß die
Schûlammitin im HL. niemals „Königin" genannt wird, ist
nach der Rolle, welche sie im Königsbuch spielt, wohlverständ=
lich. Im Laufe der Zeit traten in den Hochzeitsgesängen an
Stelle des Salomo andere berühmte Könige, heute sogar
der gegenwärtige Sultan 'Abdulhamid: Enno Littmann,
Neuarabische Volkspoesie S. 88/9.[6])

---

1) Zeitschrift für Ethnologie V S. 290 f.
2) Farâ'id al-la'âl fî magma' al-amthâl, Teil 2, Bairût 1312 h.
S. 126.
3) Kurzgefaßtes exegetisches Handbuch zum Alten Testament,
16. Lieferung, Leipzig 1855 S. 3/4.
4) Geschichte des Volkes Israel I 1887 S. 292 Anm.
5) Prolegomena² S. 227 Anm. Budde sagt merkwürdiger Weise:
„Zu Bickell's Lesung Salmâ ist kein Anlaß, auch ergiebt sie schwer=
lich einen brauchbaren Sinn." Auch Siegfried übersetzt wieder:
„Salomos Thürvorhänge."
6) Durch Freundlichkeit des Herausgebers erhalte ich während
des Druckes Korrekturbogen, bin aber nicht mehr im Stande das
reiche Material dieser Publikation in vollem Umfange zu verwerten.

Schon Wetzstein bezeichnete das HL. als eine Sammlung von „reizenden Hochzeitsliedern und Fragmenten solcher [1].“ Budde stellte diese Ansicht zunächst in einem Aufsatz des 78. Bandes der Preußischen Jahrbücher dar und das Jahr 1898 brachte 2 Kommentare von ihm und Siegfried, welche die neue Auffassung für das ganze Buch durchführten. Doch erinnern auch die neuern Arbeiten dieser Richtung, wie bereits angedeutet wurde, nicht selten noch an die Gewaltsamkeiten der Dramatiker, kranken vielfach an ganz unorientalischen Auffassungen [2], an einer Art Evolutionstheorie gegenüber dem Text, deren erstaunlichste Leistung Bickell's Bemerkung in den Akten des Genfer Orientalisten-Festes III S. 44 darstellt, und an metrisirender Textverstümmelungssucht [3]. Nur eine rühmliche Ausnahme vermag ich zu nennen: Paul Haupt, dessen Bemerkungen stets ins Schwarze zu treffen pflegen.

An einer einzigen Stelle des HL. geschieht der Hochzeit ausdrücklich Erwähnung, nämlich 3, 11:

„Kommt euch anschaun, ihr Töchter Zions, den König Salomo in einem Kranz ('ăţârâ), den für ihn seine Mutter gewunden hat am Tage seiner Hochzeit und am Tage der Freude seines Herzens.“

In der Bedeutung „krönen“, wie Siegfried übersetzt, regiert das Pi‘êl von ‘ăţar den Accusativ. Es wird also hier bei einem Kranze bleiben, der in späterer Zeit an die Stelle des wol als hohe Mütze zu denkenden pe'êr, welchen der Bräu-

1) Zeitschrift für Ethnologie V S. 291.

2) Vrgl. z. B. Budde's Kommentar S. 43: „der erste Vers läßt das junge Paar Arm in Arm näherkommen“. Arm in Arm! Welch wunderliche Vorstellung von orientalischem Liebesleben!

3) Daß die Herausarbeitung gleich langer Verse verfehlt ist, beweist der Qorân, den wir in guter Überlieferung besitzen. Littmann erklärt (Neuarabische Volkspoesie S. 88) die modernen volkstümlichen Hochzeitslieder Palästina's für Reimprosa ohne bestimmtes Versmaaß.

tigam nach Jesaia **61**, 10 trug, getreten sein wird. Ob sich in diesem Wandel der Mode griechischer Einfluß offenbart, ist mir zweifelhaft, da bei den Griechen der στέφανος, mit dem man sich allerdings nach antiker Sitte zum Feste schmückte, keineswegs, wie Graetz es darstellt [1]), ein besonderes Abzeichen des Bräutigams gewesen zu sein scheint. Die Schmückung des Bräutigams mit einer 'ăṭârâ wurde kurz vor der Zerstörung Jerusalem's abgeschafft [2]). Als Volksbrauch scheint sie verschwunden vrgl. Wetzstein bei Delitzsch S. 166: „Die Sitte den Bräutigam zu krönen besteht wol in Syrien nicht mehr", dagegen hat sie sich als kirchlicher Ritus bei Griechen und Maroniten erhalten [3]).

Gegen weitere Beziehungen auf Hochzeitsgebräuche, welche man bisher im HL. gefunden zu haben meint, läßt sich Manches einwenden. Den Schwerttanz der Braut will man in einigen Stellen von Kapitel **6** und **7** erkennen. In der That spricht für diese Deutung der Artikel in mechôlat hammachänajim: **7**, 1; der Dual, welcher wahrscheinlich auf Rechnung der Masoreten kommt, darf somit nicht verführen, an die kultischen Tänze zu denken, die nach Genesis **32** für das Machänajim benachbarte Penû'êl wahrscheinlich sind f. Gunkel's Genesis-Kommentar S. 329. Allerdings heißt es **7**, 2:

„Wie schön sind deine Schritte in den Sandalen 2c.,

während, was man nicht beachtet hat, der Schwerttanz nach Wetzstein [4]) heute mit nackten Füßen getanzt wird. Hingegen führt die Braut die Gelwe (den Paradirtanz) nach Dalman [5])

---

1) Schir ha-schirim, Wien 1871 S. 62.
2) Mischna Sôtâ 9, 14 ed. Wagenseil, Altdorf 1674 S. 962.
3) Rosenmüller, Das alte und neue Morgenland 4. Band S. 197; Theophil Löbel, Hochzeitsgebräuche in der Türkei, Amsterdam 1897 S. 141/2.
4) ZDMG. 22. Band 1868 S. 106.
5) Palästinischer Diwan S. 257.

auf hölzernen Stelzschuhen (qabâqîb) aus, die mit Perlmutter ausgelegt sind.

Bei **3, 6** ff. denken Budde und Siegfried sicherlich mit Unrecht an die Dreschtafel. Von einen Umzug des Bräutigams auf dieser, welchen Siegfried annimmt, weiß auch die Fellâhensitte der Gegenwart nichts. Aus Mischna Sôtâ **9, 14** geht hervor, daß die Braut in einem appirjôn (Sänfte) durch die Stadt[1]) (be-tôk hâ-'îr) getragen wurde. Diese Angabe genügt die Dreschtafelhypothese für unsere Stelle völlig abzuthun. Die Fiktion ist lediglich die, daß die festlich geschmückte Sänfte der prachtliebende König Salomo sich zur Heimführung seiner Braut habe bauen lassen. Das lô (sich) in Vers 9 wird traditionell dahin misverstanden, daß hier ausnahmsweise die Brautsänfte — denn das ist appirjôn — zur Aufnahme des Bräutigams dient. Bei einem Hochzeitszug, den 1001 Nacht (Bairût 1888 I S. 139) schildert, treffen wir den Bräutigam zu Pferde: râkibani 'l-farsa. Daß aber thatsächlich auch im HL. die Braut in der Sänfte gedacht wird, beweisen nicht nur die Parfümwolken[2]), welche das Nahen der Sänfte Vers 6 ankündigen, sondern ganz deutlich das mî-zôt ebendaselbst, welches Budde und Siegfried, trotzdem auch LXX τίς αὕτη liest, willkürlich in mâ-zôt verändern. Auch befürchtet man nach morgenländischem Aberglauben für die Braut ganz besonders die Gefahren des bösen Auges[3]), denen alles Schöne, Begehrenswerte besonders ausgesetzt ist. Darum müssen die Nachtunholde — das bedeutet pachad ballêlôt: **3, 8** — durch Waffenlärm und Fackelglanz verscheucht werden. Im Märchen von den beiden Vezîren Schemseddin und Nûreddîn befiehlt ein König im Zorn ein schönes Mäd-

---

1) Demnach deutet auch das appirjôn im HL. wol auf städtische Verhältnisse.

2) Vrgl. Rosenmüller, Das alte und neue Morgenland, 4. Band S. 195/6; 1001 Nacht, Bairût 1888 I S. 140.

3) Vermutlich deshalb trägt sie auch den Schleier.

chen mit einem buckeligen Stallknecht zu verheiraten. Ein
'Ifrît aber weiß am Abend einen schönen Jüngling unterzu=
schieben, den er lehrt, wenn er sich der Braut nähert, zu
sprechen: „Ich bin dein Gatte, und der König hat diese List
nur angewendet, weil er für dich vor dem bösen Auge Angst
hatte" (χaufan 'alaiki mina 'l-'ain): 1001 Nacht, Bairût 1888
Band 1 S. 141. Die Häßlichkeit des Gefährten im Festzug
soll hier also denselben Zweck erfüllen wie das bewaffnete
Geleit HL. 3, 7:

> „Siehe es ist das Bett Salomo's, umringt von 60 Helden
> von den Helden Israels",

womit 6, 8 korrespondirt. Vrgl. dazu folgende Bemerkung
Dalman's über die Hochzeitszüge, Paläst. Diwan S. 193:
„Ohne kriegerisches Gepränge sind diese Züge nicht zu denken.
In Aleppo ziehen zuweilen an hundert Krieger mit Schwert
und Schild, einige auch mit Helm und Harnisch dem Bräu=
tigam voran". Möglicherweise enthält Vers 10 eine direkte
Erwähnung der Braut in der Sänfte. Namentlich Siegfried
hat den Schluß desselben:

> tôkô râsûf ahäbâ mib-benôt Jerûschâlâjim

sehr gewaltsam behandelt. Zunächst verbessert er die „Liebe"
(ahäbâ) in „Ebenholz" (hobnîm), was ihm aber sofort neue
Verlegenheiten bereitet. Da er nämlich den Töchtern Jeru=
salem's keine Kunstfertigkeit im Mosaikpflastern zutraut, so
müssen diese überhaupt gestrichen werden. Ahäbâ steht nun
sonst im HL. in der Bedeutung „Liebchen" z. B. 2, 7. Das
würde gut zu den Töchtern Jerusalem's passen. Für râ ûf
bliebe dann allerdings, falls der Text nicht verderbt ist, höch=
stens die Bedeutung: „eingepfercht" [1]).

Eine andere Anspielung auf einen altsemitischen Hoch=
zeitsbrauch scheint mir bisher übersehen worden zu sein. Am

---

1) Eine ähnliche Auffassung vertrat, wie ich nachträglich aus
Delitzsch ersehe, bereits Schlottmann.

deutlichſten tritt dieſelbe **4, 8** zu Tage, wo nach Weiſe des arabiſchen Nasīb eine ganze Reihe von Lokalitäten in Verbindung mit der Geliebten hergezählt wird:

„Mit mir vom Libanon, Braut, mit mir vom Libanon ſollſt du kommen; ſollſt ziehen vom Gipfel Amana's, vom Gipfel Senir's und Hermon's, von den Schlupfwinkeln der Löwen, von den Bergen der Panther".

Budde urteilt über dieſen Vers[1]): „Dieſe Muſterkarte der höchſten Gebirge paßt ſo wenig hier hinein, es läßt ſich ſo wenig ein verſtändiger Sinn damit verbinden, der Vers iſt dichteriſch ſo ſchwach, daß das Mißverſtändnis und der Einſchub auf der offenen Hand liegt." Ich kenne ſchwächere Verſe im HL., deren Echtheit Budde nicht beanſtandet, und glaube, man wird bei unbefangener Betrachtung den poetiſchen Schwung des vorliegenden nicht verkennen. An der Häufung von Ortsnamen in der Poeſie nimmt nur abendländiſche Empfindung Anſtoß; ſo ſtörte Auguſt Müller dieſelbe Eigentümlichkeit in den Eingangsverſen der erſten Mu'allaqa mit Unrecht[2]). Siegfried folgt Budde und findet es merkwürdig, daß die Liebenden „ihre Flitterwochen" in einer Gegend verbracht haben ſollten, die wegen der Löwen und Pardel die denkbar ungeeignetſte war: „Das Verſtändigſte iſt jedenfalls an dieſem Einfalle die Aufforderung des Geliebten an die Braut, ſich mit ihm von dort wegzubegeben." Vermutlich bezieht ſich **4, 8** auf eine Hochzeitsſitte, welche ſich unter Beduinen nach mündlichen Mitteilungen noch heute erhalten hat und die Burckhardt, Beduinen und Wahaby S. 216 f. folgendermaßen ſchildert: „Eine ſonderbare Gewohnheit beſteht unter

---

1) Preußiſche Jahrbücher 78 S. 112.

2) Imrvvl*k*aisi Mu'alla*k*a edidit Auguſt Müller, Halle 1869 S. 1: „quattuor locorum simul commemoratorum nulloque epitheto exornatorum series inelegans versuum veritatem non admodum confirmat."

dem Stamme Mezeyne [Mezêne] in der Halbinsel des Sinai, aber nicht unter den andern Stämmen dieses Landstriches. Ein Mädchen, welches in den abba ['abâ'] des Nachts gehüllt worden ist[1]), darf aus ihrem Zelt in die benachbarten Berge entfliehen. Der Bräutigam sucht sie den nächsten Tag und bleibt oft mehrere Tage aus, ehe er sie finden kann. Ihre weibliche Freundschaft ist dagegen von ihrem Versteck in Kenntnis gesetzt und versorgt sie mit Lebensmitteln. Wenn der Mann sie endlich findet (was früher oder später geschieht, je nach dem Eindrucke, den er auf des Mädchens Herz gemacht hat), so ist er gehalten, die Ehe mit ihr im Freien zu vollziehen [vrgl. 1, 16, 17] und die Nacht mit ihr in den Bergen zuzubringen. Den nächsten Morgen geht die Braut nach Hause in ihr Zelt, um einige Nahrung zu sich zu nehmen, läuft aber des Abends wieder fort und wiederholt dieses mehrmals, bis sie endlich in ihr Zelt zurückkehrt. Sie bleibt daselbst und geht nicht eher in das Zelt ihres Mannes, bis sie in der Schwangerschaft weit vorgeschritten ist. Dann, aber nicht eher, gesellt sie sich zu ihm ... Ich hörte, daß dieselbe Gewohnheit auch unter den Arabern des Stammes Mezeyne herrschend sei, die in einem andern Teile von Hedschaz und in der Nähe von Nedschid wohnen. Unter den Dschebalye, einem kleinen Stamm am Berge Sinai von neuerem Ursprung, bleibt die Braut nach der Hochzeit 3 volle Tage bei ihrem Mann, entflieht dann in's Gebirge und kehrt nicht eher zurück, als bis er sie dort findet." An die nämliche Situation erinnern auch andere Verse des HL. z. B. 2, 14.

Nicht unwahrscheinlich ist mir ferner, daß 8, 8 ff. mit einem Hochzeitsscherz zusammenhängt, den Wetzstein in seiner Abhandlung über die syrische Dreschtafel[2]) folgendermaßen

---

1) Bei der Werbung wirft ein Verwandter des Bräutigams der Braut einen Mantel über den Kopf. Zur Symbolik dieses Brauchs vrgl. Pischel: Hermes 28. Band 1893 S. 466 f.

2) Zeitschrift für Ethnologie V S. 290.

schildert: „Darauf tritt der Ankläger vor und erzählt in
langer Rede, der König habe, wie allen bekannt, mit seinem
Heere einen Feldzug gegen eine bis dahin unbesiegte und aller
Welt Hohn sprechende Festung unternommen, um sie zu
erobern und da er wieder zurück und gegenwärtig sei, so
möge er seinem Volke zu wissen thun, ob ihm der Angriff
geglückt sei oder nicht." Zu dem Bilde der Braut als Stadt
vrgl. meine Altarabischen Parallelen zum Alten Testament
S. 16 und Tha'âlibî's Latâ'if al-ma'ârif ed. de Jong S. 102:
„Al-Ḥaggâg pflegte zu sagen: al-Kûfa ist ein schönes Mäd=
chen ohne Geld und man freit um sie wegen ihrer Schönheit,
al-Basra aber ist ein häßliches reiches altes Weib und man
freit um sie wegen ihres Vermögens."

Wenn demnach auch Verschiedenes im HL. auf Hoch=
zeitsgebräuche hinweist, so berechtigt das doch nicht Alles auf
die Hochzeit zu beziehen. Bei solchem Versuch ergeben sich
auch sofort Schwierigkeiten. Früher operirten die Theologen
mit einem der Ehe vorausgehenden Brautstand. Dem gegen=
über betont Budde[1]): „Nicht um bräutliche, sondern um ehe=
liche Liebe handelt es sich im Hohen Liede von Anfang bis
zu Ende." Dieser Satz ward zu einem verhängnisvollen
Dogma. Ein Brautstand im abendländischen Sinne ist aller=
dings dem Orient fremd. Man darf aber auch nicht die
Zustände des Islâm, der gerade auf dem Gebiete des Ehe=
lebens eine große Revolution darstellt, auf das Altertum
übertragen. Bei den vom Islâm weniger berührten Beduinen
hat das Liebeswerben und häufig auch der Liebesverkehr vor
der Ehe stets eine große Rolle gespielt[2]). Vor Allem aber
ist die eheliche Liebe in den allerseltensten Fällen Gegenstand

---

1) Preußische Jahrbücher 78. Band S. 96.

2) Bei Völkern niederer Kulturstufe muß man sich ganz beson=
ders davor hüten, geschlechtlichen Umgang und Eheschließung zu
identifiziren und von ersterem auf letztere zu schließen; vrgl. die
Ausführungen von Heinrich Schurtz, Urgeschichte der Kultur S. 194.

der erotiſchen Poeſie; aus dem nahverwandten arabiſchen
Kulturkreis läßt ſich den zahlloſen Liebesliedern, welche außer=
eheliche Verhältniſſe behandeln, kaum irgend ein Beleg für
jene Gattung gegenüberſtellen. Seltſam wäre es daher, wenn
wir im HL. nur Ehepoeſie [1]) hätten. Die Sinnlichkeit des
HL., welche den Gegenſtand der Liebe ganz wie die arabiſchen
Qaſiden zergliedert und an den einzelnen Körperteilen durch
Vergleich mit allerlei Dingen prahlende Kritik übt, würde,
dem Gatten in den Mund gelegt, wol auch primitiven Kultur=
völkern unpaſſend, geſchmacklos und töricht erſcheinen.

Sehr unbequem ſind für Budde's Lehre, daß es ſich im
HL. von Anfang bis zu Ende um eheliche Liebe handele, zu=
nächſt Stellen wie 3, 4, wo das Mädchen vom Geliebten
ſagt:

„und ich ließ ihn nicht, bis ich ihn ins Haus meiner
Mutter brachte und ins Brautgemach meiner Gebärerin“.

Nach obiger Auffaſſung handelt es ſich ja, wie Siegfried
richtig bemerkt, „nicht um eine bei der Mutter wohnende Braut,
ſondern um eine junge Frau, die den Mann doch wohl ins
eigne Haus geführt haben würde“ [2]). Die „ganz unpaſſende
Gloſſe“ iſt daher nach Budde und Siegfried zu ſtreichen. Sie
ſoll aus 8, 2 ins 3te Kapitel gelangt ſein; dort ſteht aber
in anderm Zuſammenhang: „ich brächte dich ins Haus mei=
ner Mutter.“ Die „Gloſſe“ müßte alſo ziemlich viel aus
eigenen Mitteln und zwar — wie man beachte — im Sprach=
gebrauch des Buches hinzugethan haben. Der Parallelismus
des Brautgemachs der Gebärerin, welcher auf ihre Rechnung
geſetzt werden ſoll, hat eine Parallele 8, 5 und zwar, was
beſonders ſchwer ins Gewicht fällt, außer der äußerlichen auch

---

1) Schon das Wort hat einen ironiſchen Beigeſchmack.

2) Selbſt wenn hier ein Analogon der oben erwähnten Sinai=
Beduinen-Sitte vorläge, nach welcher die Frau erſt bei vorgeſchrit=
tener Schwangerſchaft bei ihrem Manne Wohnung nimmt, würde
man doch irgendwo im Text einen Anhalt erwarten, daß es ſich um
Mann und Frau handelt.

eine innerliche, weil auch das Liebesglück der Tochter sich an demselben Ort abspielen soll, an welchem auch die Mutter das ihrige genossen hat. — Zu Vers 8, 1:

„Wärst du mir doch wie ein Bruder, der die Brüste meiner Mutter sog, fände ich dich auf der Straße, ich würde dich küssen, ohne daß man mich verachtete"

bemerkt Siegfried: „ba-chûs die Annahme ist auffällig, da sie doch den Bruder mit großer Sicherheit bab-bajit treffen konnte. Sie greift aber hier auf die Situation des Bräutigam's zurück, der ihr erst „wie ein Bruder" werden soll." Man sieht, zu welch unglaublichen Künsteleien die Voraussetzung führt, es könne sich nur um legitime Liebe handeln. Die leidenschaftliche Orientalin möchte ihren Geliebten am liebsten auf offener Straße küssen; die Rücksicht auf die Leute ist ihr lästig; deshalb wünscht sie ihn sich als Bruder; dann könnte sie ihn ja auch mit nach Hause nehmen. Die Stelle zeigt, wie die Geliebte im HL. und in der altägyptischen Erotik zu der Bezeichnung „Schwester" kam. Diese Anrede korrespondirt mit dem hier vorliegenden âch, nicht etwa, wie W. Max Müller behauptet, mit dôd, das nach ihm im HL. in der Bedeutung „Vetter" steht [1]). Abgesehen davon, daß letzterer Gegensatz schief wäre und nirgends vorliegt, korrespondirt vielmehr die Anrede dôdî ganz unverkennbar mit ra'jâtî, wie der Vergleich von 1, 15, 16, 2, 10 lehrt. Die Bezeichnung der Liebenden als „Bruder" und „Schwester" scheint auch sonst nicht auf Geschwisterehe (W. Max Müller), sondern auf freie Liebe hinzuweisen. Anders allerdings vollzog sich der Bedeutungswandel bei türkisch badschy, nach Samy: „soeur ainée; femme d'un cheikh, d'un derviche, d'un religieux; religieuse; nom que l'époux donne à son épouse par modestie".

Wenn ferner der Geliebte des HL. zu ungewöhnlicher

---

1) Die Liebespoesie der alten Ägypter S. 8.

Tageszeit vor dem Fenster der Geliebten erscheint, Einlaß be=
gehrend (5, 2 ff., 2, 8 ff.) oder sie bei Nacht, von Sehnsucht
getrieben, die Gassen durchstreift, wo sie die Wächter zu arre=
tieren versuchen, so vermag ich darin weder einen idealen Ehe=
noch Brautstand zu erblicken. Auch lassen sich diese nächtigen
Spaziergänge nicht auf die von Burckhardt, Beduinen und
Wahaby S. 67 geschilderte Sitte deuten, sondern bezwecken
offenbar Liebesvereinigung. Die von Siegfried zu 5, 6 ge=
gebene Erklärung, der Geliebte sei aus zarter Rücksicht auf
die in Vers 3 geschilderte Situation fortgegangen, vergißt,
daß es sich nach Vers 2 nur um einen Traum handelt, paßt
ferner durchaus nicht zum derben Ton von Vers 4. Bra-
chium per foramen fenestrae immissum quid significet, ex
comoedia umbratica, cui Constantinopoli interfui, intellexi.
Karagoez rarius jam phallo instructus pro actionibus ejus
brachii gestus substituit. Nur so wird Vers 4 überhaupt
verständlich. — Daß hingegen die Realität des Weinhauses
(2, 4), in welches der Orientale seine Gattin schwerlich führen
würde, um ihre Liebe zu genießen, zweifelhaft ist, wurde
S. 12 ausgeführt.

Demnach dürfte das HL. erotische Lieder verschiedenen
Inhalts zusammenfassen, was der gewöhnlichen Anlage solcher
Sammlungen entsprechen würde. Möglicherweise waren aber
auch die buhlerischen Liedchen bestimmt, bei Hochzeiten vor=
getragen zu werden. Undenkbar philiströs hätte es ja gewirkt,
wenn die Hochzeitschöre die Königswoche ausschließlich mit
dem Lob der legitimen Liebe ausgefüllt hätten. Bei solchen
Gelegenheiten bildet die Liebe überhaupt das Thema und zwar
hauptsächlich die freie, der fröhlichen Stimmung angemessen.

Daß es sich bei diesen Liedern nicht um Elaborate eines
Hochzeitspoeten handelt, sondern um wirkliches Volksgut, da=
für sprechen neben andern Anzeichen die zahlreichen Wieder=
holungen, zumal man in vielen Fällen in der Nähe derselben
noch weitere Anklänge und Berührungen findet, welche sich am
leichtesten als Reste ehemaliger Identität beider Parthien, die

demnach Varianten desselben Urtextes darstellen würden, er=
klären. So stimmen beispielsweise 2, 6, 7 und 8, 3, 4 bis
auf geringfügige Differenzen wörtlich überein. Unmittelbar
vorher ist in beiden Fällen von einem trauten Beisammensein
in einsamem Zimmer die Rede und der Liebesgenuß wird
dabei mit Wein und Erfrischungen verglichen, wobei noch
äschīschā (2, 5) an ʿāsîs (8, 2) anklingt. Vor der Wächter=
scene 3, 3 ff. und 5, 7 ff. wird uns beide Male das Liebes=
verlangen des im Halbschlaf in seinem Kämmerlein liegenden
Mädchens geschildert und die beiden auf dieselbe folgenden
Verse 3, 5 und 5, 8 beginnen mit denselben Worten. Bei
den parallelen Schilderungen der Reize der Braut 4, 1 ff.
und 6, 4 ff. decken sich zunächst im Eingang die Worte jāfā,
raʿjātî, dann werden die Augen in verschieden gestalteten
Bildern gepriesen, worauf fast völlige Identität eintritt. —
Haben wir nun Volkspoesie vor uns, so erklärt sich daraus
noch ein weiterer Umstand, nämlich die Schwierigkeiten, welche
Verse wie 6, 12 [1]), 8, 5 dem Verständnis bereiten. Jede
Volkspoesie füllt mit der Zeit die Lücken, welche das Versagen
des Gedächtnisses hinterläßt, durch mehr oder weniger un=
passende Ersatzglieder aus, die oft jeder Erklärung spotten;
das Volkslied wird „zersungen". Es ist eine bedauerliche Un=
sitte unserer Kommentare, daß sie sich verpflichtet fühlen, jeden
Vers mit einer Erklärung auszustatten, anstatt Unwahrschein=
liches zu verschweigen und Unklares als solches zu charakteri=
siren. — Schließlich sei auch darauf hingewiesen, daß die
volkstümliche Dichtung der Araber, wie sie z. B. in den
Liederzitaten der 1001 Nacht vorliegt, welche meist von unbe=
kannten Dichtern herrühren, für Parallelen zum HL. ergiebiger
ist als die Kunstpoesie.

Mit der Erkenntnis, daß es sich um Volkspoesie handelt,
verliert auch die bei biblischen Büchern meist mit großem

---

1) Der neueste Erklärungsversuch dieser Stelle bei Dvořák a. a. O.
wird schwerlich Jemanden befriedigen.

Apparat umständlich erörterte, in Wahrheit jedoch nebensäch=
liche Frage nach der Abfaſſungszeit noch mehr an Intereſſe.
Namentlich das Hochzeitszeremoniell mit ſeinen Chorgeſängen
wird nicht plötzlich erfunden ſein, ſondern eine langſame
kontinuirliche Entwickelung durchgemacht haben, ſo daß ſelbſt
für Generationen die Hauptſache konſtant blieb. Die Er=
wähnung Tirsâ's neben Jeruſalem als Vertreterin der Städte=
ſchönheit (6, 4) ſcheint mir als Zeugnis für Entſtehung jenes
Stücks zwiſchen Jerobeam I und Omri noch nicht entkräftet.
Eine gelehrte Rekonſtruktion aus ſpäterer Zeit wäre anders
ausgefallen und hätte ſicherlich Jeruſalem an erſter Stelle
genannt. Das Prädikat „lieblich" für Jeruſalem, „ſchön"
für Tirsâ ſetzt voraus, daß letzteres dem Verfaſſer großartiger
vorkam und entſpricht der thatſächlichen Wertung der Reiche
in älterer Zeit, die ſchon der Umſtand illuſtrirt, daß der Ge=
ſammtname dem Norden verblieb[1]), während der Süden ſich
mit einem Stammesnamen begnügen mußte. Ich kann mir
nicht vorſtellen, daß ein nachexiliſcher Jude die nötige Kritik
beſaß, um dieſes Verhältnis aus den bibliſchen Büchern in
unſerm Vers wiederherzuſtellen, verſteht doch LXX garnicht
einmal, was gemeint iſt und überſetzt ke-Tirsâ ὡς εὐδοϰία.
Auch die nahe liegende Möglichkeit einer etymologiſchen Spie=
lerei mit dem Namen Tirsâ erklärt doch nicht die Parallel=
ſetzung mit Jeruſalem und Bevorzugung vor dieſem durch
Stellung und Epitheton. Hinwiederum läßt ſich nicht leug=
nen, daß alle andern Indizien in eine ſehr viel ſpätere
Periode hinabführen. Die 3, 11 bezeugte Sitte, nach welcher
der Bräutigam nicht mehr wie Jeſaia **61**, 10 den pe'êr, ſon=
dern die 'ăṭârâ trug, ſcheint auf eine Zeit nach der Mitte des
5. Jahrhunderts hinzudeuten. Der weiße Marmor ſchajiſch,
ſchêſch (5, 15) wird wie Benzinger bemerkt[2]), erſt in nach=

---

1) Wenn auch daneben der Stammesname Efraim für das Nord=
reich vorkommt.

2) Hebräiſche Archäologie S. 121 Anm.

exilischer Zeit erwähnt, namentlich bei den herobianischen Bau=
ten; wir werden also bei ʻammûdê schêch (5, 15) an grie=
chische Säulen zu denken haben [1]). Der Sprachcharakter trägt
ein unverkennbar spätes Gepräge. Appirjôn [2]) (3, 9) z. B.
ist griechisch φορεῖον, pardês (4, 13) findet sich nur noch in
jungen Büchern des AT. und von Narden (1, 12, 4, 13, 14)
hören wir sonst im AT. überhaupt nichts mehr, wohl aber
im neuen (Marc. 14, 3, Joh. Ev. 12, 3). In dieselbe Zeit
wie der Wortschatz führen uns grammatische Zeugnisse hin=
unter, wie mehrfach ausgeführt ist. Demnach halte ich das
HL. für eine der Volkssprache etwa des 3. Jahrhunderts
v. Chr. adaptirte Aufzeichnung von Volksliedern, welche in
ihren ältesten Parthien bis in die ältere Königszeit zurück=
reichen mögen.

Die gewöhnliche Annahme, die Lieder seien sämmtlich an
einem Ort entstanden, ist von vorneherein unwahrscheinlich.
Sie können in verschiedenen Gegenden aufgekommen sein, in
andern hauptsächlich gelebt und wieder in andern einen Samm=
ler gefunden haben. Die Wiederholungen einzelner Verse an
verschiedenen Stellen mit kleinen Variationen deuten auf ver=
schiedene Quellen. Die Ortsnamen, welche der Text nennt,
geben keinen zuverlässigen Wegweiser ab. Erstlich könnte es
sich in einzelnen Fällen wie „Herbstzeitlose von Saron“ (2, 1),
„Zelte Qêdâr's“ (1, 5) um dichterisches Phraseninventar handeln,
wie etwa die Löwen oder Gazellen von Bìscha in einem ara=
bischen Gedicht keinen Schluß auf dessen Entstehungszone ge=

---

1) Das Bad, welches heute bei Hochzeiten eine wichtige Rolle
spielt, wird nicht erwähnt, scheint also damals in Städten, in denen
es nächtige Patrouillen gab, noch nicht eingebürgert gewesen zu sein.

2) Das Dagesch erscheint unberechtigt, da Vorschlagsalef nicht
auf doppelkonsonantischen Anlaut beschränkt ist vgl. z. B. afarsâmôn
späthebräisch = βάλσαμον. Der Übergang von φ in p war durch
die Verdoppelung gegeben, indem zunächst das zweite f in den An=
laut tretend verhärtet werden mußte und sich dann das erste assi=
milirte.

statten würden. Sodann werden im HL. Lokalitäten aus den verschiedensten Gegenden Paläſtina's und der Nachbarländer genannt. Recht willkürlich hat man einige Erwähnungen für weſentlich, andere für unweſentlich erklärt. Winckler legt den Hauptakzent auf Damascus 7, 5 und verändert das daneben ſtehende wieder nach SO. weiſende Cheschbôn in Chelbôn, eine Konjektur, die mir allerdings recht beachtenswert erſcheint. Budde dagegen betont die Ortsnamen des Südens und namentlich Jeruſalem: „Da, nicht im Norden, wurzelt das Hohelied; die „Töchter Jeruſalems" allein würden zum Beweiſe genügen." Wenn aber im Feſtſpiel König Salomo auf=tritt, ſo gehört zu ihm ein jeruſalemiſcher Chor; an ihn als den letzten Beherrſcher des Geſammtreichs konnte die Erinne=rung ebenſowohl im Norden wie im Süden lebendig bleiben. Auf eine größere Stadt deutet allerdings die Erwähnung der Patrouillen und wohl auch des appirjôn, vrgl. Sôtâ 9, 14.

Seit Herder hat man den poetiſchen Wert unſeres Buches maaßlos übertrieben; viele Ausleger ſind ganz außer ſich vor Entzücken. Driver findet [1] den Rhythmus der Gedanken an=mutig und durchſichtig, eine Phraſe, bei welcher ich mir nichts zu denken vermag. Wenn er dann noch gar die Schilderungen „in hohem Maaße maleriſch" nennt, ſo vergleiche man dazu die Jlluſtrationen bei van Veen [2]. Thatſächlich beſteht der In=halt weſentlich in einer ziemlich planloſen Sammlung grob=ſinnlicher unplaſtiſcher Bilder für den Liebesgenuß in summa oder die einzelnen Körperteile des geliebten Jndividuums. Während der Liebesgenuß durch angenehme Reizungen nament=lich niederer materieller Sinne [3] veranſchaulicht wird, beſonders

---

1) Einleitung in die Litteratur des alten Teſtaments, S. 480.

2) Ernestus Vaenius, Tractatus physiologicus de pulchritudine. Juxta ea quae de Sponsa in Canticis Canticorum mysticè pronun-ciantur, Bruxellis 1662. Ein Exemplar dieſes ſeltenen Buches be=findet ſich im Beſitze der DMG.

3) Die erſte Mu'allaqa (ed. Lyall Vers 39) verwendet wenigſtens einen grellen Lichtreiz als Vergleich für die Geliebte.

des Geschmacks (auf gute Weide gehn, Essen von Obst und Honig, Trinken von Wein, Milch[1]) und Quellwasser[2])) und des Geruchs (Myrrhe, Narde, Hennablüte ꝛc.), müssen für die Körperteile verschiedene Produkte des Tier-, Pflanzen- und Mineral-Reichs herhalten. Selbst hier wird eigene Beobachtung nach allen semitischen Analogien selten gewesen sein; man arbeitete mit einem todten Bildervorrat, den man mit geringen Modifikationen durch die Jahrhunderte weiterschleppte.

Von diesem Hintergrund, welcher dem der im Charakter engverwandten arabischen Erotik entspricht, heben sich einige uns mehr zusagende Liedchen ab, namentlich 1, 5, 6 und 8, 6, 7. Doch auch dies letztere, obschon viel bewundert, besteht, ziemlich kunstlos, fast ausschließlich aus einigen pathetischen Vergleichen und Metaphern zur Verherrlichung jenes alle Vernunft aufhebenden Liebestaumels, wie ihn der Orient gar sehr im Gegensatz zu abendländischem Empfinden zeitigt. Wie viel großartiger haben den Vorwurf, daß Liebe stärker als Tod und Flammengluten, die eddischen Sänger von Brunhild's Ende und Helfahrt, wie viel schöner hat ihn das herrliche indische Lied von Savitri zu gestalten vermocht! Die landläufige Auffassung hat überdies auch noch in den Schlußvers des Liedchens 8, 6, 7 ein gut Teil arischen Idealismus hineingebracht, der dem Original fremd ist. Wir haben nicht mit Siegfried zu verstehn:

> „Wenn Jemand das ganze Gut seines Hauses hingeben
>   wollte um die Liebe,
> Höhnisch abweisen würde man ihn."

---

1) 5, 1 (vrgl. S. 10).

2) 4, 12 ff. — Die Geliebte ist dementsprechend bald ein Garten (4, 12, 16, 5, 1), bald eine Art Speiseschrank (7, 14), bald ein Weinberg (1, 6), bald ein Weinkrug (7, 3), bald ein Brunnen (4, 12, 15); natürlich alles angefüllt mit Labung zu denken.

Vielmehr ift, wie zuerft Paul Haupt[1]) richtig erkannt hat,
bôz jabûzû Frage, und ahâbâ ſteht wahrſcheinlich wie 2, 7 2c.
für die Geliebte; an Sklavenhandel zu denken, liegt nahe;
alſo:

> „Wenn Jemand das ganze Gut ſeines Hauſes für das
> Liebchen (oder: für die Liebe) ausgeben wollte,
> Kann man ihm das verargen?“

Nach der Weltanſchauung des jüdiſchen Dichters läßt ſich alſo
Liebe doch jedenfalls mit Geld erwerben; er polemiſirt nur
gegen geringſchätzige Verurteilung der Verſchwendungsſucht für
ſolchen Zweck. Die tiefe ethiſche Auffaſſung der Liebe, welche
dieſe Verſe enthalten ſollen, ſtellt ſich demnach als exegetiſches
Kunſtprodukt dar. Schon Wahl und Beibehaltung des Sonder=
namens „Exegeſe“ deuten auf eine Begriffsdifferenz und eine
von der philologiſchen Auslegung abweichende Methode. Wenn
ich mich bemüht habe, die Poeſie des HL. möglichſt ſcharf
und unbefangen zu charakteriſiren, wolle man meine Polemik
gegen Hineingetragenes nicht mit einem abfälligen Urteil über
die Dichtung ſelbſt verwechſeln. Über das HL. als litterari=
ſches Produkt zu Gericht zu ſitzen und es wol gar mit der
Elle des antiken Schema's zu meſſen, halte ich natürlich für
einen ganz unberechtigten Standpunkt. Die Lieder werden
bei paſſender Gelegenheit mit Muſikbegleitung vorgetragen,
von fröhlichen Hochzeitschören getanzt und geſungen, die beab=
ſichtigte Wirkung nicht verfehlt haben; ihr Text aber iſt nicht
für die kritiſche Gymnaſtik des modernen Schulmeiſters be=
rechnet.

---

1) a. a. O. S. 60.

II.

Zur Erzielung von Fortschritten im Verständnis des HL. scheint mir vor allem der bisher noch kaum betretene Weg der Parallelen offen zu stehen, der langsamer aber sicherer vorwärts führt als spekulative Konstruktionen. Zunächst kommen die S. 28 erwähnten inneren Parallelen in Betracht; wie sich über die historischen Bücher durch Vergleichung ihrer Parallelberichte ungeahntes Licht ergoß, so dürfte Manches für das HL. noch aus demselben selbst zu gewinnen sein.

An diese innern Parallelen reiht sich sobann ein dem nämlichen Kulturkreis entstammendes Erzeugnis, das hebräische Hochzeitslied: Psalm 45. Leider hat dasselbe bei seiner Aufnahme in den Psalter Überarbeitung im geistlichen Sinne erfahren, indem der angeredete König, wie der Einschub ĕlôhîm in Vers 7 zeigt, auf Gott umgedeutet wurde. Die Grenzen dieser Überarbeitung dürften schwer zu fixiren sein[1]); nach 'al-kên Vers 3 erwartet man eine Fortführung im Sinne von HL. 1, 3. Da der Psalm auch andere Anklänge ans HL. enthält[2]), auf die mich zuerst mein Schüler Herr stud. theol. Auer aufmerksam machte, liegt es nahe in dem König des Psalms gleichfalls den Bräutigam zu vermuten[3]);

––––––––––

1) Auch sonst ist die Textüberlieferung eine schlechte, vrgl. die Dittographien jofjâfîtâ Vers 3, wa-hâdârekâ Vers 4, 5.

2) Môr wa-ăhâlôt nur HL. 4, 14 und Psalm 45, 9; jáfîtâ Psalm 45, 3 erinnert an HL. 1, 15, 16, 6, 4.

3) Man beachte die Parallele Vers 2: „Meine Arbeit ist für einen König, meine Zunge ist der Grabstift eines geschickten Schrift-

vielleicht war das Hochzeitslied für einen angesehenen Besitzer gedichtet und erhielt bei der erwähnten Umdeutung noch einige kräftigere Farbentöne. Immerhin würde es auch, wenn wir mit Duhm (Kommentar), Kautzsch[1] 2c. an einen wirklichen König denken, als Zeugnis hebräischer Hochzeitspoesie für das HL. von Bedeutung sein.

Ferner besitzen wir aus nahverwandten Kulturkreisen eine Fülle erotischer Texte, deren Parallelen gesammelt auf manchen Vers des HL. neue Schlaglichter werfen, vor allem aber vor jenen willkürlichen Auslegungen nach modern-abendländischer Auffassung schützen würden, von denen alle Kommentare wimmeln. Zunächst kommen natürlich die andern semitischen Völker und unter diesen in erster Linie die Araber, welche die ausgiebigste Litteratur besitzen, in Betracht. Der lange von mir gehegte Wunsch einer Aufzeichnung der modernen Hochzeitslieder Palästina's ist jetzt von zwei Seiten durch die verdienstvollen Arbeiten Dalman's[2] und Littmann's[3] verwirklicht worden.

Für die altägyptische Erotik macht W. Max Müller's zusammenfassende Bearbeitung[4] der bis jetzt wiederaufgefundenen Reste ältere Einzelpublikationen für unsere Zwecke entbehrlich. Schon lange beobachtet sind Berührungen des

---

verständigen"; die Dichtung wird hier, wie das Wort 'ét zeigt, mit einer Inschrift in Metall verglichen; borgt nicht auch hier das Volkstümliche die Maske des Höfischen?

1) Die Heilige Schrift des Alten Testaments übersetzt und herausgegeben, 2. Ausgabe, 1896.

2) Palästinischer Diwan als Beitrag zur Volkskunde Palästinas gesammelt und mit Übersetzung und Melodien herausgegeben von Gustav H. Dalman, Leipzig 1901.

3) Neuarabische Volkspoesie gesammelt und übersetzt von Enno Littmann: Abhandlungen d. K. Ges. d. Wiss. zu Göttingen. Phil.-hist. Kl. N. F. Band 5, 3.

4) W. Max Müller, Die Liebespoesie der alten Ägypter, Leipzig 1899.

HL. mit Theokrit[1]), der zeitlich und, da er längere Zeit in Ägypten weilte, auch örtlich dem Dichter desselben nahe stand. Die streitige Frage, wer Geber und wer Empfänger war, verliert an Wichtigkeit bei Erwägung, daß der einzelne Dich=ter, im Altertum immer wenig originell, vom poetischen Styl seines Zeitalters und seiner Zone beherrscht wird.

Im Folgenden gebe ich die Anfänge einer Parallelen=Sammlung, indem ich das bereits in meinen Studien in arabischen Dichtern IV gedruckte Material, so weit es sich nicht lediglich um Zurückweisung von Falschem handelt, wieder=hole und auch gelegentlich erklärende Einzelbemerkungen ande=rer Art an dieser Stelle einschalte:

1, 5.   Vrgl. Theokrit, 10, 26 ff.

Βομβύκα χαρίεσσα, Σύραν καλέοντί τυ πάντες,
ἰσχνὰν ἁλιόκαυστον, ἐγὼ δὲ μόνος μελίχλωρον.
καὶ τὸ ἴον μέλαν ἐστὶ καὶ ἁ γραπτὰ ὑάκινθος,
ἀλλ᾽ ἔμπας ἐν τοῖς στεφάνοις τὰ πρᾶτα λέγονται.

Über Salmâ f. oben S. 17, der Parallelismus ohôlê — jerî'ôt — auch Habakuk 3, 7.

1, 6.   schecharchôret schwärzlich. Die Reduplikation der zweiten Silbe bei Adjektiven der Farbe wie ădamdâm rötlich, jeraqraq grünlich entspricht der Verdoppelung, welche das Türkische im Anlaut dieser Adjektiva ein=treten läßt wie kap kara, bem bejas, ap ak, maz mavi ⁊c., mit dem Unterschied, daß hier eine Steige=rung des Begriff's, im Hebräischen eine Herabminde=rung desselben bewirkt wird.

1, 7.   'ôtejâ. Daß sich die Buhlerinnen vermummen, wird Genesis 38 berichtet. Zu einer Textveränderung liegt demnach kein Grund vor. Wahrscheinlich hängt die Sitte wiederum mit der Verschleierung der Braut zu=sammen (vrgl. S. 20).

---

1) Vrgl. Eclogae regis Salomonis. Interprete Joanne Theophilo Lessingio correctore scholae Pirnensis, Lipsiae 1777.

1, 8. hai-jâfâ (o Schöne), genau entsprechend der Anrede der Braut mit jâ meliĥa (o Schöne) von Seiten der sie abholenden Freunde des Bräutigams: Dalman S. 187. — seî lâk geĥ doch, wie türkisch bak sana sieĥ doch ꝛc.; ebenso demê-lekâ: 2, 17 (vrgl. S. 9 3. 5). Sie soll den Spuren der Heerde als göttlicher Rechtleitung (arab. hidâje) folgen, nach dem weit über den Orient hinaus verbreiteten Volksglauben an deren unmittelbarste Wirkung in den Tieren. Aus zahlreichen Beispielen, die das arabische Altertum bietet, sei nur an Muĥammed's Einzug in Medîna erinnert, der seiner Kamelin es überließ das Haus anzuzeigen, in welchem er absteigen sollte: Ibn Hischâm ed. Wüstenfelb I S. 336.

1, 9. Der Vergleich eines schönen Mädchens mit einem Roß findet sich auch bei den Arabern z. B. al-A‘schà's Mu‘allaqa Vers 2. 1001 Nacht schildert (Ausgabe Bûlâq 1251 h. 1. Band S. 55, 19. Nacht) die Aufzäumung eines Maultiers und sagt: fa-sârat kaannahâ ‘arûs maglîja (da wurde es, als ob es eine geschmückte Braut). Über die den Arabern ganz gewöhnliche Metapher „Kamel" für Geliebte s. mein Beduinenleben[2] S. 62 ff. Auffallend bleibt immerhin die enge Berührung mit den Versen Theokrit's 18, 30, 31 (Hochzeitslied der Helena):

ἢ κάπῳ κυπάρισσος ἢ ἅρματι Θεσσαλὸς ἵππος·
ὧδε καὶ ἁ ῥοδόχρως Ἑλένα Λακεδαίμονι κόσμος.

„Wagen des Pharao" war dem hebräischen Dichter eine aus dem Pentateuch geläufige Vorstellung vrgl. z. B. Gen. 41, 43; der Bräutigam kann sich als Salomo Pharaowagen beilegen mit Bezug auf I. Kön. 10, 28 ff.

1, 12. Paul Haupt belegt den Sinn von mêsab an dieser Stelle durch Talmud, Sabbat fol. 63ᵃ.

2, 6. Ein ähnlicher Parallelismus findet sich 1001 Nacht ed. Bûlâq 1251 h. S. 153:

> „Ich sagte ihr Lebewohl, während meine rechte Hand meine Tränen trocknete und meine linke Hand sie drückte und umhalste."

2, 7 u. 9. Die unrichtige Parallele bei Magnus und andern habe ich bereits Studien in arab. Dichtern IV S. 20/1 zurückgewiesen. — Das min Vers 9, welches Budde „sehr auffallend" findet, steht so wie 5, 4.

2, 12. Zur Stimme der Turteltaube vrgl. das altägyptische Lied 14 bei W. Max Müller und dessen Bemerkungen dazu, ferner Dalman S. 255 Z. 2.

2, 14. Warum sich Siegfried über das Masculinum 'âréb wundert, ist mir unverständlich, da qôl Masculinum ist.

2, 15. Vrgl. Theokrit 1, 48 ff., 5, 112/3.

3, 1—4. Eine ähnliche Scene liegt vielleicht in dem altägyptischen Liebeslied, W. Max Müller 12 vor, wenn man von den Ergänzungen des Herausgebers absieht. Vrgl. auch 14 daselbst. — Die nächtliche Patrouille scheint zum Inventar der orientalischen Erotik zu gehören vrgl. z. B. Hâfiz ed. Brockhaus Nr. 310, 5.

4, 2ᵇ. Siegfried: „Wie öfters im AT... ist hier vom Dichter das Bild über das tertium comparationis hinaus weiter geführt." Ich glaube, Siegfried hat die Beziehung nicht verstanden. Der Halbvers will besagen, im Munde findet sich keine Zahnlücke, jedem Zahn des Unterkiefers entspricht ein solcher im Oberkiefer: je zwei entsprechende Zähne sind als Zwillingslämmer oder als Mutterschaf und Lamm verbildlicht.

4, 3. Vrgl. Hans Stumme, Tripolitanisch-tunesische Beduinenlieder, Leipzig 1894 S. 106.

4, 9. Vrgl. 'Antara's Mu'allaqa ed. Arnold Vers 13ᵃ: ich tastabkâ bi-dâi ẓurúbir wa-l-llin

(als sie dich gefangen nahm durch einen Schärfe enthaltenden, glänzendweißen [Mund]).

4, 16. Nach Gesenius-Kautzsch, Hebräische Grammatik[27] S. 397
sind *sâfôn* und *têmân* weiblich, weil sie „räumlich
Umgrenztes bezeichnen". Ein Behälter wird allerdings
im Semitischen gerne als Mutterleib aufgefaßt; deshalb sind Feminina z. B. arab. ka's (Becher), bi'r
(Brunnen), delw (Schöpfeimer). Die meisten von
Kautzsch unter obige Rubrik gebrachten Begriffe gehören aber nicht dorthin; die Stadt z. B. ist offenbar
deshalb weiblich, weil sie als Mutter ihrer Bewohner
gilt und wenn irgend etwas nicht umgrenzt ist, so
sind es die Himmelsrichtungen. Die einzelnen Wind-
arten werden auch bei den Arabern weiblich gedacht.
Der konkretere Begriff der Windart war aber für den
Naturmenschen gewiß wichtiger als der durch dasselbe
Wortbild dargestellte der entsprechenden Himmelsgegend.

5, 1. Siegfried übersetzt: „Ich pflücke mir Myrrhe mit Balsam" l. „Ich sammle meine Myrrhe sammt meinem
Balsam. — Über „*laḥḥemû ed-ḍijâf* (versieht die Gäste
mit Fleisch)" als Kommando beim paläftinischen Hochzeitsschmaus s. F. A. Klein: ZDPV. VI 1883 S. 98.

5, 6. Siegfried: „Ich war ganz außer mir, als er sprach"
giebt keinen Sinn, da er fort ist; be zeigt den Grund
an: „über seine Rede, weil ich seine Stimme ver-
nommen hatte". — *nafschî jâseâ*, sonst vom Sterben
(Gen. 35, 18); so kann der Araber sagen: qad qatalanî
mich hat arg mitgenommen eig. mich hat getödtet:
Arnold's Chrestomathia Arabica I S. 46 Z. 7.

5, 7. Winckler, Altorientalische Forschungen I, 3 S. 293:
„Allgemein wird gefaßt: es fanden mich die Wächter
und schlugen mich, während doch ein Bedingungssatz
vorliegt: Wenn mich finden — so werden mich schlagen".
Zunächst würde ich lieber sagen: „Wenn mich gefunden hätten — so hätten mich geschlagen 2c." Die

Ausführung des Bildes im Folgenden macht jedoch die Bedingung unwahrscheinlich, der Vergleich mit der Parallelstelle 3, 3 zeigt die Unmöglichkeit einer solchen Konstruktion.

5, 10. Sach we-âdôm. Vrgl. Klagelieder 4, 7 [v. Orelli, Hohes Lied: Hauck's Realencyklopädie.]

5, 11. Da die Araber die Haare der Geliebten mit Dattelrispen vergleichen (Belege in meinem Beduinenleben[2] S. 46/7), schlug bereits Magnus (Kritische Bearbeitung und Er= klärung des Hohen Liedes Salomo's S. 134/5) für das ἄπαξ λεγόμενον taltallîm die Übersetzung „Dattel= rispen" vor. Beachte auch Lisân al-'Arab: „Und taltala ist ein Trinkgefäß von der Scheibe des Palm= blütenstandes, aus dem man Dattelwein trinkt."

5, 13. „Balsambeete, die Gewürze treiben" in Kautzsch' Über= setzung (Baethgen) sind ein Unding. — Maqqarî II S. 397 Z. 18 [Haupt.]

5, 14. Jâd scheint hier wie bisweilen arab. jad Arm zu be= deuten (vrgl. 5, 4). — „Elfenbeinmasse" bei Sieg= fried ist misverständlich, da wir darunter eine Misch= ung verstehn, deren Hauptbestandteil Gyps bildet.

5, 15. „Seine Schenkel sind Säulen von weißem Marmor basirt auf goldene Sockel". 'Amr nennt in seiner Mu'allaqa Vers 18 die Beine seiner Geliebten „zwei Säulen aus Kalkstein oder weißem Marmor, es klingt das Rasseln ihres Schmuckes ein Erklingen"

wa-sârijatai balanṭin au ruẋâmin jarinnu ẋuschâschu ḥaljihima 'r-ranînâ.

Auch 1001 Nacht (ed. 1311 h. III S. 286, ed. Ha= bicht 5. Band S. 312) vergleicht die Schenkel eines Mädchens mit Marmorsäulen 'awâmîd ruẋâm.

6, 2. Zu der öfters wiederkehrenden Vorstellung der Ge= liebten unter dem Bilde eines Gartens verweise ich noch auf 1001 Nacht ed. 1311 h. III S. 287, ed.

Habicht 5. Band S. 313, woselbst ein Mädchen von sich die Verse rezitirt:

Jaqûlûna fi 'l-bustâni wardum musaffafun, wa-mâ warduhu χaddî wa-lâ γusnuhu qaddî,

Idhâ kâna mithlî fi 'l-basâtîni 'indahu, famâdha 'lladhî qad gâ'a jaṭlubuhu 'indî

(Man sagt im Garten gibt es Rosen in Reihen, aber nicht ist seine [des Gartens] Rose [wie] meine Wange und nicht sein Zweig mein Wuchs,

Wenn es meinesgleichen in den Gärten bei ihm gäbe, was kommt er denn sie bei mir zu suchen.)

6, 10. kemô schâchar wie das Morgenrot. Dalman S. 193: 'arûsetu nûr es-sabâḥ (seine Braut ist das Licht des Morgens). Ebendaselbst unmittelbar vorher wird die Braut mit der Sonne, der Bräutigam mit dem Mond verglichen, während HL. 6, 10 beide Bilder für die Braut gebraucht. Vrgl. auch Theokrit 18, 26.

6, 12. Vrgl. Dalman S. 255 Z. 13/14.

7, 1ᵇ. korrespondirt als Einleitungsfrage des wasf mit 5, 9.

7, 2. bat nâdîb. Bei Dalman S. 190 heißt es von der Braut: hî ḥelwe wibnat agwâd (sie ist lieblich und Tochter von Edlen) und ebend. S. 255 l. Z. und S. 256 Z. 1 wird sie bint il-akbâr (die Tochter von Vornehmen) genannt.

7, 3. Zum ersten Halbvers vrgl. 1001 Nacht ed. 1311 h. III S. 286: wa-surra tasa' ûqîjat misk ṭîb al-ardân, zum zweiten „dein Bauch ist wie ein Weizenhaufen umhegt mit Lilien" vrgl. 'Abîd b. al-Abras (Muχtârât S. 105 V. 10): wa-kathîbum mâ kâna taḥta 'l-ḥiqâbi „und ein Sandhaufen ist, was unter dem Gürtel", worunter wir nach dem Rand-Kommentar das Gesäß zu verstehn haben. Farbe und Rundung bilden hier wol den Vergleichungspunkt. Der Unterschied erklärt sich natur= gemäß daraus, daß dem Ackerbauer die Vorstellung des Weizens, dem Wüstenbewohner die des Sandes näher lag. — Paul Haupt a. a. O. S. 68: „Thoma, Ein Ritt in's gelobte Land (Berlin, 1887), p. 40 (quoted in Stickel, Das Hohelied, Berlin 1888 p. 184), states that it is still customary to put lilies or anemones around heaps of grains of wheat in order to scare off birds." Thoma schildert allerdings in der mittlerweile (1900) erschienenen mir allein zugänglichen 2. Auflage seines genannten Buches S. 45/6 diese Sitte mit anderer Motivirung („teils zur Zier, teils um wahrzunehmen, ob nicht unberufene Hände an der mühsam erworbenen reinen Frucht sich vergreifen") und ohne Bezug auf die Gegenwart. Sein Buch beabsichtigt nämlich, wie der Titel besagt, eine Darstellung von „Land und Leuten in Palästina vor 3000 Jahren", und es ist fraglich, ob hier wirkliche Reisebeobachtung oder lediglich phantasievolle Rekonstruktion zu Grunde liegt.

7, 5. Dein Hals ist wie ein Turm aus Elfenbein „ke-migdal hasch-schên". Winckler will mit Rücksicht auf das folgende „wie der Turm des Libanon" „ke-migdal has-Senîr" lesen, was daran scheitert, daß Senîr niemals den Artikel hat vrgl. z. B. HL. 4, 8. Sodann ist gegen Winckler's Behauptung [1]): „Der „Elfenbeinturm" ist sinnlos und verdankt seine Existenz nur der Erinnerung an das bêt hasch-schên I. Kön. 22, 39" zunächst an die „Elfenbeinpaläste": Psalm 45, 9 zu erinnern. Ferner würde die Nichtexistenz einer Sache noch immer nicht die Unmöglichkeit ihrer Verwendung im Vergleich beweisen. Die goldenen edelsteinbesetzten Walzen z. B., welche 5, 14 mit den Armen des Geliebten vergleicht, werden sich auch in Wirklichkeit kaum nachweisen lassen; und ebenso malt der Araber häufig

---

[1] Altorientalische Forschungen I 3 S. 293.

im Streben nach Veranschaulichung der Ähnlichkeit
den Vergleichsgegenstand zu einem mixtum compositum
aus, das jeder realen Existenz entbehrt. — Als Pa=
rallele zitirt Graetz [1] „Anakreons Ode 29 ἐλεφάν-
τινος τράχηλος", doch findet sich der Ausdruck nicht
Ode 29, sondern ed. Rose 17, 29. Vrgl. auch ‘Amr's
Mu‘allaqa ed. Lyall Vers 13. — „Deine Augen sind
Teiche zu Cheschbôn". Tarafa vergleicht Mu‘allaqa
ed. Lyall Vers 31 die Augen seiner Kamelin mit
Wasserspiegeln; s. ferner 5, 12.

7, 6. Dallâ wird auch hier nicht Haupthaar, Locke, sondern
der eingeflochtene Faden sein. Lane, Sitten und Ge=
bräuche der heutigen Egypter, übers. von Zenker III
S. 211/2 beschreibt die Haartracht der Ägypterinnen
als aus 11—25 Flechten bestehend: „Dreimal so viel
schwarzseidene Schnuren (drei an jeder Haarflechte,
und jedesmal drei am Ende zusammengeflochten) von
16—18 Zoll Länge werden ungefähr zu einem Vier=
teil der Länge mit dem Haar zusammengeflochten, und
an einer Kante oder einem Bande von schwarzer Seide
befestigt, welches rund um den Kopf gebunden wird
und dann ganz getrennt von den Haarflechten herab=
hängt, die es beinahe versteckt. Diese Schnuren wer=
den „qaitân" genannt." Durch den Parallelismus von
kâ-argâmân (wie Purpur) wird für kak-Karmel (wie
der Karmel), obwohl ich hierzu früher arab. asch‘ar
„stark behaart, bewaldet" verglich, das späthebräische
in der Chronik vorkommende kak-karmîl (wie Kar=
moisin) sehr wahrscheinlich; dann wäre das erste rôschêk
entweder verschrieben oder vor demselben ein Wort
ausgefallen. Vermutlich ist an eine rote Kopfbedeckung
zu denken, wie sie schwarzhaarige Völker lieben vrgl.
z. B. Löbel, Hochzeitsgebräuche in der Türkei S. 135. —

1) Schir ha-schirim S. 195.

Den rehâtîm liegt vielleicht das Bild der Vogelfalle
zu Grunde, vrgl. jedoch das Lied an die Braut,
Dalman S. 258: sabâ gedâil tisbîna (sieben Zöpfe
nahmen uns gefangen). Dem Bilde der Vogelstellerei
begegnen wir in der islâmischen und altägyptischen
Erotik, bei W. Max Müller Lied 10 und 11; offen=
bar ist die gefangene Wildgans in 10 das Mädchen
selbst; wäre es eine wirkliche Wildgans, wie Müller
meint, so brauchte das Mädchen ja nicht mit leeren
Händen zu seiner Mutter heimzukehren.

7, 9: „und der Duft deines Mundes wie Äpfel". Vrgl.
al-'Abbâs b. al-Aẖnaf: Aɣânî VIII S. 19:

„dhaẖartuki bit-tuffaẖi, lammâ schamamtuhu"

(ich denke dein in Folge des Apfels, nachdem ich ihn
roch . . .),

ferner Ḥassân b. Thâbit, Dîwân Bombay 1281 S. 7
Z. 25/6 ꝛc.

7, 10: „Dein Gaumen ist wie Würzwein", wozu man bereits 5, 1
vergleiche. Zur Übersetzung „Würzwein" s. D. H. Müller:
Aus dem Anzeiger der philosophisch=historischen Classe
vom 23. April (Jahrg. 1902, Nr. X) separat abge=
druckt. 'Abîd (Muẖtârât S. 96 Vers 9): „als ob
ihr Speichel nach dem Schlaf zum Abendtrunk genom=
men hätte rötlichen klaren (Wein) mit Moschus ver=
siegelten." In islâmischer Zeit erscheint der verbotene
Wein seltener in diesem Bilde; in 1001 Nacht heißt
es z. B. von einem schönen Mädchen: „und ihr Spei=
chel war süßer als gullâb" (Enîs el-gelîs ed. A. de
Biberstein-Kazimirsky, Paris 1846 S. 8); gullâb
(Rosenwasser) bezeichnet hier eine Art Scherbet. —
Die Lesart der LXX, durch welche der Schluß des
Verses erst verständlich wird, lautete nicht, wie Sieg=
fried angiebt, sefâchî we-schinnai [am Versschluß zu
dem schinnâi], sondern sefâtai we-schinnîm, was wie=
derum nicht mit Baethgen (in Kautzsch' Übersetzung,

2. Aufl. Beilagen, S. 85), in sefâtajim we-schinnâjim, sondern in sefâtajim we-schinnîm zu korrigiren ist.

7, 14. Magnus: „Eine ähnliche Verbindung findet sich in Kosegarten's Arab. Chrest. S. 117 Z. 9, wo es heißt: „al-fâkihatu 'r-raṭbatu wal-jâbisu"."

8, 2: „ich würde dir zu trinken geben vom Würzewein, von der Muß meiner Granate". Auch in der Mu'allaqa des Imruulqais ed. Lyall Vers 81 wird gewürzter, eigentlich „gepfefferter" Wein genannt. Zur Granat= muß vrgl. 1001 Nacht, Bûlâq 1251 I S. 67 (23. Nacht): „da schöpfte *H*asan Bedreddîn eine Schale voll Granatkerne mit Mandeln und Zucker zubereitet und sie aßen zusammen" und Rosenmüller a. a. O. IV S. 201.

8, 6: „Lege mich wie einen Siegelring auf dein Herz". Schon häufig ist auf Gen. 38 verwiesen, vrgl. auch Vámbéry, Sittenbilder aus dem Morgenlande S. 12: „und mit Widerwillen greift er nach dem auf der nackten Brust befindlichen, die verschiedenen Siegel enthaltenden seidenen Säckchen, das selbst vor den eigenen Kindern verborgen gehalten, auch bei Nacht nicht vom Leibe entfernt wird".

Diese Parallelen entstammen zum Teil alten Notizen, und ich vermochte nicht immer, die Originale wiedereinzusehen, um z. B. die Zitate aus 1001 Nacht auf eine Ausgabe zu reduziren, was bei den Differenzen derselben wol auch unmöglich gewesen wäre. Es sei noch davor gewarnt, bei Anklängen sofort wirkliche Zusammenhänge oder gleiche Entstehungsgeschichte vorauszusetzen. Als Hauptzweck dieser Parallelen, den sie freilich erst bei reichlicher Mehrung erfüllen können, erscheint mir vielmehr, sichere Anhaltspunkte durch Belege des wirklich Vorkommenden zu bieten. Wie sehr das Not thut, könnte ich leicht an einer umfangreichen Litteratur, über die ich geschwiegen habe, zeigen.

Druck der Universitäts-Buchdruckerei von E. Th. Jacob in Erlangen.

Lightning Source UK Ltd.
Milton Keynes UK
UKHW020216030119
334668UK00005B/221/P

SEVEN BLACK MEN:

An ecological study of education and parenting

This book is dedicated to my parents Corinne and Cecil who met and fell in love on the banana boat that brought them both from Jamaica to England in 1953.

Special thanks are owed: to my editors Dr Barbara Spender and Fiona Thornton; to Miles Bailey and Stefan Proud my publishing mentors; to my friends and family and of course, the seven men whose histories intertwine with mine to form the heart of this book.

SEVEN BLACK MEN:

An ecological study of education and parenting

Dr Jan McKenley

Aduma Books

Published by **Aduma Books**
PO Box 2496
Bristol BS8 9AH
Tel: 44 (0) 117 925 0068
www.adumabooks.co.uk

British Library Cataloguing in Publication Data
A catalogue record for this book is available from the British Library

ISBN-13: 978-0-9551558-0-2
ISBN-10: 0–9551558-0-0

Cover design by
Stefan Proud, Hazel Design (www.hazeldesign.co.uk)

Produced by
Action Publishing Technology Ltd, Gloucester.

Aduma Books is a trademark of McKenley-Simpson Ltd which holds
exclusive rights for the manufacture and export of this book.

Contents

List of Figures

Under the most difficult of conditions and from imperfect materials that they surely would not have selected if they had been able to choose, these oppressed groups have built complex traditions of politics, ethics, identity and culture. The currency of 'race' has marginalized these traditions from official histories of modernity ...

(Paul Gilroy, *Between Camps: nations, cultures and the allure of race*, 2000:17)

Parental involvement in the form of 'at-home good parenting' has a significant positive effect on children's achievement and adjustment even after all other factors shaping attainment have been taken out of the equation.

(Professor Charles Desforges, School of Education, Cambridge University, 2005)

I think that there are not only specific, inherited chararcteristics but also fundamentals that are almost universally present in any age and any race – that's what gives me hope for the future; the destruction of prejudice is not going to be achieved by respecting differences (because that's too difficult an intellectual/emotional leap for most of us) but by recognising what we have in common, for example, love for our families, dreams, aspirations etc and the same range of physical and emotional possibilities.

(Dr Barbara Spender in correspondence, June 2005)

Introduction

The motivation to write this book was personal as well as professional. Racism has had a pervasive and corrosive impact on most black lives, particularly when we allow its negative messages to undermine our sense of who we are, what we are capable of, and our potential for making a significant difference in this, our country. But it is not the only narrative of our experience; most of us also have powerful and joyful histories, which bear witness to our heritage: the courage of our parents as economic migrants, our intergenerational aspirations to secure a better life for our children as well as ourselves, our triumphs and our struggle for social justice. I wanted to represent that different legacy.

The material was drawn from three sources: the historical research and the biographical interviews which I conducted for my doctoral study; my personal experiences as the child of Caribbean immigrants; and my subsequent experience as a parent of a daughter educated in London schools from 1987 to 2001. This book examines the extent to which the values of a 'good' education have been transmitted across three generations of black Caribbean settlement in London since 1950 and how effectively those values translated into parenting behaviours. It draws on Bronfenbrenner's (1979) ecological theory of human development to look at the experience of education and parenting of seven black men, who were educated, as second-generation immigrants, in London schools during the 1960s and early 1970s.

The first part seeks to contextualise the interplay between immigration and education policies and the experience of institutional racism in the education system through the men's lived experience as pupils.

The second part considers how those men, as fathers, exercised parental choice in the late 1980s and 1990s, and their involvement in supporting their children in English schools. Drawing on the findings from the original study, aspects of the current parenting discourse are racialised to extend our knowledge of black Caribbean 'choosing' (Gewirtz et al, 1995) – how black parents exercise parental choice; and the styles and strategies they deploy to offset the ongoing impact of institutional racism and structural inequalities on the self-esteem of black Caribbean children (Gillborn and Youdell, 2000).

The final chapter considers the implications for teachers who wish to respond constructively to the largely unmet challenges of black Caribbean pupils and their families for social justice in education.

The rationale for an ecological study

Fifty years after the docking of the SS *Empire Windrush* with four hundred economic migrants from the English-speaking Caribbean and some two, even three generations later, black Caribbean pupils are still seen as educational under-performers who pose problems of behaviour and discipline. This is evident in the consistently low numbers of pupils of Caribbean origin gaining 'the gold standard of five or more GCSE grades A*–C including English, mathematics and science' (see Clements, 1995).[1] According to recent research findings (Parsons et al, 2005) commissioned by the Department for Education and Skills, black Caribbean pupils are just over three times as likely as their white counterparts to be permanently excluded from school. Of major significance is the fact that black Caribbean boys and girls enter primary schools and perform well by comparison with their peers by the end of Key Stage 1, but thereafter, boys' attainment in particular, consistently declines relative to their peers and more worryingly, against their earlier assessed potential.

It is my contention that answers to these concerns will continue to be elusive whilst the contribution of black Caribbean pupils and their families is so under-researched (Tomlinson, 1983; Channer, 1995), and the body of research devoted to the *successful* achievement of immigrant pupils (and their descendants) remains small (Channer, 1995; Williams, 1995; Nehaul, 1996; OFSTED 2002; McKenley et al, 2003). The absence of a significant body of educational research from a black Caribbean or black British perspective (for recent exceptions, see Mirza, 1992: Williams, 1995; Channer, 1995; Nehaul, 1996: Sewell, 1997) is in the face of long-standing and clearly articulated concerns expressed as early as 1965 by West Indian community organisations about educational under-achievement and the disproportionate numbers of West Indian pupils in special schools (Coard, 1971) – concerns rehearsed in submissions to a series of inquiries held by the Parliamentary Select Committee on Race Relations and Immigration from 1969 onwards.

Explanations for the under-performance of black Caribbean pupils initially came from a social anthropological paradigm (Patterson, 1963; Morrish, 1971). Patterson's (1963) study of West Indian settlement in Lambeth is typical of the prevailing view that the educational aspirations of immigrant parents were unquestionably unrealistic, immature and inappropriate. Little respect was accorded to the cultural identities and values that immigrant families brought with them from the Caribbean, particularly their strong regard for education as a passport to economic mobility. Their aspirations for themselves and their children were infantilised and for the most part deprecated.

This book considers those early parental aspirations through the lives of seven black men and their parents as a significant and powerful discourse within Caribbean immigrant families. Through their accounts as parents we learn how the experiences of institutional racism and inequalities within the education system informs black parenting. We learn how black Caribbean parents exercise 'race'-informed choosing (Gewirtz, Ball and Bowe, 1995; Crozier, 2001) in their search for an equitable education for their children.

Few researchers have ventured into the minefield of identifying external environmental factors, such as home background, the quality of parental interventions and involvement in school as critical factors in the educational performance of black Caribbean pupils; since previous attempts to do so have drawn accusations of racism. Countering the historic hostility of the black Caribbean community to research, which appears to seek psychological, rather than educational explanations, is no easy task. As late as 1981 Professor Peter Mortimer, then Head of the Research & Statistics branch of the Inner London Education Authority (ILEA) submitted draft proposals to the Swann Inquiry to investigate the characteristics of successful black students using two groups of British-born students with family backgrounds from the West Indies and the Indian sub-continent, who had obtained five or more O level grades. However, these were dropped amid strong criticism from black and ethnic minority groups. Delsol's critical response was typical of the suspicion that such studies have engendered among black Caribbean groups. He argued that the study would 'lead to the blaming of the ills of the system on black students and their families' (quoted in the Afro Caribbean Education Resource (ACER) Follow Up Groups Report to Swann Inquiry, 1982). Nevertheless, the view that environmental factors are significant continues to hold sway, partly because the majority of successful pupils, regardless of their ethnic origin, would cite home background as a key factor.

The exhortation to schools to move beyond the school gates to engage more meaningfully with the communities they serve is enshrined in the recent *Every Child Matters* policy (Children Act, 2004). Schools are now accountable as part of a network of services for delivering five outcomes for children: being healthy; staying safe; enjoying and achieving; making a positive contribution and achieving economic well-being. Reconfiguring the boundaries between parental involvement in schools and school involvement in parenting has never been more pressing and problematic.

Policies to engage black Caribbean parents, particularly in the support of their children in secondary education, have only recently been a focus of government policy. *Aiming High* – as the Government's consultation in 2003 on the efficacy of the Ethnic Minority Achievement Grant is known – was tacit recognition that successive policies to raise the achievement of some ethnic minority groups, including black Caribbean pupils, had failed. Since then two pilot initiatives (Aiming High: African Caribbean Achievement Pilot and Key Stage 3 Ensuring the Attainment of Black Caribbean Boys) to raise the achievement of pupils of Caribbean heritage have operated, both with a commitment to increase the participation of black parents. The learning from both pilots underpins a new approach delivered through the National Strategies; the Black Pupils' Achievement Project will run in over eighty secondary schools nationally.

Designing an ecological study

Cross-generational or longitudinal biographies, family histories over time, systematic attention to transformation of cultural themes would all be useful approaches. (Finkelstein, 1983:314)

My reading of the literature on the educational achievement of black Caribbean families in England revealed a long expressed need for more longitudinal, generational studies to examine the phenomenon of black Caribbean under-attainment over a longer time frame. As early as 1982 the Afro Caribbean Education Resource (ACER) Project in their submission to the Rampton Enquiry: *Racism and the Black Child* reported that the key to successful or unsuccessful educational achievement in black families of Caribbean heritage was complex and required a broad focus. This study was a response to that plea and to Finkelstein's proposition for cross-generational research (1983). Her contention that very little is known about the intergenerational effects or consequences on immigrant families of educational processes that were intended to 'de-tribalize the young' (Finkelstein, 1983:310) remains the case. Finkelstein poses a number of critical questions about how the experience of education transformed relationships in immigrant families. She wonders, for example, whether 'arguments between parents and children were intensified by the experience of children in school or were generational relationships cemented and revalidated?' (op cit). Finkelstein argues for the importance of looking beyond power and structures in studying urban educational history and suggests that answers to such questions will require 'the exploration of data that will reveal the educational experience of children within families, churches and neighbourhoods, as well as within schools' (op cit).

Further reading demonstrated that the role of black parents in supporting their children's academic achievement in secondary education was under-researched, particularly from the viewpoint of fathers. Dr Tony Sewell has written extensively on the 'crisis' of under-achievement of black Caribbean boys and his belief that there is 'an anti-education culture' in the black Caribbean community evident in the fact that:

So many black boys are brought up in fatherless families, which deprive them of other masculine role models. (Sewell, *Sunday Times*, December 2002)

However Majors and Mancini-Billson contend:

With few exceptions, social scientists have tended to ignore middle-income, educated and successful black males. They have tended to neglect father-present families and to ignore the positive aspects of a male's presence, even when he is not living in the household. (Majors and Mancini-Billson, 1992:106)

Most urban school ethnographies include sections or chapters on the parental backgrounds of minority ethnic pupils, but these are usually based on structured interviews and used by the authors to support or refute the impact of negative stereotypes and teachers' racism on black Caribbean pupils (see Smith and Tomlinson, 1989; Sewell, 1997). Channer's observation that the 'examination of British African Caribbean family culture from the viewpoint of the subjects has not been successfully explored' (Channer, 1995:85) is still relevant. There has been some qualitative research on the contribution of black parents to their children's education in England (see Williams, 1995 on the contribution of black mothers; Nehaul, 1996 on black parenting in general; Sewell, 1997 in the context of a discourse on black masculinities; Gewirtz et al, 1995 as part of a wider sample in their work on parental choice and Vincent, 2000 on parenting styles).

I wanted to design a study which would do justice to my belief that the disaffected black teenager can transform him or her-self in adulthood; disillusion is not inevitable. What seemed catastrophic at 14 looks very different in retrospect ten, fifteen, twenty years later. This was borne out by my professional experience of teaching and youth work in Hackney over a twenty-year period. Many of the students I worked with in boys' schools in the 1980s experienced disaffection and despair during their compulsory school years. Girls too experienced the same sense of alienation but their responses were different (see Fuller, 1980; Mirza, 1992; Mac an Ghaill 1988). However, my later meetings with those former male students as adults and parents confirmed how the opportunities for young women and men were radically changed by further education, employment and family responsibilities. Nevertheless, in conversations about education, many of those same fathers use their experiences as children to inform their perspective as parents, when their own children appear to be faltering educationally. It was the challenge to design a study that tried to mine this richer, deeper vein of generational complexity that led me to consider an ecological approach.

Bronfenbrenner's ecology of human development

In his book *The Ecology of Human Development: Experiments by Nature and Design* Bronfenbrenner outlined his basic theoretical concepts as a series of eleven definitions and one proposition, which built on the earlier work of Barker (1968) and Doyle (1978) in introducing the role of ecological approaches. Bronfenbrenner's work is dominated by two key research interests: firstly the extent to which human beings adapt to, tolerate and create the ecologies in which they live and grow. Arising from the first research interest was a particular focus on the ways in which the 'next generation' is brought up. A second key research interest was the extent to which public policy has the power to affect the well-being and development of human beings 'by determining the conditions of their lives' (Bronfenbrenner, 1979:xiii). This led Bronfenbrenner to focus his research efforts to change policies that could influence the lives of children and their families where, he perceived, the interface between developmental research and public policy is most critical. His central thesis is that:

> The ecology of human development involves the scientific study of the progressive, mutual accommodation between an active, growing human being and the changing properties of the immediate settings in which the developing person lives, as this process is affected by relations between these settings, and by the larger contexts in which the settings are embedded. (Bronfenbrenner, 1979:21)

Bronfenbrenner conceives of the ecological environment as a set of nested structures (Figure 1).

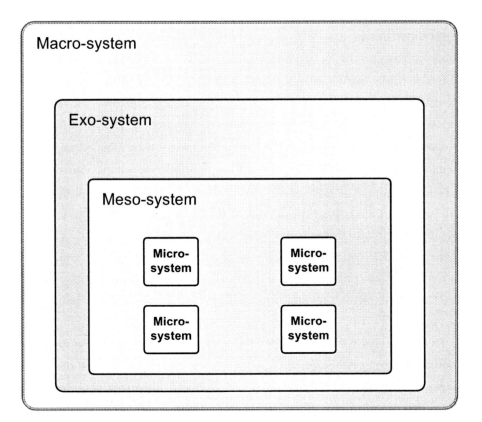

Figure 1: Bronfenbrenner's model of systemic influences (Thomas, 1992)

An alternative metaphor evoked by Bronfenbrenner is to see the individual's development as a set of 'Russian' dolls with each setting adding a layer of contextual experiences contributing to the individual's growth. However this metaphor infers a determinist approach, which does not capture the fluidity and increasing hybrid nature of identities, which form and re-form in the course of an individual life. I was more interested in the theoretical significance of overlapping contexts as they impinge on human development.

Adapting the ecological model

Figure 2 demonstrates how the model was modified for use in the study to look at the ecological environment of the formative adolescent years of the seven black men.

At the innermost level is the black Caribbean parent in the immediate setting of the home considered in two time frames, first as a child of immigrant parents, then later as a parent themselves. The next step is to look beyond the single settings to the relations between them. It is these inter-connections – the interplay between the school and the home – that Bronfenbrenner sees as having the decisive impact on development. The third level of the ecological environment goes beyond the immediate to settings in which the person is not even present, in this instance parents' employment, to explore the inter-connections between work, immigration, race relations and education policies. Bronfenbrenner contends that the extent to which parents can perform their child-rearing roles within the family depends on role demands, stresses and supports emanating from these other settings.

The same approach is adopted to explore the ecological environmental settings at play in the development of the seven men as parents and 'choosers' of secondary education, and the extent of their involvement in the education of their child at home and at school (Figure 3).

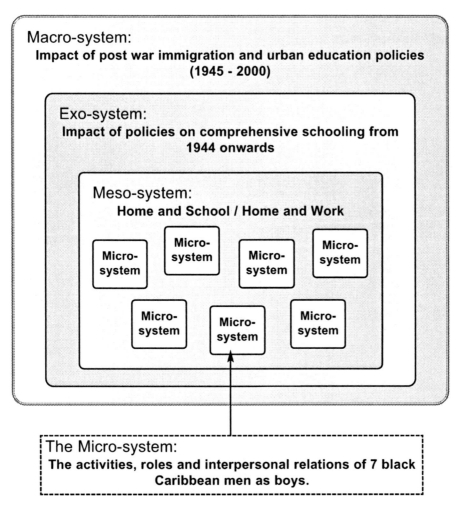

Figure 2: The ecological environment for the seven men as children of first-generation immigrant parents.

Of relevance and resonance is Bronfenbrenner's contention that 'within any culture or sub-culture, settings of a given kind – such as homes, streets, or offices – tend to be very much alike, whereas between cultures they are distinctly different' (op cit: 4). This struck a chord. Why, despite similar homes and schools, does the achievement of black Caribbean pupils continue to be variable and highly problematic? Poverty is not the overriding factor since there is no

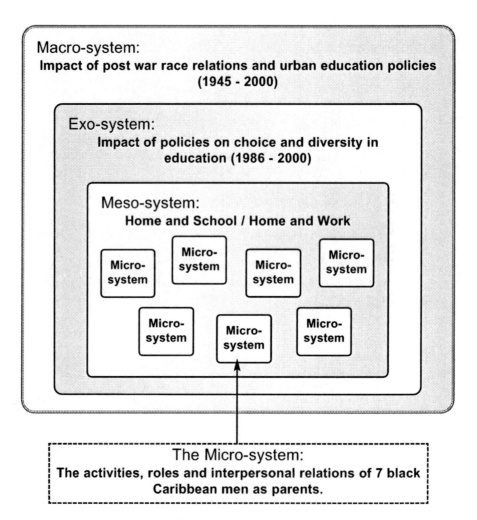

Figure 3: The ecological environment for the seven men as second-generation parents.

discernible difference in the achievement of black Caribbean pupils eligible for free school meals and their more advantaged counterparts (see PLASC data produced annually by the DfES). The detection of such wide-ranging differences becomes possible only if a model can be designed that permits these phenomena to be explored.

Few studies have followed the ecological approach outlined by Bronfenbrenner (1979); however Ogbu's (1974) ethnographic study of the interrelations between the school and other settings in the wider society in Burgherside – a community of predominantly black and Mexican-American families – comes closest to Bronfenbrenner's construct. Entitled *The Next Generation: An Ethnography of Education in an Urban Neighbourhood*, Ogbu's study of 'academic death at an early age' (Ogbu, 1974:147) was cited by Bronfenbrenner as 'truly an ecological study of school effectiveness at the level of both the meso- and exo-systems in which schools are embedded' (Bronfenbrenner, 1979:254). In his findings, Ogbu is careful to discriminate between the experiences of urban African-Americans – 'involuntary migrants' and the very different economic reality afforded to blacks of Caribbean heritage living in the US who are seen as hard working 'voluntary' migrants. It is the African-American children of Burgherside who perform poorly in school. Ogbu notes three typical explanations: cultural deprivation, weaknesses in schools and genetic inferiority; however he rejected these in favour of a fourth explanation. He demonstrates that school failure is an adaptation to the barriers of discrimination, occupational and social achievement; a response to those limited opportunities available to groups, whom Ogbu terms 'subordinate minorities', as opposed to their white middle class counterparts whom he calls 'taxpayers' to denote their superior power. Ogbu's conclusion that African-American pupils have internalised the lack of economic opportunity echoes Willis's earlier UK study of working class boys entitled *Learning to Labour*, published in 1977.

Kevin Marjoribanks (1980) used an ecological model in his work on ethnic families and children's achievements where he developed the concept of an 'ethclass' whose boundaries are stratified both horizontally into social status groups and vertically into ethnic groups. His research explored the relationship between the academic performance of different ethnic groups, the biographies of children, and the various settings that impact on their lives.

Marjoribanks's central thesis is the importance of analysing family learning environments when developing educational policies to address underachievement. He developed a theoretical tool for measuring the extent of support using the variable constructed earlier by Dave and others (see Marjoribanks, 1980:36) of 'presses'. Marjoribanks uses three 'presses' to measure parents' achievement orientations: first, the extent to which parents discuss their child's progress; second, the use of English within home and family reading habits and third, the extent to which parents expect that their children will become more self-reliant and independent.

Ogbu has developed a 'cultural ecological' theory (1981) to explain the underperformance of some minority groups in the US school system. He uses the concept of *the system* to depict the way minorities are treated and the factors affecting educational policies and pedagogy. He uses the term *community forces* to define a second set of factors to describe how minorities respond to their treatment in *the system*. Ogbu then analyses these forces and their implications for the schooling of minority groups. This 'cultural ecological' approach (1981) has been further refined by Ogbu's collaboration with Signithia Fordham in supervising her ethnographic doctoral study of a Washington DC school. Fordham applied the 'cultural ecological' model in her study of disaffection and alienation among African-American working class pupils in urban high schools. This was later published in 1996 under the title *Blacked Out: Dilemmas of Race, Identity and Success at Capital High* and is a study of how African-Americans at Capital High and in the wider community 'conceptualize and internalize the school experience' (Fordham, 1996:11).

Both Ogbu and Fordham confidently assert that racism is not the only determinant in defining why black working class American pupils do less well than their peers. But how relevant are these ecological studies to an English setting? I am not aware of any comparative studies on the correlation between the history of the black Caribbean community's settlement in Britain in the second half of the twentieth century and the experience of African-Americans whose descendants were brought against their will to the United States as part of the Atlantic slave trade.

However Fordham's description of the childrearing practices of the parents, 'how they connect with and abrogate the dominant imaging and imagining of African Americans' (op cit:11) does resonate and echoes concerns raised in the quote below.

We tended to expect that coloured children born in this country would grow up to be 'coloured English children', but this has seldom proved to be the case ... perhaps this is largely the consequence of 'second generation immigrants' being nurtured in home environments produced by 'first generation immigrants' and it may only be that when our 'second generation immigrants' establish their own homes they may be productive of coloured children who are more attuned to the cultural norm of this country. (Memorandum submitted by the National Association of Schoolmasters to the Select Committee on Race Relations & Immigration Fifth Enquiry on Education 1972–73:23).

Although Fordham does not cite Bronfenbrenner, she echoes his concerns about the psychological development of parents bringing up the next generation of African-Americans and their experiences in US public schools. In a chapter on 'Parenthood, Childrearing and Male Academic Success', she presents her findings on the interconnections between parenthood, childrearing and academic success in two separate chapters on female and male students. Fordham concludes:

Like the parents of female students, the parents of male students are impaled on a fulcrum of resistance. Consciously and unconsciously they teach their sons through the use of a particular linguistic code to survive by resisting claims regarding the Black Self; they teach them to both conform to and avoid socially defined race and gender roles. (Fordham, 1996; see also earlier studies by Willis (1977), Fuller (1980) and Mac an Ghaill (1998))

I was interested in exploring further how family learning environments are constructed in second-generation black British households (Marjoribanks, 1980).

Populating the settings – historical and archival research

Thompson, in his description of 'oral history' considers the 'difficulties of capturing the important elements in the inter-generational transmission of many families' (Thompson, 2000:302), which he acknowledges 'can take practical, cultural and emotional forms'. He makes a powerful claim:

It is only by tracing individual life-stories that connections can be documented between the general system of economic, class, sex, and age structure at one end, and the development of personal characters at the other, through the mediating influences of parents, brothers and sisters and the wider family, of peer groups and neighbours, school and religion, newspapers and the media, art and culture. (Thompson, 2000: 304)

The research plan for the study sought to model the multi-dimensional approach encapsulated in both Thompson's and Bronfenbrenner's conceptual frames. The aim was to generate rich archival and qualitative data on first-generation Caribbean immigrant life, particularly in relation to educational opportunity in the 1950s and 1960s and similarly for second-generation black

Caribbean parents in the late 1990s, which would populate the various settings identified earlier in Figures 2 and 3.

The study began with a chronological review of the early studies of Caribbean immigrants and their families, their reasons for leaving the Caribbean and the cultural identities they brought with them, and how settlement in London shaped and re-fashioned. A mixture of first level data sources was used: documentary data – primary and secondary sources found in local and national newspaper reports, Education Committee papers and LEA in-house publications concerning immigration and education matters; individual biographical accounts found through the survey of the literature and autobiographies of black Caribbean writers; case studies drawn from fiction – plays, films and novels.[2] These were then underpinned by a review of the most relevant studies on schooling, immigration and education policies, including parenting choice and parental involvement in schooling as they related to the experiences of black Caribbean pupils and their families.

In seeking to generate a deeper understanding of the different environments affecting black British Caribbean families, primary and secondary sources have been interwoven with the empirical data of the biographical accounts to model the interplay between those ecological settings in which the individual is directly involved (the micro-system and the meso-system) and those where they are not (the exo-system and the macro-system) .

Designing the life history interviews

The interviews were designed using McCracken's 'long interview' four-step model (McCracken, 1988): first an exhaustive review of the literature is conducted not only to immerse oneself in the field in order to create the relevant categories for the interview but also to create an appropriate distance from the interviewee. Second, a review of cultural categories is conducted using the self as an instrument of enquiry – I maintained a journal and reflected on my autobiography. Third, the construction of the life-history interview, which builds on the cultural categories developed in the first two steps. Fourth, the analysis of the qualitative data through the use of taped interviews and where possible verbatim transcripts. The schedule was ordered chronologically to add experiential data to the archival research I had already undertaken.

Researching subjects with racialised identities – terminology

The blurring of cultural identities and official classifications in terms of citizenship and nationality recur as a leitmotif throughout this book. The term **Caribbean** is used extensively to refer to the ten island countries of the English-speaking Caribbean region, namely: Antigua, Barbados, Dominica, Grenada, Jamaica, Montserrat, St Kitts & Nevis, St Lucia, St Vincent, Trinidad & Tobago, plus Guyana on the South American mainland (Nehaul, 1996:12). The term is highly problematic since most immigrants from this region conceive of their heritage as derived from the individual islands; the concept of a federal Caribbean has never taken hold among the islands themselves. **West Indian** poses a similar dilemma reflecting both the geographical and colonial designation of the islands and was widely used until the 1980s. Stuart Hall reflecting on the *Windrush* celebrations in a special edition of the journal 'Soundings' on his early experience of settlement in London wrote:

> I had met very few West Indian people other than Jamaicans before I came to London in 1951, when the black migrant presence was still extremely small … This *is* the paradigm diasporic experience. The plain fact is I became 'black' in London. (Hall, 1998:190)

As a matter of academic courtesy I reflected the definitions of my sources and did not attempt to impose any standardisation, hence the plethora of terms used in a study spanning fifty years. The term **coloured** was generally used to describe non-white British residents in the early period of West Indian migration to Britain in the post-Second World War period but was overtaken by the term **black** from the late 1960s onwards.

All these terms suggest a homogeneity, which does little justice to the increasingly complex and diverse British population. Like the identities they seek to represent, the descriptors of lived experience remain stubbornly fluid. I have deliberately used the wide range of definitions in contemporary usage to define the black British community during this period because non-white identities remain contested and deeply sensitive. My preferred self-definition and that of many younger black people is **black British,** which reflects the category in the 2001 national census. Nevertheless among my over-40 peers I am in a minority, the terms **African Caribbean** or **Afro Caribbean** are more widely used by both black British subjects of Caribbean heritage and in official terminology. I believe the experience of people of African heritage in this country is significantly different from their Caribbean counterparts and so the term **black Caribbean** is used to reflect the census categories in the Pupil Level Annual School Census collected annually by the DfES.

According to the national census data published by the Commission for Racial Equality (Connections, Spring 2003) the Black British population of Caribbean heritage comprises 1.1% of the total population of England and Wales. There is now an official designation of **Mixed**,[3] which is further broken down to include White and Black Caribbean; 0.5% of the population used this category in 2001.

The term **racism** is used to signal **racial prejudice and discrimination** but wherever possible, I specify the perpetrator/s and the victim/s, although this was not always easy to achieve. **Teacher racism** recurs as a theme or concern of researchers in this field but is often unspecified and to some extent has been overtaken by the term **institutional racism**, which has become more widely used since the inquiry into the death of Stephen Lawrence by Sir William Macpherson of Cluny (1999).

> Institutional racism consists of the collective failure of an organisation to provide an appropriate and professional service to people because of their colour, culture or ethnic origin. It can be seen or detected in the processes, attitudes and behaviour which amount to discrimination through unwitting prejudice, ignorance, thoughtlessness and racist stereotyping which disadvantage minority ethnic people. (Macpherson, 1999:321)

But I was also mindful of an earlier polemical definition by Humphry and John:

> Institutional racism – manipulating the bureaucratic system to outflank the unwanted. (Humphry and John, 1971:112)

Profile of the Seven Black Men

Seven biographical accounts of first- and second-generation education and parenting comprise the core of this book. The seven men either joined or were born to parents who had migrated to England in the 1950s and early 1960s. All are black Caribbean fathers who ranged between 40 and 48 years old when they were interviewed between 1997 and 1999. Three of the subjects were born in London while the other four were born in the Caribbean and came to England as primary-aged pupils. They joined fathers, who came from manual, unskilled backgrounds, although one was formerly a policeman in the Caribbean. Their mothers had held domestic service roles, such as seamstresses or caterers as well as housewives, but on arrival in England, with one exception, both parents secured employment in mainly low-skilled work in factories, or in public services. The experiences of the men in this study, both as sons and fathers, challenge the gender-stereotypes of black Caribbean families and deepen our understanding of the roles adopted by immigrant mothers and fathers.

ARRAN: 56^4 years old, born in Trinidad. His mother emigrated when Arran was 5 years old while his father stayed to look after the family. Arran came to England at 11. Arran has three children: two daughters aged 22 and 15 and a son aged 17. Arran is an Educational Psychologist and lives in a shire county in the south of England.

ERROL: 53 years old, born in St Lucia. Father emigrated first. Errol came to England with his mother and his siblings. Errol has one son aged 20. He is a freelance Management Consultant and lives in South London.

DEVON: 49 years old, born in Montserrat. Father emigrated to England first, followed by his mother in the early 1960s. Devon joined them a year later, aged 8. Devon has three sons aged 16, 14 and 11. He is Programme Director of a leadership organisation and lives in an outer London suburb.

DENNIS: 49 years old, born in London. His father emigrated from Jamaica first and joined his brother who was already in England in the early 1950s. Mother followed soon after. Dennis has a son aged 26 and a daughter aged 21. He is a Management Consultant and entrepreneur. He lives in South East London.

OWEN: 49 years old, born in Jamaica. His father emigrated first but was soon joined by his mother in the early 1950s. Owen came to

England at 8. He is father to four children and grandfather to one. He is a Librarian and lives in South London.

COLIN: 47 years old, born in London. His parents emigrated separately from Antigua; his father in 1955, mother in 1956. They met in Hackney. Colin is the father of two sons, aged 26 and 11. He is a Youth Project Manager and lives in East London.

CARL: 48 years old, born in London. His parents emigrated from Jamaica in 1950s; father first. He has a daughter aged 8 and a son of 6. He is a Senior Social Worker and lives in South East London.

The seven men attended one of the two London boys' secondary schools (High Towers and Home Beech) featured in this study from 1960 onwards; the youngest left school in 1976. Six are parents of children in compulsory education, although one has since educated his son at an alternative black school, which he helped to establish with other parents. I have included the professional role held by each of the men at the time of their interview. However this does little justice to the circuitous route by which some, but not all, came to their current employment. In common with many members of the black Caribbean community who were at school during the 1960s and 1970s, the men experienced first hand, or have close peers and family members who were involved in or touched by, the English criminal justice system. This rich hinterland was not the major focus of the original study, although clearly such experiences form part of their individual biographies and are central to their analyses of the interplay between institutional racism and equality of opportunity.

How the rest of the book is organised
Part One: Seven Black Men as Children introduces the biographical accounts of the men as the *children* of economic migrants from the

Caribbean to the United Kingdom in the immediate post-*Windrush* period 1955–1975. Their experiences as pupils of primary and secondary schooling in London are covered in Chapters 1 and 2.

Part Two: Seven Black Men as Parents explores their experience as *parents* of pupils in compulsory education in the second time frame from 1992 onwards in Chapter 3. This period coincides with the advent of parental choice as a central concept of government policy, articulated in the Parents' Charter initiative of John Major's Conservative administration in 1992 and continues through both the first Labour administration (1997–2001) and its second (2001–2005). The concept of 'black Caribbean choosing' (building on the work of Gewirtz et al, 1995; Vincent, 2000; Ball, 2003) is examined through the experiences of the men who are now parents of children in the English education system themselves. Chapter 4 develops this further and looks at how reflexive and critical those choices have been and the extent to which they echo or challenge the educational values of their immigrant parents.

In the concluding section, the policy implications of involving black Caribbean parents more equitably in the education of their children are considered in Chapter 5.

PART ONE:

Seven Black Men as Children

In order to understand low performance in our urban education system we must acknowledge that for years, the British education system was designed to socialise white working class people into having low aspirations. Our experience in the Caribbean was different. Even the most illiterate farmer would expect his children to succeed in the education system so that they could better themselves. When we came to Britain we found that there was a fundamental difference. It is clear that we have moved away from what education originally meant for us. We now have a generation of black parents who were failed by the education system and are not sure what direction they see for their children in that system.

(Professor Gus John, speaking when Director of Education, Hackney at a conference on black achievement in 1994)

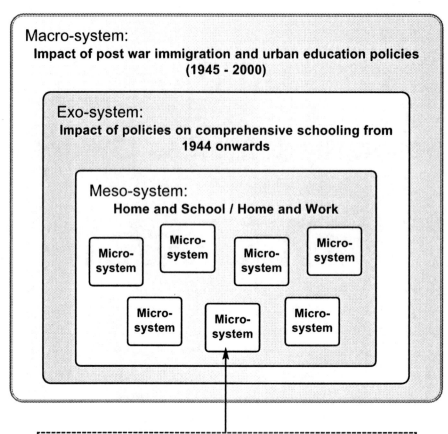

The ecological environment for the seven men as children of
first-generation immigrant parents.

Chapter One

Migration and Settlement

The interplay between post-war immigration and urban education policy

> I have crossed an ocean, I have lost my tongue. From the root of
> the old one, a new one has sprung.[1]

This chapter examines the early experiences of migration and settlement in London for the families of the seven men. Their accounts
recall the consequences of British immigration policy in relation to
the Caribbean as it impacted on the lived experience of seven immigrant families, particularly in the areas of housing and employment.
These socio-economic experiences of immigration are also interwoven with the education policy environment, which provide the
context for the men's experience of primary and secondary
education.

Six of the seven men attended primary schools in London: in some
cases within days of arriving from the Caribbean to join their families. They reflect on the impact of racism and prejudice, and their
parents' response to those challenges. The effectiveness of these
parenting styles and interventions are also reviewed. The chapter

concludes with the recognition that the temporary nature of black Caribbean settlement in London had become an illusion for many of those first-generation immigrants and explores the generational consequences of those failed parental aspirations for their children's development as they progressed from primary to secondary schooling.

Arrival and settlement

What a joyful news, Miss Mattie;
Ah feel like me heart gwine burs –
Jamaica people colonizin
Englan in reverse.

By de hundred, by de tousan,
From country an from town
By de ship-load, by de plane-load,
Jamaica is Englan boun.

Dem a pour out a Jamaica;
Everybody future plan
Is fi get a big-time job
An settle de motherlan.

What a islan! What a people!
Man an woman, ole an young
Jussa pack dem bag an baggage
An tun history upside dung!

What a devilment a Englan!
Dem face war an brave de worse;
But ah wonderin how dem gwine stan
Colonizin in reverse.[2]

The first major wave of immigration from the Caribbean in the late 1940s consisted initially of young adults, predominantly male. However under the Imperial Act of 1914, every person born in a British colony was deemed to be a British subject (Verma and Darby, 2002). Layton-Henry reminds us that Britain has always been involved in migration, but emigration rather than immigration, as a consequence of its colonial heritage. The economic depression between the First World War (1914–1918) and the Second (1939–1945) changed this balance for a time but as the economy recovered after 1945, emigration began to increase. The demand for labour had been fuelled by the needs of the Second World War. Britain, unlike Germany, had been able to call on its imperial resources. Offers to sign up for military duty were not consigned solely to the British Isles; willing conscripts besieged consulates across the Commonwealth. Initially, all three branches of the Armed Forces operated a 'colour bar' and entry was restricted solely to people of 'pure European descent' (Layton-Henry, 1992:23). It was the Royal Air Force with its need for trained pilots that first accepted West Indian subjects as officers, pilots and ground crews; the Army and the Royal Navy did not lift the 'colour bar' until 1948.

A significant proportion of the adults on the *Empire Windrush* in 1948 included men whose experience of military service in the Second World War had made them unable to 'demob' and settle to the relative poverty of Caribbean life (Phillips and Phillips, 1998). West Indian pilots had enlisted in the Royal Air Force and were stationed in Britain (Dickinson, 1982). Others on the ship had caught their restless fever or had a youthful appetite for adventure.[3]

I don't really know why they came. My father had a profession.

(Devon)

However the individual details differ, the prime motivation for many was economic advancement. Lawrence notes that unemployment stood at 40% in Jamaica in 1948 and those in work earned less than £2 per week (Lawrence, 1974:15).

> My mother was very aware of her poor status in Trinidad. Raising the funds to pay for the passage was an effort. I have no memory of a discussion that suggested there was any other choice available to her. (Arran)

Most authors refer to the SS *Empire Windrush* as the first significant crossing but Nehaul notes that the previous year, 1947, one hundred Jamaicans travelled on the SS *Ormonde* (Nehaul, 1996:1). Many male West Indians responded to the call for Commonwealth labour to aid Britain in its post-war construction of the Welfare State, but Britain was not the first choice destination (Davison, 1962) for the majority. In the immediate aftermath of the Second World War, West Indian economic migration was primarily to the United States until severe restrictions on entry were placed with the passing of the McCarren-Walter Act in 1952 (Tierney, 1982; Dodgson, 1984), which reduced West Indian immigration from 65,000 to 800 per year (Cross and Entzinger, 1988). This was the case for the fathers of Carl, Owen and Devon, but also unusually for Arran's mother:

> Originally my mother wanted to go to America but at that time migrating to the UK was easier. She went to school in Barbados until she was 14. She had basic skills and advanced literacy. On arrival to the UK she was a caterer. She did not have a job waiting for her. She got a job working at Dr Scholl's shoe factory and did more catering courses until she acquired the skills to become a housekeeper and migrated to the US when I went to university.
>
> (Arran)

Working on large US fruit farms as temporary contract labourers had given their fathers the opportunity to experience, first hand, the racial segregation of the Southern States and to contrast and compare both their colonial Caribbean conditions with those of working life in England.

> My parents came in the 1950s to better themselves. My father, before coming to Britain, had been to the States a few times and worked as a contract labourer so he had travelled out of Jamaica before. He heard there were opportunities in England so decided to give it a try. He came first, then sent for her. They got married then. (Carl)

> My father was floating really. He went on contract to America first when he was very young to pick oranges. I think he went back to Antigua and then came to England. (Colin)

The post-war Caribbean economy on many islands could not sustain the ambitions and aspirations of its inhabitants (Davison, 1962).[4] A better English education was a powerful motivator, not just for their children, but for themselves too (Lawrence, 1974), since the overwhelming majority of the early Caribbean immigrants were unskilled, manual workers.

> My mother's background of illegitimacy, the daughter of a maid, stayed with her as an experience. It pushed the importance of a good education and the opportunities opened because of one. She wanted that for her children and this was her driving force. My mother's work in the UK financed our education. (Arran)

> My parents were educated up to the minimum. Mum was a seam-stress and she was brought up in the tradition of sewing clothes, which she made for the family. (Owen)

Few small children came initially, as it was common practice for immigrant parents to leave their young children with their grandparents until employment and accommodation had been sorted and then children were 'sent for'. Philpott describes this phenomenon as 'migrant ideology', which saw no harm in leaving children behind and was not considered a signal of irresponsibility within Caribbean culture (Philpott, 1977:115).[5] In the early years of Caribbean migration to the UK, most came on freight ships, not just the proverbial 'banana boats'. The majority of the early accounts focus on the experiences of adults, but children shared the journeys too (Arran, Devon, Owen and Errol).

> The journey had some of my most powerful life memories. Seeing dolphins swimming was one of them. The boat just felt gigantic, huge. We packed tins of biscuits, water biscuits for the journey. I remember my brother knew more English than all of us. My mother couldn't speak English well [only St Lucian French patois] but my older brother could, so he roamed the boat, talking to white people and bringing back all the gossip. I was too intimidated by it all. We had a cabin and we had bunks. I remember one particular incident when the boat announced a fire drill or a sinking drill or whatever it is they call it on a blasted boat. My mum rushed into the cabin and we could hear announcements 'Don your lifejackets and report to _____'. There were only three lifejackets in our cabin and herself and four children. I saw my mum look at her four children. She felt she had to make a choice. Then my older brother came back and rescued us with the truth. But that look on my mother's face has always stayed with me as a powerful memory. (Errol)

> My parents nominated someone to look after me on the boat, which was a Portuguese passenger vessel carrying freight. It was

my first time travelling and my memories were of awful food, sickness and boredom. There were only two other kids of my age, the rest were predominantly young adults, male from all of the Caribbean islands. (Arran)

The impact of the decision to emigrate on the children and families *left behind* depended largely on the extended family support networks 'back home' and the level of contact maintained between the absent parents and their children.

To Arran, the youngest of five sons, the loss of his mother was devastating.

My mother emigrated to England in 1956. I was 8 years old at the time. I felt a mixture of excitement and at the same time my world was collapsing because my mother was at its centre. (Arran)

For Devon, the close contact with his grandparents was sufficient compensation.

My childhood in the Caribbean is something I have held onto. I have a very strong and active memory. I was the first grandchild and allowed a lot of freedom. I do not have any memories of my parents in the Caribbean, just the picture on the wall. (Devon)

Generally links between 'back home' and the UK were ritualised and very strong.

Our parents would send barrels and write regularly. I remember dictating inputs into letters to parents. They would send things for us kids like toothbrushes. There was no question of pining for parents. We felt like a natural belonging, a sense of history and community. (Owen)

Even when contact was meticulous through weekly letters and the occasional exchange of photographs, it still did not compensate for the shock of reconciliation.

We unloaded at Southampton and took the boat train to Waterloo. I was met by my mother. I could barely recognise her; she looked so different from three years earlier when I had last seen her.

(Arran)

I saw people waving at me. But the interesting thing is I didn't recognise my mum because I only knew her from photos. (Devon)

Most Caribbean immigrants arrived by boat to working docks such as Tilbury, Essex in the case of the SS *Windrush* but also to Avonmouth (near Bristol) and Southampton. From there the destination was usually by rail in the early 1950s to mainline stations in London or the Midlands.

We arrived in the night time. I believe it was Southampton and we got a train to London and all my uncles arrived to meet us. We brought pillows, potties from St Lucia. They greeted us like long lost Gods and they carried us on their shoulders and they were so proud. (Errol)

Not everyone came by boat; by the 1960s it was not uncommon for children to come by plane (Owen, Devon), which was seen as a signal of increasing prosperity.

We came on a British Overseas Airways Corporation plane in 1965. The flight was from Kingston to New York and from there to Heathrow but it developed a fault in New York and we had to stay over in a hotel which was a big thing. (Owen)

I came in 1966. My sister and I came alone by plane. It was no big deal. (Devon)

Immigration policy with respect to West Indian migration

The migration of black colonial subjects was a matter of serious political concern during the Second World War and in the post-war period. Despite the experience of those returning West Indians who had served in the Armed Forces, it was clear that the initial settlement in the late 1940s was for the most part spontaneous and unplanned. Verma and Darby (2002) note that two days after the *Windrush* landed, eleven Labour MPs wrote to Prime Minister Atlee expressing their concern. Controls to review the immigration of 'coloured' peoples were discussed by the Cabinet in March 1950, following a report from the Colonial Office on the numbers involved. It was agreed that since the numbers consisted of, at most, 4000 people, the Labour Government would take no action but would consider future legislation to restrict entry should numbers increase dramatically (Layton-Henry, 1992).

The newly elected Conservative Government of 1951 followed a similar public line but concerns began to rise in 1954 when the impact of US immigration controls became apparent in increased West Indian immigration to the UK. Figures presented at a Cabinet meeting on 10 July 1956 noted the rise of coloured immigrants from 3000 in 1953, to 10,000 in 1954 and to 35,000 in 1955 (Layton-Henry, 1992:34). The Commonwealth Immigration Act 1962 was the successful culmination of a concerted campaign to restrict immigration, which was waged throughout the 1950s. The Act established what has become the prevailing argument to justify immigration controls: namely the importance of assimilation and the need to reduce numbers to make that process easier (Verma and Darby, 2002:14).

Early settlement

By the time the parents of the seven men arrived in London, they were joining newly established communities in North and South London. Police estimates produced at the request of an inter-departmental working party of civil servants in January 1953 set the number of non-white communities in London as 19,000, from a total of 40,000 for the country as a whole (Layton-Henry, 1992).

Perceptions of the new immigrants were encapsulated in the early anthropological studies of West Indians in London. Patterson's account (1963) is typical of the period in which she presents a fascinating, if somewhat painful picture to the contemporary reader, of the social and moral values, which the 'host' community attributed to 'coloured' immigrants. Based on a study of settlement in Brixton undertaken between 1955 and 1958, Patterson conducted her fieldwork accompanied by her husband as she reported 'some difficulties of contact with less settled male migrants who tended to classify white women as welfare worker or potential sex partners' (Patterson, 1963:39).

Patterson's uncritical and somewhat essentialist use of racist and sexual stereotypes to describe her research is not atypical for her race *and gender* and has to be seen as an accurate depiction of the prevailing views of that time. Immigrants from Africa, India and the Caribbean were viewed by many British people through the lens of an imperial education, which depicted subjects of the British Empire as inferior and backward. In a chapter entitled 'Images for confident control' Mangan argues that a major purpose of this education was to inculcate in the children of the British Empire appropriate attitudes of dominance and deference. There was an education in imperial schools to shape the *ruled* into patterns of proper subservience and 'legitimate' inferiority, and one in turn to develop in the *rulers* convictions about the certain benevolence and 'legitimate' superiority of their rule. Imperial education was very much about establishing the presence and absence of confidence in those controlling and those controlled. (Mangan, 1993:6). Many West Indian migrants expected a different future in Britain based on their colonial education, which had stressed superior British concepts of justice and fair play (Layton-Henry, 1992).

Patterson saw West Indian migrants as drawn from 'a semi-rural colonial proletariat, which has left a distinctive mark on working habits, family organisation, religious practice and attitudes to authority' (op cit:17). Those views are to some extent both confirmed (Errol, Dennis, Colin) and refuted by the accounts (Carl, Arran, Devon, Owen) in this study. Few middle class black Caribbean families emigrated in the early 1950s and 1960s, although intellectuals such as E K Brathwaite and George Lamming came to Britain in this period.

> My mother could just about read and write. My father could not and cannot to this day. (Dennis)

> My mother was a peasant. My father left school to look after his family when his mother died. (Errol)

> My father had a profession. He was a policeman in the Caribbean.
> (Devon)

Throughout the post-war period those MPs whose constituencies included West Indian settlers tabled motions about the consequences for race relations. Anti-immigration speeches had been a consistent undercurrent of political and social life in the post-war period. As stated earlier, the Labour Cabinet debated immigration controls in 1950. Four years later Sir Winston Churchill's concerns about black immigration were placed on the record when he described immigration as the most important subject facing the country and deplored his inability to get any of his ministerial colleagues to share his concerns (quoted in Layton-Henry, 1992:31). It is not unsurprising to find that anti-immigration formed the central tenet of the emerging British National Party, which was established in 1960 as the result of a merger between the White Defence League and the National Labour Party. Six years later the National Front was formed.

Enoch Powell's 1968 'Rivers of Blood' speech was therefore not an isolated incident. Immigration from the New Commonwealth had significantly increased the numbers of non-white settlers in urban conurbations in England in the 1960s. The exodus of East African Asians posed a new challenge, against which both Duncan Sandys and Powell were keen to campaign. They succeeded, and in 1968 the first immigration control bill to include an element of 'patriality' – the unconditional right of entry restricted to those with close ties to the UK by birth, naturalisation or descent – was passed.

Race relations policy

It would be wrong to present the response of the English public to West Indian immigration as universally hostile; quite the reverse in many individual cases (see McKenley, 2002), however anti-discrimination policies in the form of Race Relations Acts in the post-war period were unable to protect West Indian immigrants from racist and discriminatory practices in housing and employment (Mullard, 1973). Levels of discrimination were recorded in a number of studies; the first and most influential of which, 'Population and Economic Planning' (PEP), was published as 'Racial Discrimination in England' in 1967. Researchers found evidence of widespread discrimination in all areas of employment and housing which demonstrated the inadequacies of the provisions of the 1965 Race Relations Act. This Act had sought to make discrimination in public places and incitement to racial hatred illegal in speech and written material but was largely ineffective as evident in the rising number of complaints lodged with the newly established Race Relations Board (see Layton-Henry, 1992). The Race Relations Act of 1968 made it unlawful to discriminate on grounds of colour, race or ethnicity in employment, housing and other services. Racist advertising was banned and the Race Relations Board was given powers to investigate claims of racial discrimination. The Community Relations Commission was created to act in an advisory capacity on behalf of the Home Secretary and replaced the National Committee for Commonwealth Immigrants.

Social relations with the host community: housing and employment

These linked tenets of government policy: immigration and race relations formed two key contextual settings, which directly affected the seven black men and their families as they were trying to secure decent employment, housing and education. Employment and housing provided a key context for the limited contact with the white community in the early days of settlement and was an important element in the construction of social relations with the 'host' community.

My parents were very clear about how the English might grin their teeth at you but there's no substance behind it. I would describe my parents as very conscious, politically very conscious and very rare. That comes from my father having gone to America and seen what racism was like in America and then come to England. He was able to compare what it was like under white people in Jamaica, what it was like going to America and what it was like coming to England. What were the differences in terms of the nature of racism. As a child I grew up with that understanding about what was happening and why we were being treated in this way. I was quite privileged that my parents were able to answer those questions and explain what was happening.

(Carl)

For others, housing helped to sustain an identity, which remained culturally Caribbean and fundamentally different from that of the host community.

What has become clear to me is my parents have a disdain towards 'whiteworld'. They came here to earn money. They came for no other reason. They don't trust white people, they don't engage with them more than they have to and certainly school was a white institution. And so on reflection recently I realise that contact was minimal; it was a black world. The guy stepping through the door selling insurance may have been white but otherwise nobody white had any engagement with us, we were in 'Jamaica' at all times – Clapham was seriously black. It was not as white as it is now and they moved to Brixton to my regret. I could retire now on the house we owned then. (Dennis)

Housing

At a ministerial symposium on ethnic minority achievement in July 2002,[6] Diane Abbott, one of the first black British Members of Parliament recalled her parents' experience of trying to find accommodation in North Paddington and repeated her memory of the signs in windows: 'No Dogs, No Coloureds, No Irish' that were almost iconic in their depiction of London in the 1950s and 1960s. Similarly pictures of the first *Windrush* embarkees housed in fomer air raid shelters in Camberwell (South London) were also given a new airing in the recent *Windrush* fiftieth anniversary celebrations (Phillips and Phillips, 1998). The brief accounts of those years presented in this book provide another set of insights into how both parents and children experienced immigrant life in London. Many of the Caribbean immigrants maintained their kinship and 'locality bonds' (Cropley, 1983:78) with relatives in their country of origin. Yet the notion of a 'Caribbean' identity or heritage would be an over-statement since most immigrants identified most closely with their island of origin and more particularly with their village or parish. Even now some fifty or more years on, at the level of lived experience, 'Caribbean heritage' remains a problematic concept and is essentially bureaucratic in its origins.

> My mum came to people from her village [in Antigua] and they met her at Victoria Station. My dad's story is more vague. I know he lived with some friends from his village as well and they all lived and worked together at the same place. (Colin)

Undoubtedly accommodation was a struggle for the majority. Stories of immigrants living in squalid, over-crowded rooms are well chronicled but their impact on parents and children were different. Access to public housing in the early years of settlement was very limited and most immigrants were in the rented housing sector, particularly in London where landlords used West Indian tenants to realise higher rents and property values. A number of London Labour MPs raised these concerns in an adjournment debate led by Marcus Lipton, MP for Brixton, under pressure from his white working class constituents (Layton-Henry, 1992:37).

The inter-connectedness of immigrant life has not always been given sufficient attention. Many black Caribbean families initially rented accommodation from Jewish landlords in North London. These landlords were the recent descendants of Jewish migrants who fled the anti-Jewish pogroms in the Soviet Union and Eastern Europe between 1870 and 1914 to settle in the East End of London.

We lived in a house, a massive house on the Common [Clapton] with five flats. Lovely house, massive flats we rented from a private landlord called Mr Silverstone owned the house, little Jewish man, very nice man who bought us Christmas presents as kids and used to give you sixpence behind your mum's back.

(Colin)

The first thing that struck me was the terrace housing, all stuck together; I thought it was one house. We lived in Dunsmore Road in the middle of the Orthodox Jewish community which I took as normal. (Devon)

We arrived at Downs Park Road, Hackney where we lived in one bedroom – aunts, sister, mum and her boyfriend. We shared a kitchen, toilet and bath with the rest of the house. (Arran)

House ownership of the kind we see today was not yet established among the 'host' community in the period after the Second World War.[7] Immigrants were often forced to buy houses with older 'sitting tenants' (residents with security of tenure until they died, or who could be bought out for a price once the house was purchased) because this was the only part of the market in which they were able to participate.

We lived in Clapton in Hackney. First of all they shared a house, then they bought their own house with a sitting tenant. It was difficult for black people to buy houses then in the early 1960s and the only way they could get a house was to buy one with a sitting tenant in it. They live in the same house to this day. (Carl)

For others like their white working class counterparts, a council house signalled a change in fortunes.

I remember the day. My dad had gone to work and we got the letter saying we'd got a council house. We had spent years living in a one room flat in Brixton with mice and all kinds of things. My mum got one of us to read the letter then we all hugged up and danced round in circles. Round and round jumping up and down.

(Errol)

Property did not hold the same mystique for those Caribbean families (Dennis, Carl, Owen and Errol) who came from rural farming backgrounds and were used to 'leasing' land.

We always had property. So we have land in Jamaica and property here. My father has always encouraged us to buy our own homes. (Dennis)

Social relations and networks within the community were also defined to a large extent by the intimacy of cramped housing. Co-operative group rituals around food, hair and celebratory events such as weddings and christenings, were ways of keeping the cultural connection between Caribbean life back home and in London.

My mum had a reputation as a good cook, so did a few of the women who lived together, my aunt and my godmother lived together in this one flat and the men would come round with some meat and rice and they [the women] would cook for them. People was always round their flat, I think that's how they [my parents] met. (Colin)

For others, such rituals were sustained by the Church. This was, in the eyes of their children, both their salvation and a burden.

> My parents came as churchgoers. Roman Catholic. My father still goes to church every Sunday now. I've got all the guilt, which is the advantage of being a Catholic. (Errol)

> My father was deep in the Church – a deacon. My father's interpretation of the scriptures was narrow. The Church was not a catalyst, not an enabler, because of its accommodation, its complacency and deference, which was not helpful. (Dennis)

To a certain extent the early experiences of housing would have differed little from the cramped shared living spaces of urban and rural Caribbean life. It was perhaps in the experience of employment that conditions differed significantly.

Employment

> My dad's profession was a stonecutter and my mum, on my birth certificate, it says her first job was as a linen maid at St Bartholomew's Medical College where she worked until her retirement. (Colin)

The colonial call for labour to support the reconstruction of England after the Second World War is well chronicled (John, 1981). However about 1000 West Indian technicians and trainees were recruited earlier to work in munitions factories in Manchester and Lancashire and a further 10,000 recruited to work as ground crews on Royal Air Force bases across the country (Layton-Henry, 1992). The period of economic prosperity which emerged after a decade of post-war austerity was characterised by an acute shortage of labour in the UK and contrasted radically with the continuing economic deterioration of the Caribbean economy. The London Transport Executive began recruiting first in Barbados in 1956,[8] then later in Trinidad and Jamaica. Although John reminds us that the visit by the London Transport Executive was 'not altogether unconnected with the industrial action the company had been experiencing with its indigenous workforce' (John, 1981:34).

Both Rex (1973) and Tierney (1982) note the creation of a set of low status menial jobs in English metropolitan towns and cities, which white working class people no longer wanted. Nevertheless Carter recalls that there were many one-day strikes by Transport and General Workers' Union members against the employment of black transport workers (Carter, 1986: 25).

Black immigrants to England received a mixed reception as the racial disturbances in Nottingham and Notting Dale (a district in North Westminster now better known as Notting Hill) London in 1958 attest. These were not isolated incidents. These and other disturbances were not unrelated to tensions arising from the post-war increase in unemployment among the white working class as well as xenophobia and colour prejudice (Lawrence, 1974) or as Layton-Henry acknowledges:

> Even when recruited as a replacement labour force to do the work that the natives rejected and to occupy inner-city accommodation that the natives wished to leave, they could still be seen by those who remained as competitors for jobs, housing and their scarce resources. (Layton-Henry, 1992:19)

Disturbances were reported in Liverpool in July 1948; in Deptford, South East London the following year; and in Camden Town, North London in August 1954. Hostile crowds of over a thousand were involved in the Nottingham disturbances. Smaller crowds in the hundreds were involved in Notting Hill with some 1400 people arrested in the four main days of disturbances between 30 August and 3 September. A year later Kelso Cochrane, an Antiguan carpenter was murdered by six white youths who were never caught.

The impact of employment on gender relations within the Caribbean community

What is less well articulated is the impact of employment on gender relations within the Caribbean community. The experience of Caribbean immigration and settlement undermined fixed notions of masculinity and femininity in terms of domestic roles and expectations.

> My mum was a bus conductor. She was always good educationally, intelligent and incredibly charming. Her dreams were put on the back burner. (Devon)

> My parents both got jobs with London Transport. Father came in 1958 and mother in 1959. They worked on the Underground as ticket sellers. (Owen)

Working mothers, shift work patterns, shared parenting, were factors for the majority of first-generation Caribbean households in London. Bagley (1975) in a survey of 54 West Indian parents of 10-year-old children (at the end of Year 5) attending local authority schools in Southwark, found that scarcely any of the West Indian families had non-manual jobs and only a fifth of West Indian mothers were housewives compared with nearly half of the 97 parents interviewed. He also found that amongst those who had jobs, the West Indian mothers worked for longer hours (Bagley, 1975:284).

The differentiated experiences of black men and women in Britain in relation to their white peers are reflected in education and employment terms. Economically and domestically post-war experiences differed for white and black women. The Rampton Inquiry noted that a disproportionate number of West Indian women are forced to go out to work because of their economic circumstances and quoted the 1971 census data which showed that 68% of West Indian married women went out to work, compared with the national average of 42% (House of Commons, 1981:15). Similarly goffe's poem reminds us of the multi-task gendered experience of working class immigrant life:

My mother is a seamstress
A humble stitcher joiner
Of things

First she cuts the pattern
From paper lays it on the
Cloth probably a loud cotton
Anniversary

Then she chalks it up and down
A curve for the neck and arms
A little off the waist
A little on in Edna's case

Then she cuts the goat from
Head to toe and
Blows the flame alight and
Soaks and sprinkles
White pepper black pepper
Salt time thyme
Cash and carry curry and
Coconut cream for the rice and
Peas

She leaves a note for janet
on the door "'Finish the dinner tell
Tony to do the dishes empty the
    dustbin
behave till I come
Mum."

She goes off to work on a red eighty
Five seat nineteen fifty-three double
decker bus five pound weight steel
ticket popper strapped across the
Brace of her back and
London Transport thanks her

When the pound shillings and
    pence
And octgonal-headed three penny
Bits are counted and the last bus
Checked she can leave

Next the pattern must be pinned and
Hung round the dummy standing in
The corner of the room.[9]

Like some of their white peers during the war, black Caribbean women in the post-war period took up employment in jobs previously restricted to men, as well as more traditional areas such as nursing and clerical work. White women were 'demobbed' from that work after the war and expected to return to more feminine duties; no such expectations were held about black women. West Indian women were heavily over-represented in the lower echelons of the National Health Service as nurses and domestic auxiliary workers, reflecting the direct recruitment from Barbados and Jamaica. Many but not all Caribbean women worked throughout the late 1950s and 1960s at a time when full employment was a feature of the economy, but others like the majority of white women, did not hold full-time jobs outside the home.

> When they came to England, father worked in a variety of different places: as a porter cum helper in a local swimming baths, then he worked for a long time in precious metals in a foundry, then he worked with furs, taking their skins off. Mother initially looked after kids and did some small jobs part time. (Carl)

The hardship of immigrant life and its consequences

Regardless of gender, an enduring feature of adult immigrant working life was its hardship. Harsh working conditions were a common experience for mothers and fathers, but as children, the seven men remember their fathers tired at the end of a day's work. There was an unspoken recognition within the family of the hardship the men faced working in low status jobs for which they were generally paid less than their white counterparts for the same work, and often in discriminating, hostile environments.

> My dad worked at lots of different places as a stoker – Gas Board, Royal Mint, the majority night work or shift work. Hard work.
> (Colin)

Caribbean immigrants were recruited as a replacement labour force (Tierney, 1982) but the economic prosperity of the 1960s was short-lived. West Indian immigrants had obtained work in mainly unskilled or semi-skilled jobs, although by the 1970s the spread was more even and West Indians were well represented in skilled manual occupations. West Indians were poorly represented in non-manual and executive roles unlike some of their Asian counterparts (Layton-Henry, 1992). The experience of working life provided evidence of the impact of racism, discrimination and prejudice on the lives of Caribbean families, informed by the increasing radicalism of the American Civil Rights movement and its influence on black British communities.

The economic hardship and the psychological impact of racism on their aspirations for themselves and their families had negative consequences, not least in securing an acceptable standard of education in the poor disadvantaged working class communities in which they settled.[10]

> And I think that what I look at now is that I had a childhood. I ran about, over the parks a lot, over the marshes, scrumping. But my childhood was changed by meeting some white men who used young kids to break into houses. My cousin got involved and he had money, so I wanted money too. But from there childhood started to go out the window. Some of the older white families of kids who used to go to my primary school starting calling you 'black bastard' and wanting to fight you so you'd have to fight. Then I went to secondary school. (Colin)

The powerful but potentially destabilising concept of 'back home' also took its toll since it contributed to the notion that this life in England was temporary and that long-term settlement was not planned for by the first generation of immigrants. Brah in her important research on the experience of East African Asian migration to the UK poses and answers her own question:

'Where is Home?' On the one hand, 'home' is a mythic place of desire in the *diasporic imagination*. In this sense it is a place of no return. (Brah, 1996:192; emphasis added).

Rosen too reminds us that:

a memory becomes collective because it emerges from the constant negotiation of conversation. (Rosen, 1998:132)

For Colin, the memories had indeed become mythic, ritualised-remembering of crowded Sunday dinners of stewed peas and rice, jerk chicken, fried fish and macaroni – 'telling stories, keeping back home alive' (Colin) – when the uncles, aunts and cousins came round and the stories of back-home-life and right-now-strife were told and retold. Its key recurrent theme was that this life in England was temporary.

Not so much about going home but they talked about 'home' constantly and there was a sense of home was where we belonged and here wasn't where we belonged. But they were still trying to achieve something here – a very temporary state. (Carl)

As far as I'm concerned, my mum was always talking about going 'back home' but it was getting further and further away, just surviving. (Colin)

Linked to the temporary nature of settlement was the view that the hardship of their London life was for a purpose and therefore supportable – a short-term project to earn enough money to go back home, which some, but by no means all, achieved.

My parents bought a house in the UK and at the same time began laying the foundations for a new house in Jamaica on the family land. There was always a sense of them going back. I wanted them to go back. Both my parents are alive in Jamaica, they went back in 1979, they got their shit together. It was part of their plan. They were very practical and matter of fact but in the everyday decisions was an underlying logic. (Owen)

Even so Owen's family took twenty years to achieve their goal, but for others – the majority – the experience was much less positive. Housing also defined the choices of education available and since the majority of West Indian families lived in the poorer areas of London, they shared their schooling with their white working class counterparts.

The experience of primary education

As stated earlier, once the first wave of early settlement was over, better education opportunities (and the doors such an education would open) became a key motivator for West Indians to uproot and leave children, often in the care of grandparents, to emigrate. To Arran, Devon and Owen, the importance of education was already evident in the attitudes to education expressed by their families before migrating.

At home [in Trinidad] there was always a great stress placed on good presentation, homework, looking studious. Money was saved to buy books and uniforms. A Caribbean education was very much for the rich. For the poor the only route to education was to gain a scholarship. There was an island-wide competition for scholarships. I have a strong memory of my older brother trying for one of these scholarships. He had to have a tutor and eat special food – the sacrifice to support this permeated the whole household. (Arran)

Although the main focus of the study was the experience of secondary education in the UK, accounts of early experiences of primary education (in both England and the Caribbean) were also generated.

> I've held on to my Caribbean schooling memory. I come from a strong extended family. My dad was Antiguan but he was stationed in Montserrat. My mum was from Montserrat. Caribbean schools are always formal. My school was very strict with high expectations by the whole community. Headteacher Mr Morgan came from the village. Most teachers came from the local village. (Devon)

> Apparently I did go to school in St Lucia but I can't remember a thing about it except one memory of being under a house with a blackboard and some other kids. I must have been because when I came to England, I knew my multiplication tables, I could write and I knew my alphabet. (Errol)

Immigrant parents and children began to present themselves at English schools in growing numbers through the late 1950s and early 1960s. Once they arrived in the UK, most immigrant children went to the local primary school in closest walking distance from their new homes. This to varying degrees was the experience of Arran, Owen, Errol and Devon.

> I went to school within a month of arriving. (Arran).

> We were met at Heathrow and it seemed almost the next week that I was sent to school. No time lapsed as both my parents were working. (Owen)

> I went to school within days. (Errol)

A significant number of immigrant families settled in London, with sizeable populations in Haringey, Brent, Ealing and the boroughs of the Inner London Education Authority (ILEA). Of the 146 English LEAs in 1970, only 48 authorities had more than 1000 immigrant pupils; 79 had less than 500 pupils and of those 48 LEAs had less than 100. (Townsend, 1971). At that time, children of Caribbean origin comprised just under half of the numbers of immigrant pupils. As changes took place, the teachers and administrators of the schools involved became increasingly concerned to make special provision for their ethnic minority pupils. Driver observed that 'the problem appeared dramatic to those involved but it was a localised phenomenon' (Driver, 1979:132).

> In my year there was one other black person, from an African country, but as I went up the [primary] school, more came and the dynamics of the school changed dramatically. We were all 'Jamaicans' then regardless of the island you came from! (Errol)

Government policies on the education of immigrants
There was little intervention by central government in the early days of settlement after the landing of the *Windrush*. Local education authorities were left to handle the unexpected, and consequently unplanned for, number of West Indian pupils on an individual basis (Bhatnager, 1970). As Nandy wryly observes:

> Through the 1950s Britain acquired a coloured population in, so to speak, a fit of absence of mind. Since the process of immigration was not planned, it was on the whole no one's responsibility in particular to anticipate and to provide for the foreseeable consequences of the process. (Nandy, 1971:7)

Hawkes also notes:

> Apart from occasional bursts of publicity in a few areas it was a
> local, semi-secret affair, a worry to sub-committees, the object of a
> few items in the local or educational press, and principally, one
> extra problem for already hard-pressed teachers. (Hawkes,
> 1966:1)

The first formal item of governmental policy from the Department
of Education & Science on the placement of immigrant children was
not issued until 1965. Circular No. 7/65 *The Education of Immigrants*
(DES, 1965) instructed local authorities to avoid the over-concentra-
tion of immigrant children in one institution by a policy of dispersal
by 'bussing' – providing transport to ensure that the numbers of
immigrants were distributed across a range of schools and so did
not rise above one third of the total school population in any school.
In practice this meant educating a significant number of immigrant
pupils outside of their local area.

Few authorities adopted this approach, although certainly in the
early sixties there was some political support for the policy of
dispersal. Indeed Education Survey 13 *The Education of Immigrants*
by HM Inspectorate states that the policy of dispersal identified in
Circular 7/65 emerged as a result of a 'potentially serious situation'
(DES, 1971b:16) in Southall in 1963. After a meeting with white
parents, who were protesting about the adverse impact of large
numbers of Indian children on the education of white children in
certain local primary schools, the then Minister of Education, Sir
Edward Boyle, agreed that a limit of thirty per cent was advisable.
Nevertheless the Inner London Education Authority was not alone
in rejecting this advice, which was judged to have been ill
conceived, particularly with regard to primary age pupils (Maclure,
1970). Statistics compiled in February 1969 for the Parliamentary

Select Committee on Race Relations & Immigration (House of Commons, 1969) suggested that only a quarter of the authorities which had more than 2% of immigrants on the school roll complied with the instruction. Townsend (1971) notes that the dispersal strategy did not tend to apply to West Indian pupils but to pupils with obvious linguistic difficulties.

The psychological impact of racism and prejudice

A number of local enquiries into the education of black Caribbean pupils were commissioned during the late 1970s stimulated by the work of the Parliamentary Select Committee on Race Relations and Immigration. The enquiry into the under-achievement of West Indian pupils in Redbridge in 1978 is typical in involving the local Community Relations Council. The enquiry noted:

> We were disturbed to find that on a number of occasions when discussing this Enquiry in the Borough that the names of Jensen and Eysenck[11] were mentioned quite spontaneously by local teachers. Although no teacher admitted to believing in the genetic inferiority of black people, the claim by Professor Arthur Jensen to have shown that negroes were of lower intelligence than whites was clearly close to these teachers' thoughts. (Black Peoples Progressive Association & Redbridge Community Relations Council, 1978)

Examples of racial prejudice on the part of teachers, pupils and the wider community were a shared theme of the seven black men during both their primary and secondary education. Teachers' accounts indicate that doubts about the IQ or perceived ability and potential of West Indian pupils had become, for some, an uncritical part of the educational discourse in the early years of West Indian settlement (Drew, 1995). As Mac an Ghaill pointed out:

These racist stereotypes were not simply locked away in individual teachers' heads. By the end of the 1960s they were translated
into social and material responses. (Mac an Ghaill, 1988:42)

Mirza makes a similar point arguing that the work of the scientific
racists had permeated the thoughts and beliefs of some of the teachers
in her study (Mirza, 1992:60). For all seven men, the emotions of their
London primary school days still evoke feelings of public humiliation.
They also contributed to a deep-seated distrust of teachers, which
informs their parental involvement in their own children's schooling.

There was an immediate negative impact on arrival. I was made
to say my alphabet, which we already knew at 8 but they said it
so slow like a song that I was completely confused. There were
lots of clashes as I was coming to terms with what we had to do
and the teacher often spoke aloud to the rest of the class about me.
(Devon).

I went to school within days [of arrival]. I knew I was smarter
than the white kids but that didn't last long because I have memories of the teachers constantly undermining me in a range of ways.
I had a way of putting my jumper on which the teacher ridiculed
and said I was an idiot. (Errol)

I had to reckon with being called names and teased which was a
new experience. I remember thinking to myself – they can do and
say whatever they like, I'm better than this. I remember that same
thought while doing the third year of my degree. Same solution.
Define your own self worth. (Owen)

For others, the feelings of rejection by their white peers were more
complex and their responses more pragmatic.

I loved [primary] school, loved, loved it, loved it. It was great. There were little silly things that I didn't like to talk about them. There's something in me where I knew that in Kiss Chase, the girls didn't want the black boys to catch them and stuff like that so after a while you didn't play with them no more. There was no black girls, just white girls, so after a while you found out why you wasn't going out with them. You know you was popular, you was in the football team, you was in the top class so wha' a gwan here? And then you kinda realise what's going on. (Colin)

Most, but not all of the immigrant parents of the men felt ill-equipped to make sense of the accounts of prejudice at primary school and in the neighbourhood that their sons brought home to them at that time. Their experiences of education in the Caribbean differed so radically from their English reality; the location was so different from the close knit extended family networks from which the majority of Caribbean immigrants derived their experience of schooling and their generally non-racialised identity.

It was the local school, the closest school, the nearest school. See now I think about it because in Antigua when they went to school, there was no doubt that people wanted you to learn. There was nothing about racism. If you went to school, you did something wrong, you teacher would beat you, your brother would beat you, your mum would beat you and your father would beat you last. My school Tyssen [here in London] was lovely. I had the same teacher in the infants all the way through and the same teacher in the juniors all the way through. When I was young I was the only black guy in my year at the primary school, and my sister and my cousin were the only black youths in their year. I was a Cockney, a Cockney Rebel. For my first years at Tyssen, I didn't even realise I was black. It was just Colin, Michael, Rochelle, Michelle,

Nicholas but as we got older, 8 or 9, people started calling us 'wog' as they passed and looked round, and I'd look round as well. But then older people started abusing us, calling you names Chalkie, Jungle Bunny. But it still didn't really worry me because my friends were my friends and they were alright. (Colin)

I remember being asked if I could swim and saying 'Yes' [in the Caribbean sense of playing in the sea]. I jumped into the pool and nearly drowned. And I remember the following year a boy from St Vincent did exactly the same thing. When he was asked and said 'Yes I can swim' I wanted to put my hand across his mouth and shout 'No you can't.' And he jumped in too and nearly drowned. Déjà vu. (Devon)

Little prepared them for the increasingly hostile environment many Asian families already faced and that Caribbean immigrants and their children came to face with much harsher intensity in the second half of the 1960s. Powell's 'Rivers of Blood' speech made in Birmingham in 1968 put paid to any sense of ease or rightful belonging that they might have regained after the disturbances of the 1950s (see Humphry and John, 1971).[12]

'Choosing' secondary schools

Contemporary concepts of *parental choice* did not pertain for many Caribbean immigrant families at the time when their children were entering urban secondary schools in the late 1950s and early 1960s. For the older research participants (Errol, Arran), the degree of choice available for secondary education was determined by their performance in the 11-plus examination.

I didn't have much choice, I failed the 11-plus and joined my older brother at High Towers. (Errol)

However, towards the end of the 1960s, the 11-plus was abolished as the principal means of defining by ability whether a child qualified to go to a selective grammar school or the local secondary modern or technical school. Dennis, some three years younger than Errol, did not sit the 11-plus examination but felt the outcome would have been irrelevant because of his parents' illiteracy.

> I am sure no research was done by my parents, I just went to High Towers. No other schools visited, no discussion about the virtues of mixed schools or otherwise. We were surrendered to the wiles of this society. (Dennis)

As comprehensive schools became the norm, unofficial hierarchies of schools by their former status and reputation remained and pupils of Caribbean heritage found it difficult to gain entry into those former grammar schools which still had a strong academic cachet. For many Caribbean immigrants whether their children 'passed' or 'failed', the end of primary school assessment was the first real test of whether their children were doing as well as they hoped. For the majority of the men, such assessments were problematic and as indicated earlier, the stakes were high. What appeared to be a neutral assessment led to outcomes which surprised almost all of the seven men and their families, despite, in at least four cases, memories of being academically successful in primary school.

> I was in the top class at school and I was doing well. There was some people who were very very clever and I was very clever but on some things they were ... Anne she could spell! Jeremy could add up! We had this mental arithmetic thing that the teacher did every day. 8, 9 10/10 was no problem to me but I couldn't sustain 10/10 every day like Jeremy and Anne. They'd be at the top and I'd be third or fourth. (Colin)

Whatever the rationale for explaining the results of the 11-plus, not all the parents were persuaded of its objectivity; its impact on their children was equally significant. Carl's parents went up to his primary school to complain but to no avail.

I went to Millfields Primary School with my sisters. When I was 11, I put my name down with my friends who were mostly white at that time, for the grammar school. I wasn't successful and I remember being upset about that and one of the reasons cited was that they didn't take many black children and there weren't many black children in the school at that time. And I thought that it was because I was black and my parents were black. It was a significant occasion for me because I was in the top band of the school and we used to have special classes with the headmaster in English, maths, reading and arithmetic. So you was sort of being groomed in that sense so not to get into grammar school was quite traumatic. (Carl)

Colin had a place at another school but begged to go to Home Beech, the same school as his mates from primary school.

I used to go round with the Stamford Hill mob. I had Dr Martens, Levis at 6 and a Ben Sherman shirt and braces. I was like the mascot and they'd put me on a wall, then fight and then pick me off the wall and they'd take me home afterwards. So I knew them and I knew I'd be protected. I just wanted to go there [Home Beech] and be with the big boys. It's funny because some of them was just about to leave, they were so old. They were in the Fifth as I was just reaching and I hadn't counted on that. And by then some of them was bunking off bigtime by then so by the time I got there, it was like I was by myself. (Colin)

Devon's family circumstances affected his ability to take up a grammar school place.

My parents split up so I got carted off to another school. I was 10. I had joined Cubs in the local area, which was familiar from Montserrat. So just as I was settling in, learning the territory, I had to move house to Walthamstow and went to Henry Maynards Primary School. And this school was a fairly well-to-do Church of England school, traditional with a uniform. It was a single sex boys' school with a girls' school on the same campus, which was literally next door. My first trip to Europe was with that school – Germany, Belgium. Then we had to move back to Hackney but I stayed at the school so I was constantly late, given the journey. I struck up a good relationship with the headteacher. He knew I was having a difficult time so I was allowed to arrive late with the agreement of the headteacher. I would have gone to grammar schools in Walthamstow but we had to move again to a Council estate in Homerton and I went to Home Beech. These were huge decisions dictated purely by circumstances and my mother's personal life. (Devon)

For Owen the abiding memory is one of perplexity.

We did cross-country for the first two weeks [of secondary school] in Epsom and Ewell where the school had a track. It felt like five miles, ages more than two miles. Everyone did it but later in the intervening years I've thought: 'Could they make me do that now?' I ran as fast as I could and the 11-plus was like that; no memory of any preparation – its significance only clear later. (Owen)

Commentary

The ecological approach provided a framework for exploring the interplay between the policies that determined the predominantly hostile environment in which the seven families lived, and their *actual experience and behaviours.* A number of themes emerge in this chapter from the accounts of the early years spent in the Caribbean, the impact of migration, arrival and settlement in London and insights into the housing, employment and primary school experiences. Many, but not all, were coloured by the negative effects of racism and prejudice. The transmission between parents and children of the importance of education as the prime tool for aggrandisement and self-improvement was problematic. The clarity of the signals, the degree of interference and the power of the message were all factors which affected the reception.

Firstly, the communication from parent to child of the value of education was not always consistent with the degree of parental involvement, understanding of the English education system and/or the levels of literacy needed to engage with and support their children's education. For Owen and Carl, there was no dissonance between their parents' behaviours and their values.

My parents were farmers, down to earth, not bourgeois. They went to school and valued the English education but they were also heard praising the Jamaican system. (Owen)

How did they show that they valued education? By asking us how we were doing at school. Not so much sitting down and helping us because although they had some basic education, they weren't highly educated. We had to do all our study before going out to play. They put a lot of store in education, faith in education but they also understood that here was not like back home. Even back home they knew there were issues about skin colour. (Carl)

They continually stressed the importance of school. They did not intervene but were encouraging. I took their involvement for granted. (Owen)

Carl and Owen perceived that their parents were *actively and consciously* engaged in their children's schooling. This engagement was characterised by consistency between the high aspirations articulated and their behaviours. They adopted a reassuring approach, which acknowledged the hostile racist environment in which their children's education was being framed but at the same time worked hard to build a critical awareness of those factors in their children. Critically their children perceived their parents as *authoritative* and *influential*. Devon's parents would have conformed to this model but their domestic instability militated against their ability to provide a consistent approach. In retrospect, Errol and Colin's parents appeared *passive and naïve* to their children in their assumption of trust and deference to the 'benign' authority of the teacher in the English system, to much the same degree that they would have assumed in the Caribbean.

They never thought they should sit down with us when we got home from school. The school's job was to educate, our job was to learn and so he [father] only ever got involved when we got our reports and they weren't good enough and he would shout and scream and beat us. (Errol)

Secondly, there was ambivalence about whether an English education was an entirely benign or wholly desirable process.

My parents would say things like: 'Don't let knowledge turn you fool.' There was a tension between wanting you to learn and recognising that education was having a disorienting effect for some children in trying to balance the Whiteworld and the Blackworld. (Dennis)

Dennis's parents understood the hostile context of life in England and were *instinctively distrusting*. However their behaviours demonstrated their powerlessness to exercise any influence over that context, because they lacked the levels of literacy, confidence and awareness to fully engage with their children's education. They had few dealings with the 'host' community and sought recourse in separate, parallel lifestyles.

The early days of arrival and settlement described in this chapter were characterised by initial optimism and worthwhile sacrifice for the parents of the seven men. But already by the end of their primary education, there is evidence of the hard impact of ignorance, prejudice and racism, together with the class realities of employment and housing in post-war London, beginning to take their toll.

One thing I regret about coming is that no one said when I was leaving: 'When you go, make sure you come back.' No one said this is only temporary. I regret that it was not explicit. In hindsight I wish that had been firmly implanted in me. (Devon)

The desire of most economic migrants from developing countries – to build a brighter future for themselves and their children – was clearly shared in the hopes and aspirations of the parents of the seven, but was transmitted in varying degrees of success by their behaviours to their children. As those primary years passed by and settlement took on a more permanent form, the hopes, for many but not all, turned to a frustration, which is captured in the unforgiving tone of some of the memories.

My mum would come home and she'd be washing and cooking and I'm saying 'Mum' and she'd be trying to read it [my home-work] while I held it. By the time she was finished, she was tired so I didn't really bring them stuff home, I dealt with it by myself.

(Colin)

For Dennis, Earl and Colin, whatever was happening in the wider world, at home it seemed to the children that their parents needed all their physical and much of their emotional energy to survive the often-challenging working environments they faced.

Summary

In this chapter, the seven men reflected on their experience of primary education as first-generation black Caribbean immigrant pupils and their acculturation in education, housing, employment and social relations. The effects of structural inequalities in the education system had only become apparent towards the end of primary schooling when, despite the advent of 'comprehensive' schools, access to high status, high performing secondary schools proved difficult.

Many of the negative themes consistently expressed as factors contributing to the underachievement of black Caribbean pupils in recent official contemporary accounts (see Gillborn and Mirza, 2000; DfES, 2003) were also the common experiences of the seven black men and their parents, for example: high parental aspirations meeting low teacher expectations; acute awareness of racism (insti-tutional and teacher); equality of access to effective high-performing schools; levels of parental involvement; and negative parent–school encounters.

In the next chapter, the experience of secondary schooling is laid on the primary foundations and examined through the seven men's secondary education at **High Towers** and **Home Beech** boys' schools. The impact of the post-imperial independence movements around the world, the US civil rights movement and the offshoots of black and women's liberation had particular implications for comprehensive education in Britain with the increasing politicisation of the teaching profession in the 1970s, particularly in terms of race and gender issues. This period also saw the emergence of black political and cultural voices in the UK modelled on the civil rights struggles of the US, Africa and the Caribbean: A Sivanandan at the Institute of Race Relations; Darcus Howe, Faroukh Dhondhy and Linton Kwesi Johnson from the Race Today Collective; Gus John and John La Rose of the Black Parents Movement.

Immigrant pupils and their parents were trying to steer a course through a secondary education system in turmoil and transition. Pupils and their families were also affected since literally outside the school gates the ferment of the Sixties was unfolding.

Politically it was '68 revolution time, it was Civil Rights, it was clenched fists at the Olympic Games. (Dennis)

Chapter Two

The Secondary Years

The interplay between post-war race relations and urban education policy

The contrasting backdrop of home and community (where their parents could exert influence) and education policy (over which their parents exercised little power) were manifest in the experiences of the seven black men in the newly-formed comprehensive schools. Their accounts are considered from their first impressions as 11-year-olds through to the often painful exit following un-instructive and often openly discriminatory careers advice. The interplay between the macro- and the exo-system – 'one or more settings that do not involve the developing person as an active participant, but in which events occur that affect or are affected by, what happens in the setting containing the developing person' (Bronfenbrenner, 1979:26) – is explored through the experience of attending **Home Beech** and **High Towers** Schools and the interaction between home and the wider community.

The changing policy context of secondary education with the advent of comprehensive schooling in the mid-1960s is considered as the *macro-system*. These changes together with the impact of immigration on inner London secondary schools, its consequences for teachers and the structural inequalities of the early models of comprehensive schooling form a rich ecological background to the construction of parenting and educational values among the seven black men.

The policy setting – the changing face of secondary education

> Extra resources should be applied where required, but no attempts made to turn 'geese' into 'swans'. It is cruel to try and make a non-academic into an academic whether at a middle class fee paying school or a down town comprehensive or primary. 'Geese' are more use anyway to those who have eyes to see, in their own habitat just as beautiful. (Memorandum from the Chair of Haringey Community Relations Council to the Parliamentary Select Committee on Race Relations and Immigration, 1973)

What is often omitted from accounts of 'race' and the education of immigrant children in the post-war period is their location within a wider social and educational debate on the merits and demerits of comprehensive secondary education, which was at its most intense after the Second World War. The 1944 Education Act laid down no rules governing the pattern of provision to be made for secondary education. However the Ministry of Education in the late 1940s was insistent that comprehensive schools must be large schools of at least 1600 pupils to be able to serve the ability profile of 'grammar, technical and modern' in a similar ratio as they existed at that time. This required a minimum of ten forms of entry divided, typically, into two grammar streams (for those who had passed the selective 11-plus exam), two technical streams (for those opting for a more vocational training) and six or seven modern streams for those wanting a general education. Nevertheless as local education authorities began to work out their development plans, some, including London, opted for 'multilateral' schools – which catered for pupils of all abilities; others proposed 'bi-lateral' schools of various types, for example, grammar–modern, technical–modern. As Rubenstein and Simon note:

> The mid-1950s were marked by a series of conflicts between local authorities wishing to establish comprehensive schools, and the Ministry wishing to prevent this development except on its own terms. (Rubenstein and Simon, 1969:73)

Government policies on immigrants and education were ostensibly non-interventionist for much of the post-war period. However the Race Relations Act 1968 which heralded the formation of the Commission for Racial Equality also signalled a shift in educational policy towards ethnic minorities in general, and West Indian pupils in particular. These developments were chronicled in the deliberations of what was to be the highly influential Parliamentary Select Committee on Race Relations and Immigration.

The impact of the Parliamentary Select Committee on Race Relations and Immigration

Established in 1968, not only did the Committee receive a wide range of submissions and personal testimonies, but they also commissioned and published a series of reports from 1969 onwards (for example, Townsend, 1971), which reveal the government's laissez-faire approach to the education of immigrant pupils. In his evidence to the Select Committee on Race Relations and Immigration on 14 May 1969 Sir Herbert Andrew, Permanent Under-Secretary of State for Education replied thus to a question about the absence of leadership by the department:

> I do not think we are in a position as a Department to give lead-

ership except that we might encourage sensible and rational and humane tolerant attitudes within educational institutions. I think the Department is not so much leading as in part following.

The monitoring of Britain's school population by ethnicity has long been problematic. For many years, an accurate picture of the number of black pupils of Caribbean, Asian and African origin in English schools was not possible, primarily because of the definition of 'immigrant' favoured by the Department of Education and Science (DES). Taylor (1981) in her review of the research into the education of pupils of West Indian origin notes that in 1972 the DES data defined 'immigrant' pupils as:

> Either children born outside the British Isles who have come to this country with or to join parents or guardians whose countries of origin were abroad [or] children born in the UK to parents whose countries of origin were abroad and who came to the UK up to 10 years before the date to which the figures apply.

The figures *excluded* children of mixed immigrant parentage and all pupils of secondary school age born in the UK. Indeed such were the difficulties entailed in using the DES statistics to conduct any meaningful analysis of numbers of West Indian pupils in English schools, that the Parliamentary Select Committee on Race Relations and Immigration was driven to rebuke the Department on a number of occasions: first in 1968 while investigating 'the problems of coloured school leavers'; and more notably in 1973 when the committee was able to secure an admission from the Secretary of State for Education that the Department continued to collect the data knowing not only that the figures were unhelpful and difficult to collect, but virtually unusable. As a consequence, the Chair of the Committee concluded that:

'... much of our inquiry [involved] taking detailed evidence about statistics, assembled with great labour and no doubt some embarrassment by teachers and local education authorities, which have served little or no practical purpose. (House of Commons, 1973:46).

Similar points were made by members of the Rampton Inquiry, commissioned by the Parliamentary Select Committee in 1981, which noted that their task in preparing the report *West Indians in Our Schools* was made more difficult by the absence of statistics on the distribution of West Indian children. Although schools collected statistics on the ethnic origins of their pupils, there was little uniformity in the classifications used. The final report reiterates these points and concludes:

By implication these statistics suggested that after ten years in Britain an immigrant family would cease to suffer from any educational difficulties that could be attributed to immigration and racial difference. (House of Commons, 1981:95)

However this needs to be seen in its political context; particularly at the level of expediency, as Hawkes observed earlier:

The main hindrance to public concern has been the unwillingness of national and local authorities alike to reveal the extent of the 'immigrant problem' at all. Because of the atmosphere which tends to surround the immigration issue in this country (Hawkes, 1966:18)

Throughout the preceding decade, the Government was under considerable pressure from its right wing to respond to the issue of immigrants in schools as outlined in the previous chapter. DES

Circular 7/65 recommended that numbers of immigrant pupils should not rise above one-third of the roll of a school. Enoch Powell MP, whose infamous anti-immigration speeches in 1968 had shaken Government complacency, also raised concerns about the impact of immigration on education. In 1971 Powell wrote to the Secretary of State for Education challenging the DES statistics on immigrant pupils as 'phoney', drawing a written parliamentary reply, in which the Secretary of State indicated that the DES would follow the Select Committee recommendation that schools should record parents' country of origin in order to give a more accurate picture of the numbers of immigrant pupils in the population.[1] Had this recommendation been implemented (it was not) the recorded numbers of immigrant pupils would have been significantly larger than the statistical data collected by the DES indicated.[2] Clearly this would have had political ramifications and might arguably have aided those politicians and extreme-right organisations which were campaigning for an end to immigration. Nevertheless, the consequence was that many schools had to work out their policies and strategies for teaching and supporting immigrant pupils at best locally but more often on their own. The Select Committee on Race Relations and Immigration's fifth report on education stated categorically:

> If, after our enquiry, one conclusion stands out above all others, it is that we have failed to grasp and are still failing to grasp the scale of what we have taken on. Far too many who are closely involved show reluctance to assess it realistically. (House of Commons, 1973:55)

Trevor Burgin, headteacher at Spring Grove, Huddersfield noted the high level of local as well as international interest in their approach as the designated school in the area for receiving and integrating immigrant children. Yet he observed wryly:

> Throughout these days of experimenting, of accepting or discarding, of formulating and pioneering, help and guidance from the Ministry of Education, now the Department of Education and Science, has only occasionally been in evidence. This might possibly be because the education of immigrant children is a completely new field. However six years is a considerable time, and our experiences have shown that the problem shows no sign of decreasing in size. Discussions with colleagues who have faced similar problems show complete agreement that a strong lead from the 'top' is vitally necessary. (Burgin and Edson, 1967:87)

The impact of immigration on urban secondary schools

Within the space of a few years the source of intake of some schools changed radically, all the more noticeably because of colour. Townsend reported that, not only were there disparities in the distribution of immigrant pupils between LEAs, but within individual LEAs, only some schools were affected. (Townsend, 1971:22).

In September 1958 one Birmingham secondary school had one 'coloured' boy on roll; three years later Commonwealth immigrant pupils represented thirty per cent of this school's roll (DES, 1971a). Headteacher George Meredith recalls with painful honesty, in a chapter entitled 'The Changing Response of a Secondary Modern School in Handsworth, 1958–1970':

> During the first two or three years when our school became a multi-racial one, the predominant feeling of the teachers was one of considerable dismay. (Meredith, 1971:88)

A similar transformation took place in a significant number of London's secondary schools. J R Roberts, headteacher of a Haringey secondary school wrote in 1967:

> At assembly I often look at all the various faces in front of me and think: What have we done to deserve this? How have we been able to avoid racial trouble? The answer is briefly that we have always tried to face every issue as it comes. (London Council of Social Service, 1967: 79)

This sense of transition was equally evident to pupils at Home Beech and High Towers Schools. Arran remembers his first days at the school in 1955.

> Home Beech was an all boys' school and there were four other black boys. (Arran)

Ten years later the ethnic profile of the school was markedly different.

> At the time in Hackney, there were two schools, which were predominantly for black children. Clapton Park for the girls and Home Beech for the boys. (Carl)

Similarly at High Towers in 1968 Dennis recalls joining a school in transition:

> There were whites in the years above but they were fading whereas with my intake it was black. By the fourth year (1972) the school was 60% black and teachers were just in control, but losing it. (Dennis)

The impact of black Caribbean immigration on teachers

It was hardly surprising that in the absence of any central direction for the previous decade, by 1970 a culture of 'blaming the victim' was in place with regard to the education of immigrant pupils. Gibbes quotes an unnamed Caribbean teacher in her pamphlet 'West Indian Teachers Speak Out':

> When I came back to London in 1965 I thought that my qualifications which were all from London University – the BA, PGCE and later the MA would stand me in good stead, together with my experience. But to my surprise I was told that I had to start at the bottom of the ladder. I was given a class of twenty-five West Indian louts, as the teachers called them. They were really dreadful girls. Coming from the West Indies, I myself was horrified when I walked into that school and that class because it was the first time I had come face to face with really rough West Indians, and at that time I did not have the experience, which I now have. I couldn't understand why those black children were like that. Now I understand it because I am like that myself. I can fight and turn and burn down buildings and do anything now. I feel that way. Unfortunately for the children, at that time I couldn't really sympathise with their feelings. (Gibbes, 1980:16).

As Nandy accurately asserts:

> The real responsibility lies with the policy of *laissez-faire* which characterized the whole field of race relations and immigration, and it is well to remind ourselves that *laissez-faire* is not the *absence* of policy so much as a policy *not* to have a policy. (Nandy, 1971:10)

Nandy is echoed by one of the seven-strong National Union of

Teachers (NUT) delegation, which submitted evidence to the House of Commons Select Committee on 7 May 1969:

> There is a row of teachers here and not one of us has been trained to look after immigrants. We just got ourselves involved in it. It is a climate of opinion among the whole public, of which the teachers ought to be leaders, that makes people get themselves involved in things.[3]

All seven would attest to the absence of specialist training and the lack of cultural awareness of many teachers. Errol remembers that at the end of one assembly, all the 'Jamaican' boys were asked to remain behind.

> I was leaving 'cos I ain't Jamaican [I'm from St Lucia] and I was going out of the place and a teacher stopped me. Apparently somebody had nicked some cakes out of the bakery down the road so, and the person was black and they couldn't tell whether the person was in the first year or the sixth form! All the black kids in the school were lined up in a big long row, right and this teacher right, old military man, he walked along the row putting his hands on our hearts and anybody's heart who he felt was beating too fast was pulled out and questioned right. It could never happen now man. Yeah I remember that. (Errol)

Although the DES did fail to provide a lead, that is not the same as saying the government made no contribution to the debate on the education of immigrants; their interventions were subtle. For example, much of the text in Education Survey 13 *The Education of Immigrants* (DES, 1971b), written by HM Inspectorate, appears to be taken up with justifying the lack of policy direction. However its main purpose is to shore up the teaching profession against charges of racism in its treatment of black pupils. By its fulsome and uncritical praise of teachers for their excellent work with immigrant children, it is intolerant of any suggestion of racism on the part of teachers.

> Where teachers occasionally show biased attitudes towards coloured peoples these probably result largely from a lack of knowledge of the pupils' cultural and social background and from the sense of bewilderment they experience at not knowing how to set about the job of teaching these pupils. (DES, 1971b:11)

Concerns about the educational achievement of West Indian children were considered by the Parliamentary Select Committee on Race Relations and Immigration. They were the subjects of various Department of Education reports (1965, 1971a, 1971b, 1972) throughout the period during which the seven men were at secondary school. However it was not until 1981 that the interim findings of the first significant Committee on educational achievement (chaired by Sir Anthony Rampton) were published under the title 'West Indian children in Our Schools'. The committee's final report 'Education for All' was published in 1985 after the Committee was reconstituted controversially by the new Conservative administration and placed under the chairmanship of Lord Swann.

Not everyone had seen the arrival of immigrants as negative or problematic. In his personal evidence to the Select Committee on Race Relations and Immigration on 1 April 1969, the headteacher of Clissold Park School (a 1000-pupil mixed Hackney secondary school with an immigrant intake of some 60%) said:

> May I add something which is not always realised: one great benefit which large numbers of immigrant children bring to a school such as mine is that almost every single one wants to stay on at school after the statutory leaving age. They create in the

school the tradition of staying on and by doing so they draw up with them into this the white boys and girls from the area who otherwise would have gone as soon as the law allowed. So quite an extraordinary percentage of all nationalities do stay on beyond the leaving age – 90 per cent in my own school, which, in an area like this, is remarkable. (House of Commons, 1969: Vol 1–2)

Clearly some teachers shared the colour prejudice endemic in the wider indigenous community at that time. A decade later, the Rampton committee (House of Commons, 1981) devoted a section of its report to the impact of teacher racism on the education of West Indian children; largely because of its frequent citation by West Indian pupils and their parents as a significant factor. To summarise: the Inquiry found evidence of teacher racism, whether intentional or otherwise, in low expectations, negative attitudes, perceptions of West Indian pupils as inevitably causing difficulties and stereotypic assumptions of low attainment in academic subjects in contrast to physical education, drama and art. The Inquiry also noted the wide discrepancy between the positive and considered submissions by teacher unions at national level with regard to the educational needs of minority ethnic groups and the often negative responses and practice by their members at local and school level (House of Commons, 1981:74).

Numbers of immigrant pupils placed in special schools

The placement of a high proportion of pupils from black Caribbean backgrounds in special schools in the early days of post-war Caribbean migration was not the focus of this study. As evident earlier, the impact of immigration on urban schools was a largely unsupported affair. Teachers could hardly be blamed for *initially* seeing the arrival of immigrant children as 'problems' (Nandy, 1971) given the leadership and tone demonstrated by the Department of Education:

> The needs of immigrant children in their early days in school are often as much social and medical as educational. (DES, 1965:2)

Anxieties about the over-referral of West Indian children to special schools had been expressed by members of the North London West Indian Association as early as 1965 (Taylor, 1981). Bernard Coard's highly influential pamphlet 'How the West Indian Child is Made Educationally Sub-normal In The British School System' published in 1971 is the most cited critique of this outcome of educational policy on immigrant pupils and was based on his analysis of the 1967 ILEA Language Survey.[4] For example, the ILEA Report of 1967/8 on Norwood Girls' School in Lambeth included a table of the proportion of immigrants in other local secondary schools, based on the 'Form 7 immigrant return' for 18 January 1968. Norwood is recorded as having 21.5%; but the highest return was for Parkside, the local special school with 55%.

Since few studies use black Caribbean parents as primary sources, there is very little evidence of the impact of such high numbers of first-generation black Caribbean pupils being educated outside mainstream education. Such research might begin to explain the continuing reluctance of the majority of black Caribbean pupils and their families to reflect on their experience of education. Bryan et al (1985) quote anonymous testimonies:

> At first I didn't realise what was going on because I really thought they were sending her to a 'special' school. The school sent me a letter telling me they were going to transfer her and that she'd get more attention, they never spelt out what kind of school it was. As soon as I saw that most of the other kids there were Black, I knew

something was going on ... I didn't know what to do, I was so angry ... But I went along to this meeting one Sunday and there were a lot of people there with kids in ESN schools who felt the same way. That's how they came to set up the Saturday School, because everyone was saying if the schools wouldn't educate our children, we should do it ourselves. (Bryan, Dadzie and Scafe, 1985:71)

Little consideration has been given to the negative impact and stigma associated with attending special school for many of the black Caribbean pupils, who are now parents themselves (McKenley, 2001). The impact is under-researched although the numbers were such as to indicate that a significant minority of black Caribbean pupils were placed in special schools for reasons which had as much to do with institutional racism as their special educational needs (Coard, 1971).

The secondary schools attended by the seven black men

Home Beech School, North London and **High Towers School**, South London were just two of the new London multi-lateral comprehensives described earlier and typically streamed by ability in academic subjects with vertical House systems for pastoral and sporting activities. Arran was in the first intake of pupils to Home Beech School:

There were four Houses: Newton, Stephenson, Kevin and Faraday. There were vertical tutor groups, house captains and head boy. Each year was set. The school was secondary modern. My mother liked the look of it because it was new and without reputation. Another memory I have is of the headteacher showing me the blank leavers board for future graduates. (Arran)

Arriving nearly a decade later Carl remembers his parents were less impressed than Arran's mother had been:

At the time in Hackney, there were two schools, which were predominantly for black children ... and my parents were very clear on this and thought why are all the black kids going to these two schools? Why aren't they going to university? They wanted me to have what they thought was a better education by not going to that school. (Carl)

High Towers School, South London opened in September 1956 with a roll of 1622 boys; most of whom had transferred directly from three existing local schools, Santley School, Stuart School and the Brixton School of Building. The rest came on voluntary transfer from other secondary schools and the remaining one-quarter direct from local primary schools. Its first headmaster was formerly deputy head of a prestigious boys' public school. Staff appointed to the school came from all over Britain. Sited on the playing fields of a former local grammar school, High Towers school was unique in architectural design: a nine-storey purpose built comprehensive. Boys were prepared for university, the professions, industry and commerce. The school was divided into a lower and upper school for administrative purposes. Games and social activities were organised on a House system. Each boy on entry to the school was attached to one of eight Houses, named after famous South Londoners. Most of the former pupils in this study joined the school a decade later but Errol recalls:

The intake included a lot of middle class kids whose parents were committed to the comprehensive ideal. (Errol)

The organisation of the study schools

A typical entry in the ILEA Secondary Year Book (1956) conveys a sense of the curriculum and ethos of a multi-lateral comprehensive:

> During the first three years, the boys follow a curriculum which is designed to give them a broad general education and includes English, history, geography, religious education, mathematics and science, handicraft, music, art, physical education and games. French, Spanish and Latin are included for those boys who are capable of profiting from work in these subjects.
>
> In the upper school, specialist studies are added according to the interests and abilities of the individual boy. These studies include physics, chemistry, biology and zoology; engineering and building; German, Greek and ancient history; economics and accountancy ...
>
> Boys can prepare for such professions as architecture, surveying, engineering and commerce.

Whatever the rhetoric of comprehensive education policy, in the early years of Caribbean immigration, few immigrant children were to be found in the 'grammar' streams of the multi-lateral comprehensives described above; neither on the whole were their poor white counterparts.

> The school was seriously streamed. Those who did Latin were at the top, I was in the middle. (Dennis)

Its inequalities were transparent. As Colin (Home Beech) sums up so succinctly:

> Top stream – two black kids – expected to take O levels; second stream expected to do mostly O levels, some CSEs; third stream –

each stream had six classes, expected to do half and half – was 60% black and the bottom stream had only one white kid. You could tell what stream you was in by the colour of the class and the work they were doing. (Colin)

Clearly the organisation of both schools had a significant impact on the choices available to pupils as they progressed through the school. The rigidity of the streaming arrangements was a significant constraint and belied the empowering rhetoric of comprehensive education. Arran's experience at Home Beech was typical:

Within the first day it was clear that I was much too able for the remedial set into which I had been placed. I have memories of working hard despite the behavioural difficulties of the white working class boys. I was put up one set in the next year and subsequently it was not until the Fourth Year that I got into the right set for my ability. One casualty of this was my French which was only available for top sets and so I was disadvantaged, not having studied it earlier. The teacher made fun of my accent and to this day I have found it difficult to learn languages. O levels, A levels these were available to us only in the Sixth Form because of the streaming of the school. (Arran)

For Owen the structures of High Towers were bewildering:

I was shocked that some black pupils were doing Greek and Latin. I thought no one asked me if I wanted to do Greek and Latin. I was aware of streams in different subjects which suggests fluidity but becomes a physical structure you're in. (Owen)

Those structural inequalities contributed to a profound understanding of institutional racism in education – which is evident in the parenting accounts presented later in this book – but also a deep sense of injustice on a subjective personal level as evident in Errol's contribution:

> The grammar kids didn't use the woodwork and the metalwork blocks in my memory and the rest of us did. The grammar stream was white. And the F stream, I think it was F for failure but I'm not sure, was significantly black. (Errol)

Trevor Carter recalls his first impressions of teaching in his autobiography *Shattering Illusions*:

> When I became a teacher in the early Seventies the image I formed of the academic structure of my first school, in which the majority of pupils were black, was of a snow-capped mountain. At the top, the white headteacher and most of the staff [I was the only West Indian teacher]. Immediately below, the white children. Then the black children, concentrated at the base of the mountain, a long way from the snow. (Carter, 1986:88)

The Caribbean Teachers' Association was formed during this period, in 1972. Carter defines the Association's aims as not just for mutual support and solidarity but also

> to provide role models for black children, to help black parents develop their involvement with their children's schools, and to provide a positive image for white people too, combating their stereotyped images of black people. (Carter, 1986)

The group worked alongside other anti-racist teachers' associations such as All London Teachers Against Racism and Fascism (ALTARF) and the National Association for Multi-Racial Education;

latterly the National Anti-Racist Movement in Education. Faroukh Dhondy was a founder member of ALTARF and taught in South London:

> Remember that at the time I read in the newspapers, almost every day, that the Labour Government of Harold Wilson was giving every child in Britain a new opportunity of equality through schooling. I read this on the bus to school and when I actually went to teach, I saw that all the top classes or forms in the school were exclusively white, and all the bottom forms, including the two, X and Y, which were composed of all the trouble-makers who wouldn't take instruction in the other forms, were black. (Dhondy, Beese and Hassan, 1982:9)

For Carl, the experience was completely different:

> I was in the top band when I got there and in the top band when I left. There were three or four black kids in the top stream at most. (Carl)

Colin also began his school life in the top stream at High Beech but could not resist the temptations of the alternative curriculum which operated beyond the classroom:

> Educationally I was OK because I was in the top class for the first two years. I wanted to work. I never got into trouble in my actual lessons. I got into trouble between lessons, at lunch times, at break times. I got dropped down in my third year and then I had problems because I don't think they expected anything of us. There were more black kids in these classes and we got lots of silly new teachers that had no chance in Home Beech. (Colin)

School daze[5] – first impressions of the study schools

Like their junior school equivalents today, the seven men were apprehensive about the transition from primary to secondary education.

> Usual fears that your head would be flushed down the toilet
> (Dennis)

> Some of the older boys said it was alright. And some of them got exams as Home Beech had an alright academic reputation.
> (Colin)

Arran recalls his mother had already done her research on Home Beech before his arrival from Trinidad and decided that it conformed to her expectations of a place in which her son could do well.

> My mother had seen Home Beech being built. We were interviewed by the headteacher and I was admitted to the lowest set of the first year. (Arran)

Arran's mother had been doing other kinds of research as well:

> I was warned by my mother about racist names. I remember her going through them with me as preparation in order that I would not be shocked and get into a fight. I survived without fighting for one week, trying to appease my mother, but I was badly losing face, becoming a target to be spat at, to have my book scrawled on – incidents which the teachers never appeared to see. I knew this could not go on or my life would be hell so I took on one of the leaders and that sorted that out. (Arran)

Errol recalls the initiation ceremony for first year pupils at High Towers:

> High Towers had a ritual. All new kids got thrown off the terrace which was about 10 feet high and it sloped. I learned something about myself that day. I never allowed anyone to push me over. I fought and fought and I wouldn't let anyone push me over. (Errol)

Owen remembers 'teachers wearing dracula gowns' at High Towers. For Colin, his first day at Home Beech was a rude awakening.

> That first day, the place just looked massive. I still kept my friends from primary school but at Tyssen we all looked out for each other. If someone fought one, they fought everybody. I got my briefcase and some sixth-former ran and jumped and went boom in my chest and then played football with my briefcase and all my little white friends watched, they couldn't do anything. And I got up all ready to go, expecting *us* to go and nothing happened. I thought all right and I got up and asked for my things back and the boy said 'Shut up you litttle black ...'. Then one of the big boys I knew, came and gave the boy a spanking. But what was in my mind, was my friends didn't help. I cut off my white friends from primary school because I felt betrayed. I avoided some of them for years because of that. (Colin)

Mike, a white Irish contemporary of Errol's, joined High Towers in September 1965. He recalls a school of nearly 2000 boys stratified by colour and ability, with twelve forms of entry divided into four bands: Blake, Brunel, Dickens and Faraday ('IB1 grammar; 1B2 modern: 1B3 not bright') with a school motto 'Omnes Ad Unum' – working together to one goal. Similarly Errol remembers:

being intimidated by this large school, which felt like another planet – so huge, so regimented, so organised. At one time we had 1700 boys singing hymns loud in assembly. (Errol)

Three years later Dennis arrived to a school in transition, which he remembers was:

Big like a factory and felt like a battlefield. It shifted from a high brow school, where you could be put into detention by prefects, to an uncertain comprehensive. (Dennis)

Curriculum debates

The turbulence of revolutionary and liberation movements in the US, Europe and Africa, and the increasing politicisation of debates within education, fuelled a deeper desire for recognition and a growing group/cultural identity. This was reflected in the potency of debates about the relevance of the curriculum. Professor Chris Mullard, born in Hampshire in 1944 and one of the first black British academics in the field of race relations, wrote in his autobiographical account *Black Briton* that:

Many of the books used were out of date, reflecting attitudes reminiscent of the colonial era, this bolstered up the feelings of insecurity and inferiority which many black children already felt.

(Mullard, 1973: 44)

Urban secondary schools like High Towers and Home Beech were at the forefront of debates on mixed ability groupings, remedial education, compensatory curricula and Black Studies. Tensions between teachers and older pupils were the inspiration for the seminal publication 'Black Settlers in Britain 1555–1958' (File and Power, 1981). This was one of the first secondary history textbooks to provide source material which proved the existence of black settlers in Britain much earlier in English history. It was written in response to pupils' demands for a more representative curriculum and Black Studies.

> Defining our own history because as it was taught, we were absent. The great challenge and support came from Y who took on board our concerns and rethought what to do and he pushed others to do the same. (Dennis)

The increasing radicalism of the pupils as well as the staff was also in evidence (Goffe, 1984). Post-war socialist ideals of equality and working class empowerment were contested in staffrooms and classrooms across the country. Leslie Goffe remembers joining High Towers School in 1970:

> Four-foot Afros were everywhere, as were the badges which flashed clenched fists and the demands 'Free the Soledad Brothers', 'Free Huey' ... The term 'coloured' which served my parents well enough was giving way to 'black'. When it was not petitions to get James Baldwin's work on the A level syllabus, it was a campaign for the 'The Brockwell Three' or to 'Stop Sus'. (Goffe, *Guardian* 16.08.1988).

Dennis saw the debates about the relevance of the curriculum as critical:

> What Black Studies gave us around the Fourth Year was a sense of purpose, direction, energy and drive, which we took into other lessons. This was triggered by older black boys who had contact with the Black Panthers. We followed their lead. (Dennis)

Relationships with teachers

There were teachers who saw the newly-formed comprehensives as an opportunity to put their educational ideals into practice. This was evident throughout the history of the two secondary schools; not only at the outset, where the emphasis was on bringing the best of the English public school curriculum into mainstream comprehensives.

> The teachers were all post-war trained and passionate believers in education; some were Oxbridge graduates. (Arran)

Former pupils and teachers at High Towers School cite a classroom debate during a religious education lesson on the merits of passive resistance versus armed liberation as the catalyst for change. Errol describes this lesson as a turning point in defining his identity as a black man and group member:

> I remember the RE teacher who was this great Liberal guy who was very progressive. He wanted us to have a discussion about whether the Black Panthers [a revolutionary Marxist group which began in the USA] were right to pick up guns and he talked about the Panthers to engage us, but basically his message was the same as anybody else, which basically violence was wrong and so I wanted to agree with him, because I do believe violence is wrong, but I said to him, 'Why are you condemning the violence of the Panthers but not the violence of the Police?' and he said but they're both wrong. I said, 'But if they're both wrong, why are we talking about condemning the Panthers for violence, why aren't we having a discussion about the Police Force in America and what they're doing to black people?'

I hardly knew anything about what the police were doing to black people, but somehow from this discussion it came up and then other black guys came in and gradually, what happened was that the class polarised, and every single black person in the room was for the Panthers, or at least for not condemning the Panthers, and all the white kids were being good liberals and condemning violence in an abstract kind of way. That lunch time when the lesson was over all of us as black boys got together and walked down to the park, Brockwell Park. We didn't go back to school for the rest of the afternoon, and we just stayed there and talked. It was a very significant moment, because those guys who were in the classroom, who I walked down to the park with, are my friends today. We stayed together ever since. (Errol)

The power of the pupil–teacher relationships described in this study was captured in Arran's account of what he perceived to be a critical moment in his secondary schooling:

I have no recollection of us black boys being unruly, although I can remember an incident where the headteacher called me to his office. He wanted me to tell the other black boys in the school to stop jumping over the flowerbeds while playing 'He'. The head said, 'I know that you boys aren't used to flowerbeds but please stop.' Now in the school everyone who could, black and white, jumped over the flowerbeds because it gave you an advantage when being chased. So I and the other boys who were Fourth Years at the time called a meeting of all the black pupils in the school, by then about 200.

Everyone came. I recounted the head's conversation and his view of the black pupils being the only ones to jump the flowerbeds. I used this as an example of the challenge we faced, what we were up against and to remember to concentrate on our education, inferring that no one would do it for us. The Head of the House, in whose main room the meeting was held, must have passed and observing some 200 black boys in a meeting addressed by other black kids, started to intervene. I replied that the Head had asked me to call this meeting. I can still remember the look on his face. That was a very important moment for me.

Later when I began to truant as I was fed up and disaffected, the same Head of House came and had a word with me and made common cause with his Jewish immigrant experience and mine and the value placed on education by his family and my mother. He talked about my mother's sacrifice and that he thought I was letting her down. He made a direct link and that was a turning point – the intervention of a teacher as a human being who knew about discrimination and education was important. It was as if seeing me addressing that meeting had changed his view of me and after that I felt he looked out for me and argued my corner. He saw me as an individual from that moment on. (Arran)

Mention has to be made of both the negative 'tyranny' of PE teachers in schools such as High Towers and Home Beech, and the positive opportunity to broaden pupils' horizons that PE and Games afforded. The special privileges that those boys who were talented sportsmen enjoyed in such schools at this time were also extended to pupils of Caribbean heritage.

I remember getting in trouble and being suspended and I had a football match. The PE teacher came round my house to tell me that I wasn't suspended anymore. Nuff man in trouble and I've seen the Sports Master almost fight the teacher that suspended you. He'd be shouting at the teacher, 'You'd better get it sorted.' And that gave us a false sense of power. Yet having said that I did fencing at Home Beech. I fenced in some funny schools with wood-panelling everywhere, dark musty places. (Colin)

Undoubtedly, the arrival of Caribbean pupils changed the sporting reputations of many schools during this period. It provided some of the few opportunities where black pupils were able to exert bargaining power and influence. But even here, schools often exploited the talents of black Caribbean boys to suit the school's purposes, rather than the interest of boys. Boycotting PE to focus on their academic studies in the Fifth Year is a common theme for black pupils educated in comprehensive schools at that time.

The school wasn't responsive enough ... I remember abandoning sports and through Black Studies a mass of us left for college because school was not an environment for learning. (Dennis)

Crimes and punishments – formal and informal disciplines

The corporal punishment ethos of a boys' school in the post-war period is clear from the extracts below and reinforced in some cases by the social anthropological perspective adopted by early researchers on West Indian immigrant life.

The West Indian child is used to being told what to learn and how to learn it ... He is not expected to have a naturally inquiring mind, perpetually demanding to know answers to his search questions. On the contrary he is expected to respond to a heavy discipline with the threat of flogging if he doesn't do as he is told or learn what he should. (Morrish, 1971:89)

Mr F was a good headteacher, but if he caned you, you laughed and there were other teachers who you had to sit in a basin of cold water after. (Colin)

However a cautionary note has to be struck since this was the prevailing view on maintaining boys' discipline at that time; notwithstanding its impact on pupils and teachers alike.

> I think in Home Beech you had an old school of teachers, old middle-aged white men who didn't want to be there, ran the school, were House Masters. There was a younger generation of teachers who would talk to us. But there were others who would do some dark things in cupboards. But when I went home and told my mum, she said, 'You lie, teachers don't do that.' So you couldn't go home and tell them. I've seen geezers from Trinidad, not born here, big muscular guys who wouldn't take any shit, fighting teachers all the way down the corridors. (Colin)

Playground discipline had its own rules with territories and boundaries clearly outlined.

> I remember once I was in the toilets and this guy came to mug me for my money and he slapped me on the back of my head while I was drinking water so I banged my mouth on the tap. I was very upset. He asked me for the money and I don't know what came over me but I punched him and ran, ran, ran into the playground. I thought I'd got away from him, then bouf! This white guy landed on top of me and started to beat me up. And all of a sudden this guy got picked up and carried over to Niggers Corner. The playground was divided into Niggers Corner, Smokers Corner and the white bit in the middle. The black kids used to hang out in Niggers Corner and Smokers Corner was where the hard white guys used to hang out. And these black guys carried this kid into Niggers Corner and he never troubled me again. (Errol)

Errol remembers being told by friends that 'some sisters at the local girls' school had been banned from wearing their hair Afro style' and that the next day *every* black girl in the school came in with her hair in an Afro. Carl recalls a similar situation in Home Beech.

At first the school had banned us having Afros and you couldn't bring an Afro comb but eventually they relented reluctantly. The school found it difficult to deal with the idea of strong black men. They believed in the comprehensive ideal but it had its limits.

(Carl)

The interplay between gender and ethnicity evident in these school biographies is complex and worthy of more in-depth consideration than can be afforded in this book. Gillborn's two-year ethnographic study conducted in 1984 and 1985 at City Road comprehensive found that behavioural rather than educational factors operate for many teachers in multi-ethnic classrooms (1990:23) He analysed all aspects of the school's sanctions, not just exclusions, and found that

during their school careers a much greater proportion of Afro-Caribbean pupils in the age group received at least one report card: 37 per cent of Afro-Caribbean pupils compared to 6 per cent of all other ethnic origins. (Gillborn, 1990: 34)

This continues to be the case (see the recent report by the London Development Agency, 2004) – black boys continue to be disproportionately represented in school exclusions (formal and informal).

Involvement of parents
The growth in political consciousness stimulated by the Civil Rights movement in the United States and anti-imperialist liberation struggles worldwide led Dhondy (1982) to argue that:

> There was a black movement in education in this country from the time that our children began to be schooled here. Its spokesmen were the parents of the young blacks who were born here or brought from the West Indies, from India, Pakistan, Bangladesh and Africa, as dependents. (Dhondy et al, 1982:11)

This radical picture is only partly reflected in the experience of the seven men. The patterns of parental involvement that had been established during their time at primary school continued into secondary school, albeit in keeping with their white peers, in a more reduced capacity. Carl, Arran and Owen felt their parent/s were generally active in their involvement, not just in terms of attendance at key school events but in their attitudes toward supporting their sons.

> My mother always went to Parents' Evening. My father did shift work and would join her when he could. They played an active role. Anytime there was a problem, they came up to school – always a back up for me. (Carl)

Errol and Dennis, however, had parents whose levels of literacy ill-equipped them to engage critically with their sons' education. In this regard Dennis felt that, in common with many of his peers as he observed, he was basically on his own.

> They came to school once and realised it was not for them. They had no ability to intervene. We conducted our own pupil–teacher debates about our welfare because they [my parents] couldn't do it. (Dennis)

For Colin, his mother's involvement in school was solely in response to misdemeanours and sanctions.

I got suspended five times and my mother had to come up lots of times. She'd come and then she'd say, 'Do you want to come back to the school? Then hush your mouth!' Except one time, when two teachers were beating up my cousin and I steamed in to help and we both got suspended, my cousin went home with the same story and my mother said, 'But wait, it truth him talk all the time deh?' Mum came up the school and said 'How come Terry [my cousin] bruise up and how come Junior always tell me these stories – is lie him so lie?' So she said 'Are you taking him back or should I report this to somebody?' They took me back but after that it got more subtle. Eventually I was expelled. (Colin)

Tomlinson (1987) admits that much of the educational research literature of the 1960s and 1970s was devoted to discussing the 'unrealistic' aspirations of immigrant parents for their children. There is no evidence to suggest that parental aspirations of the families diminished with the advent of secondary education, but nor were there any discernible changes in the behaviours established in Chapter 1. Parental participation of families in the governance of schools was not generally a Caribbean experience at that time; domestic commitments and working patterns militated against such involvement by parents.

Towards the end of the 1970s, concerns about black Caribbean achievement or as depicted then, *West Indian under-achievement*, take on a different gloss with the emphasis shifting from immigrants failing to fit into the 'host' society, to a more social class-based perception that along with white working class children, schools were failing to educate disadvantaged pupils.

This is a criticism of the system not of the victims of that system.
(CRC, 1974)

Following the Rampton report (1981) authorities such as the ILEA began to address the issue of black underachievement from a wider perspective. No longer seen as the domain of a minority of multi-ethnic schools, authorities began to incorporate system-wide, anti-discriminatory policies; these developments were hard-won.

> It must be remembered that anti-racist policies were not adopted as something desired by the white administration at County Hall [headquarters of the ILEA and Greater London Council]. They were fought for by black parents and teachers who saw and opposed the damage a racist education system was doing to black pupils. (Gus John, quoted in Williams, 1990:113)

But by then the former pupils had long since left school.

> High Towers wasn't a place you felt you'd come out as part of the New Britain. This was about endurance. (Dennis)

> Having said all of that, I loved it at Home Beech. I didn't want to miss it because there was excitement every day. Sometimes I'd be sick, wheezing, mum would say that I couldn't go and I'd be there at home wondering what everyone was getting up to, and me begging to go to school. (Colin)

Post-compulsory education?

The main focus of the ecological study was to examine the educational biographies of seven first-generation immigrants from the Caribbean, the parenting they received and how they reflect on that experience when they consider their own parenting of children who are currently at school in the UK. However, I have included this section as a bridge between the experience as pupils and the later experience of becoming parents. It demonstrates how educational values were sustained in the face of considerable challenge for some, but not all of the seven black men. Paragraph 11 of the memorandum submitted by the DES to the Select Committee observes that:

> There is a tendency, especially noticeable in some thickly populated West Indian areas, for a higher proportion of coloured than white pupils to stay on beyond the statutory leaving age to give them better employment opportunities ... this sometimes stems from parental aspirations which are far beyond the qualifications their children are likely to obtain, in which case it can give rise to disappointment and resentment. (House of Commons, 1969:100)

Ten years later, members of the Rampton Committee took a different view:

> One of the strongest impressions which we have formed from our visits and discussions has been of the wide gulf in trust and understanding between schools and West Indian parents. In some cases, however, the expectations, views and worries of West Indian parents about their children's progress seem to be misunderstood and sometimes, as we have found, even disregarded by teachers. (House of Commons, 1981:41)

Preparation for working life – the role of the Careers Service

Concern about racial discrimination against the 'West Indian School Leaver' was one of a number of recurring themes throughout the period of schooling considered in this book. Each major inquiry merely served to restate concerns, foreshadowed in early research studies, about the poor standard of careers information and guidance available to West Indian pupils at school. These included the widespread discrimination in the job market and the mismatch between options available on leaving school and the likelihood of being directed towards meaningful employment. The Rampton Inquiry (1981) found a lack of serious attention given to the importance of careers education for West Indian pupils. There was little evidence of systematic monitoring by the Careers Service of the vocational opportunities and job destinations of pupils from black Caribbean backgrounds. Four years later, the final report of the Swann Committee identified institutional racism as:

> the way in which a range of long-established systems, practices and procedures, both within education and the wider society, which were originally conceived and devised to meet the needs and aspirations of a relatively homogeneous society, can now be seen not only to fail to take account of the multi-racial nature of Britain today but may also ignore or even actively work against the interest of ethnic minority communities. (House of Commons, 1985:28)

These sentiments are echoed by a number of black and anti-racist researchers. Verma and Neasham (1990) analysed the findings of the Brent Independent Investigation Team who collected evidence from local parents over a three-year period from 1981 to 1984. The team's terms of reference were to assess the standards achieved in the authority's secondary schools with an emphasis on the concerns of parents, particularly black parents, about levels of provision and achievement. Verma and Neasham analysed the sample of 700 interviews and 1200 parental questionnaire responses; the ethnic breakdown of the sample was 40% white, 35% Asian and 24% Afro-Caribbean. The researchers found that Afro-Caribbean parents felt their children were:

> All too often steered towards *soft* subjects when it came to making 4th and 5th year curriculum choices, thus reducing their career opportunities. (Verma and Neasham, 1990:74).

Verma and Neasham's research (1990) also stressed the reliance that ethnic minority parents and their children, unlike their white counterparts, placed on institutions like the Careers Service for advice and placement; access to informal networks was limited.

> School actually put me off work to an amazing degree. I was totally confused. My parents' notion of a good thing for me to do as an educated person would be to become a lawyer or doctor or a minister of religion. Nobody at school expected anything of the kind and this made for a ridiculous disjunction between who I was at school and who I was at home. (Mike Phillips quoted in Green, 1990: 237)

The National Union of Students convened a group of students of Caribbean and African origin to give evidence to the Swann Committee on their formative school experiences. The extract below gives a flavour of the issues pupils faced at this time:

> The type of advice I was given by my careers teacher at school when I stated that I wanted to become a lawyer was, 'Work in Woolworths where you can meet people.' I was so amazed I couldn't be bothered to say anything else to her. (House of Commons, 1985: 103).

The seven men reserve their most vitriolic scorn for the Careers Service. A recurring theme is the sense of anger at being abandoned by the school at such a critical time, of being so poorly prepared for the racism in the work place and the hard realities of finding meaningful employment as a young black man in London. The tone of Owen's account is illustrative:

> Of all sections in High Towers, the failing of the Careers Service

was the most damning. There, gradation was most apparent. Black pupils were seen as fodder. The Careers officer asked what did I want to do on leaving school. This man I'd hardly met. I remember saying that I wanted to be a radio and TV engineer but I received no response to my request for advice on how I might go about that. He actually said 'You're a tall lad, have you thought about joining the Police Force or the Fire Service?' Given the racism of the time, it was clearly a question of going through the motions. Surprise, surprise ten months of looking for job after job – dejected and rejected. (Owen)

These disappointments and failures were a source of deep sadness and humiliation in many immigrant families and are a theme in many of the plays, films and literature of this period.[6] For Errol's family, the consequences were tragic when his older brother did not do well academically.

A big fight ensued and a sadness which permeated the house. Father felt that his eldest son, his pride and joy had failed. He blamed the son not the school. Mother did not feel like that, just love him still the same. My brother has never had children. (Errol)

Only Colin had a different perspective:

I didn't do my O levels. In my last year of school, I punched a teacher, I was playing cards and he tried to get them off me. I was about to get suspended and my maths teacher pleaded for me and so I was allowed to exams and if I stayed out of trouble. I mucked about in one exam and that was that. I went to work, there was work then. (Colin)

Higher education?

As reiterated earlier in this chapter, the structure of the multi-lateral comprehensive with its bands, streams and setting and its differentiated curriculum meant that acquiring the qualifications required for higher education was highly problematic. Only Arran and Carl went to university directly on leaving school. Of the seven accounts Carl's experience of school was the most atypical. Of the seven he was the only one who *began and ended* his schooling in the top set.

> A lot of people left and went to college. I stayed on at school. I did fairly good but I could have done better. I think I should have got three A levels but I failed my best subject so I was a bit disappointed. But I was able to go on and do a degree as my sister had done. All four of us did degrees. My parents publicised our achievements in the Jamaica Gleaner (weekly broadsheet newspaper published in Jamaica). They did the same when my sister got her Master's Degree. I'm doing one at the moment. (Carl)

Pictures were also sent home of Arran's achievement in going to university although his route to higher education was less direct than Carl's. Having started school in the 'bottom' set, he moved 'up' incrementally each year and was only able to recover his options by staying in the Sixth Form for three years. But Arran did eventually fulfil his mother's 'unshaken belief' that he would attend university: 'No matter what they throw at you, you're going to university.' Arran left Home Beech to attend the University of Kent in 1975; he was 20 years old.

Holberton (1977) provided one of the few taxonomies of black achievement, which appeared in the ILEA's weekly in-house newspaper *Contact*. Arran and Carl were the closest match to 'the achiever' at the end of their secondary schooling; with Errol and Dennis perhaps more akin to his alter ego.

The Achiever

Finds home a place where he can follow interests and hobbies.
Has grown-ups who are prepared to spend time with him.
Wants to stay on at school to see how far he can go.
Prefers university or college to employment at school-leaving.
Receives the support of his parents in these aspirations.
Has parents who do not mind an argument about some things.
Does not feel unfavourably compared with other children.
Does not spend a great deal of time with his peers.

The Under-Achiever

Has parents who are too busy to spend time with him.
Gets into trouble for asking questions and for arguing.
Has only restricted discussion with his parents.
Has parents who make rules and take decisions without
    reference to his opinions.
Is allowed to make few decisions.
Has a home in which there is a strong tendency towards
    distinct role-taking.   (Holberton, 1977)

For the other participants the path to higher education was more circuitous, with periods of unemployment, low paid, low status work and further education. Professional vocational qualifications were achieved on the job or as part time evening study (Dennis, Owen, Errol, Colin and Devon).

Second chance – the transformational role of adult and further education

The importance of adult and further education colleges for black and white working class people is well known. Mabey concludes her article 'Black pupils' achievement in inner London' by acknowledging that much of the research has suggested that the causes lie in the individuals themselves and are beyond the power of the school or LEA to affect, but she argues that her research points firmly to 'two areas and to two stages of pupils' educational experience where the quality of education is critical: in the teaching of reading in the primary school *and in the nature and scope of post-16 provision'* (Mabey, 1986; emphasis added).

Attending 'night school' or doing vocational day release courses for apprentices were still a strong theme of British culture at this time. Adult education provision was described as the 'jewel in the crown' of the ILEA provision when the education authority faced abolition in the late 1980s. Further and continuing adult education (FE) played and continues to play a transformational role in the lives of the seven black men and their families. FE had an added dimension for the black men of this study: not only did it provide a 'second chance' of securing a decent education, it also provided a more relevant political education for the times and strengthened an emergent self-help networking approach to accessing educational opportunities. Owen's account is illustrative:

> A chance meeting with LB, then President of the Afro Caribbean Students' Society at Kingsway College, he had left school and gone straight to college and suggested that I do the same. (Owen)

Dennis and Errol followed a similar route:

> I did Sociology at South West London College but was trying to

define my own learning; then Law, which I hated. I worked at the Stationery Office and studied at Kingsway College in the evenings. I was working Saturdays well outside the boundaries of Brixton. I worked in a men's shop in the Walworth Road for a Jewish chain. (Dennis)

Errol was able to get work in the offices of a graphic design company, where he changed the water pots and bought sandwiches for the workers, but returned to High Towers to run the after-school Black Studies group, until a trip back home to St Lucia inspired him to do teacher training.

Commentary

The experience of secondary education has clearly been a powerful element in the formulation of identity for the seven black men. The narrow constraints of the curriculum as well as its power to expand horizons were experienced differently as demonstrated in the extracts from the seven participants.

It was a school that believed in the comprehensive ideal, which some teachers personified. We learned French, Rugby, Boxing, Fencing, Archery. We had national champions, kids going to the Olympics, London champions. It was a high achieving school on reflection. Academically, there was a list of people going to university, as well as on the sporting field. I was in the top band throughout. (Carl)

The subtle and overt power relations between pupils and teachers was evident in both the formal and informal structures of the school. The positive interventions by teachers, in which individuality and shared humanity were affirmed, are central common themes in the accounts of epiphany, those defining moments of school life (Denzin, 1989; Bronfenbrenner, 1979) where 'respect' is mutually accorded and becomes transformational. For Arran and others, the act of survival as an individual was important and part of a family discourse. A key element in all the accounts is the importance of group survival and self-empowerment which were unintended and powerful responses to the challenges and inequalities they faced as young black men in what they experienced as hostile environments.

In the Fifth Year a lot of the black children in the school came together as a larger entity and became a force, who have been my friends for life. We bonded as a group, went on field trips and got to know each other more. We raved outside together. It wasn't about *sets*, it was all about being black in the school. Some are now in prison, youth workers, social workers, teachers, in housing, one is a doctor, in the legal profession – all are beginning to achieve.

(Carl)

But this too had its negative downside as the impact of the institutional racism in the structures and processes of school life also took their toll. Carl described his Home Beech experience very differently to Colin.

Home Beech taught me a kind of terrorism, that's what it taught us. I think other people had a different experience, some of the older pupils but for us in our year, there was a lot about fighting, a lot about standing up for yourself. This black bastard thing this don't happen no more but then it was 'Whappen Chalkie?' and them was from people who liked you, and I wasn't able to do something about it then, but later I was and that was what Home Beech taught me. (Colin)

The schooling experiences of the seven black men echo long-standing concerns about the access of black Caribbean pupils and their families to an acceptable and equitable standard of education. These continue to be the subject of research studies. For example: concerns about the impact of ability groupings on equality of educational opportunity (Gillborn and Youdell, 2000); the relevance of the curriculum and teacher racism (Gillborn, 1990); group identities and black masculinities (Sewell, 1997; Mac an Ghaill, 1999) and Black Caribbean achievement (Channer, 1995; Gillborn and Gipps, 1996; Nehaul, 1996; Reay and Mirza, 1997; OFSTED, 2002).

The accounts of secondary education in this chapter provide important contextual data, which underpin the expectations of these seven fathers, when engaging as parents themselves. To what extent and how powerfully is demonstrated in the next two chapters. The virtue of a 'good' education as the key to social mobility was a powerful factor for many Caribbean migrants in deciding to emigrate, starting families and/or arranging for their children to join them in England. I examine how strongly these values of a 'good' education are held by the second-generation black Caribbean parents of children in the education system currently, and consider the positive as well as negative effects of their own secondary education experience on the transmission of the seven men's values and behaviours.

The interplay between the education and immigration policy impacted in diverse ways on the lives of the seven men and their parents. For the most part, the importance of education as a tool for self-improvement has not been eroded by the experience of institutional racism in both schooling and employment. But already confidence in the capacity of the English education system to deliver equality of educational opportunity has been undermined.

Mixed emotions and more and more as I've learned and become aware what should have taken place at school, I've become more and more resentful. (Colin)

The extent to which those experiences of schooling translate into values of education and are transmitted as an intergenerational discourse is considered in Part Two where the focus shifts from the men's retrospective memories of childhood and adolescence to their present experiences as *parents* of second-generation black Caribbean children currently in the English education system. The taken-for-granted importance of education as a key value of immigrant families is evident in all seven accounts, yet the transmission of its importance from parent to child was not always effective or demonstrable, for example in the degree of parental involvement at home or at school. Transmission had to be achieved in a highly charged environment where the consequences of institutional racism in employment, education and prejudice within the community took their toll on family life. The sheer effort to survive is evident in the reflections of Colin, Errol and Dennis.

My mum would come home and she'd be washing and cooking and I'm saying 'Mum' and she'd be trying to read it [my homework] while I held it. (Colin)

The school's job was to educate, our job was to learn and so he [father] only ever got involved when we got our reports and they weren't good enough and he would shout and scream and beat us. (Errol)

Our education was a painful grounding. We could have become accepting of the poverty, we came out with a sense of challenge.
(Dennis)

Clearly the effects of this environment had differential consequences since some immigrant families were successful at this
transmission (Arran, Carl, Owen and Devon) and yet they thrived as
young men in different ways in the short term as evident in the
differing educational outcomes achieved at the end of their secondary schooling.

> When I left school I went to College and did a course which was
> a chore – sociology, history – eurocentric and dry as hell at a time
> when I was alert and active. I went through the motions, unmoti-
> vated. (Owen)

> I think I should have got three A levels but I failed my best
> subject so I was a bit disappointed. But I was able to go on and
> do a degree as my sister had done; all four of us did degrees.
>   (Carl)

Summary

The inter-connections and implications of post-war urban education
policies and the experience of their implementation in the new
comprehensive schools are central in the biographies of the seven
black men. The extent to which these experiences contribute to the
formulation of parenting strategies is considered in the next chapter.
The ecological frame suggests that when the connections between
the impact of the different settings on the schooling experience of
the child are made explicit by parents, this transmits very positively
to their children and raises their self esteem. Thus the ability of the
first-generation parents to display agency and influence is seen by
their children as affirming and critical in their sense of security and
well-being. This was evident in the accounts of Arran, Owen and
Carl. The converse also pertains – the powerlessness of parents

contributes to the less consistent transmission in the case of Dennis, Devon, Colin and Errol; all of whom are critical of their parents' inability to 'protect' them from the impact of education policies and guarantee their access to 'good' schooling.

PART TWO:

Seven Black Men as Parents

Having gone through High Towers School on exit I had to make choices about my life and my kids. Black liberation in America and Africa emphasised education as key component. I wanted my children to leap those hurdles that had defeated or stunted our growth. I was aware that people had been failed by the system, unable to read or write. I was keen to make sure that those things were beyond the realm of possibilities for my children. (Owen)

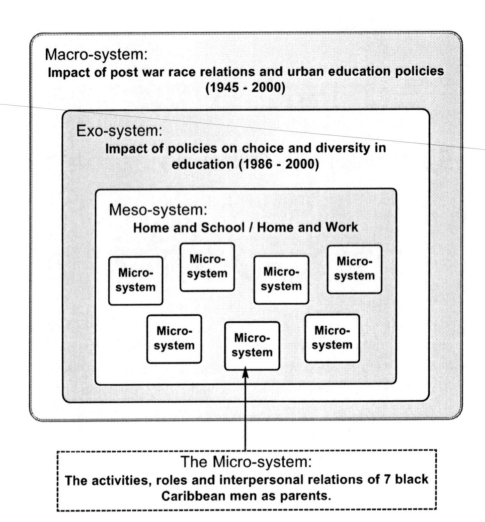

The ecological environment for the seven men as second-generation parents.

Chapter Three

Home–School Relations

The interplay between education policies on choice and diversity in schooling and the expectations of black parents

They seem to absorb something of the nonchalance of the native-born English in fact so there is a decline in aspiration.[1]

This chapter explores the parenting accounts of the seven black men who are parents of children currently in the English education system. Their accounts demonstrate how the problematic interplay between aspirations and engagement, both in the school and the home, underpin choices about the education of **their** children.

Experiences of *'black Caribbean choosing'* (see Ball's concept of 'race'-informed choosing, 2003) are considered within the wider settings of school reform, which characterised the second and third Conservative administrations: the introduction of the National Curriculum; local management of schools flagged in the Education Reform Act (1988); the policy and practice to increase the information provided by schools, including the formation of the Office for Standards in Education (OFSTED); and the annual publication of school performance tables in the Parents' Charters of 1991 and 1994. All had an impact on the range of choice and diversity in school provision, particularly in London. The educational choices of the seven men are considered in the light of recent studies of parental engagement and reflect some of the diverse strategies adopted by black Caribbean parents in their pursuit of an equitable education for their children.

The ecological approach

One of Bronfenbrenner's key research interests expressed in the preface to his text *The Ecology of Human Development* was the extent to which 'public policy affects the wellbeing and development of human beings by determining the conditions of their lives' (Bronfenbrenner, 1979:xiii). The interaction between the two settings of home and school is explored as the 'meso-system, which comprises the interrelations among two or more settings in which the developing person actively participates' (Bronfrenbrenner, 1979:25). This approach is used to consider the adaptive strategies adopted by second-generation black Caribbean parents to tackle the lived experience of institutional racism and its effects on equality of educational opportunity. The policy context is the exercise of parental choice from pre-school through to secondary education, where the decline in the successful attainment of black Caribbean pupils is most apparent (DfES, 2003).

The policy setting

The changes in educational policies enacted in the Education Reform Act (1988) were heralded in the manifesto commitments of the Conservative Party under the leadership of Margaret Thatcher, and were clearly attractive to the electorate; the Conservatives won the General Election of May 1979. By that date all seven men had completed their secondary education and were following the path from further education to employment described in the section on post-compulsory education in Chapter 2.

The 'social and political maelstrom' of their school days had given way to worldwide economic recession signalled by the decline in manufacturing industry, the backbone of British industry. Mass unemployment in the mid-1970s, particularly youth unemployment, became a reality for the first time since the economic depression of the 1930s. This proved a difficult period for young people generally, but particularly those young men from traditionally working class areas, where the adverse consequences of this structural unemployment were manifest. In urban areas black youth unemployment was disproportionately high and contributed to the vulnerability of young black Caribbean males, typified in the disproportionate numbers of black men 'stopped and searched on suspicion' and prosecuted under what became known as the 'SUS' laws.[2] There were widespread community campaigns against the racism of the police and the continuing growth of nationalist right-wing fascist and anti-immigrant groups such as the British National Party and the National Front. It was no surprise when the turbulent 1970s culminated first with the election of the Conservative leader, Margaret Thatcher, as Prime Minister in 1979 and then the following year with a series of riots, rebellions and uprisings in those areas of English cities where black Caribbean communities had settled. Major disturbances began in the St Paul's area of Bristol in 1980, followed by unrest in Toxteth, Liverpool 8; Handsworth, Birmingham; Brixton, South London; and Tottenham, North London.

Around that time I was involved in community struggles around policing, housing, Afrikan Liberation organisations, rebellions across the Continent on our agenda and involved in community politics – educational experience through political involvement.

(Owen)

The Conservative Party had been voted in on a landslide of working class disenchantment with the Labour Party. Their promises of the benefits of a different capitalist, monetarist alternative to the management of the economy clearly touched a chord. The manifesto pledges included a commitment to increase consumer choice, first with the privatisation of previously nationalised industries for the production of utilities such as gas, electricity, coal and telecommunications; then secondly with the wide ranging 'reform' of the public services such as transport, health, education and the police. The twin tenets of these policies were choice and diversity. The objective was the radical application of the market to all areas of public life and the destruction of the so-called 'nanny (welfare) state'. A key strategy was the reform and reining in of trade union rights, which had been so instrumental in the downfall of the previous Labour administration.

Changes in education policies

Education was affected detrimentally during the early days of the new Conservative administration in 1979 with a series of acrimonious disputes between teachers and their employers, which led to the withdrawal of goodwill by members of the main teaching unions, particularly in urban areas. Reform of teachers' pay and conditions was clearly signalled in the Conservative manifesto for the second term of the Thatcher government, which pledged the abolition of the Greater London Council (GLC) and by default its education function which was discharged through the ILEA. By 1989 both the ILEA and the GLC were abolished. Both High Towers and Home Beech had closed by this time.

THE LEGISLATION

- 1980: The Education Act allows parents to express a preference for the school of their choice, and establishes the Assisted Places Scheme. Parents are given increased representation on governing bodies, and the right to information concerning the curriculum and organisation of the school.
- 1981: The parents of children with special educational needs (SEN) are given the right to participate in the assessment of those needs, and in an annual review of the statement of special educational needs.
- 1986: The Education Act (No. 2) describes parents' responsibilities within school governing bodies, and institutes an annual school governors' report to parents at an obligatory meeting.
- 1988: The Education Reform Act, through establishing open enrolment, strengthens parents' rights to choose their children's schools, and to appeal should a school refuse to admit their child. Schools are required to give parents more information concerning a child's programme of work, and his or her progress within it. Parents are given the right to vote their school out of local authority control.
- 1989: The Children Act gives priority to the welfare of children, and outlines parents' rights and responsibilities.
- 1991: The Parents' Charter. Parents are to be given information on their child's progress, and are able to find out how the school is being run and to compare all local schools.
- 1992: Parents are to be consulted before schools are inspected by the Office for Standards in Education (OFSTED).

Source: OECD, 1997.

Figure 4: Key educational reforms enacted by the Conservative government from 1979 to 1992.

Education reform was all encompassing with parental choice at its core. The publication of the Education Reform Bill in 1986 and its enactment in 1988, led to the introduction of local financial management for schools, the deregulation of admissions criteria and the creation of new kinds of schools. Schools were allowed to 'opt out' of local authority control and become grant maintained (GM) schools. The Act allowed City Technology Colleges (CTCs) to be established which were independent of the local authority and sponsored by businesses. Provision for assisted places was made to provide financial assistance to the parents of able pupils who had successfully secured a scholarship place at an independent school.

The Education Reform Act was followed swiftly by the introduction of a National Curriculum with national public examinations at the end of each of its Key Stages at age seven (Key Stage 1); eleven (Key Stage 2), fourteen (Key Stage 3) and sixteen (Key Stage 4). Lastly came the introduction of the Charter Initiative across all major public services, manifest in education with the publication of the Parents' Charter by the Department of Education. Of particular relevance to this study was the requirement for all schools to publish their end of Key Stage test results annually and report these to parents; and regular inspection on a four (now six) yearly cycle of all maintained education institutions by the newly established Office for Standards in Education (OFSTED). Many of the changes were welcomed by black and minority ethnic parents because of their emphasis on transparent procedures and public reporting of an individual school's standards and academic performance.

I considered CTCs and GM schools because I feel they embody a success culture and are well-resourced. (Errol)

The London context

The implications of these changes to British society were far-reaching and nowhere more so than in London, following the abolition of the GLC in 1986. Three years later the ILEA was abolished and reconfigured into thirteen education authorities (including the Corporation of London) with significant consequences for urban education in the decade that followed. Many of the schools in the capital were blighted by a long and ultimately unsuccessful campaign to save the ILEA, which resulted in low morale, discord and uncertainty across inner London. Once it became clear that the breakup of the ILEA was inevitable, some boroughs welcomed the opportunity to plan and experiment. For example the Liberal Democrat local administrations in both Tower Hamlets and Islington introduced radical neighbourhood planning and renewal strategies, in which local schools were central; councillors in Wandsworth and Westminster saw themselves as standard bearers for the new Conservative education policies and published plans for specialist magnet schools, new teachers' pay and conditions arrangements. Local authority school support services were reorganised into self-financing business units. Others, for example Hackney and Lambeth, found the transition very difficult.

Furthermore traditional admissions criteria and local agreements were challenged by the Greenwich judgement of 1989 which established that LEA maintained schools could not give priority to children simply because they lived in the authority's administrative area (DfES Circular 12/88); parents could only express a preference but could not be guaranteed the place of their choice.[3]

Exercising parental choice – 'black Caribbean choosing'[4]

The choices exercised by the seven black men illustrate the difficulties of securing an acceptable standard of education and bring a different perspective to the concepts of 'choosing' and 'privilege'.

Arran: Arran's <u>1st daughter</u> was born in Hackney in 1983. She attended a local community nursery until she was four and a half. She entered reception (YR) not at a local primary school, but at one favoured by middle class parents a short bus ride away. She stayed until Year 4 but was moved because she appeared to be making little progress and was about to have an inexperienced newly qualified teacher for the third year running despite expressed concerns. The school was heavily involved in 'Save ILEA' campaigns and hostile to the new National Curriculum. Both parents tried to get their daughter into a well-regarded primary school in the more affluent neighbouring LEA but they lived too far outside the catchment area. In desperation they moved their daughter to a second more local primary school in Year 4 where the headteacher expressed surprise at the decision of 'middle class parents' to choose his school.

She moved after two terms to a fee-paying, black-owned independent school in South London (1 hr travelling distance by bus and tube accompanied by either a parent or grandparent; occasionally driven in a car by mother before going to work) and spent two successful years making up the gaps in her basic education, skills and self-esteem. Her mother attended the open days of a number of high performing selective schools a year early so she could assess what their daughter would encounter the following year. The local Hackney mixed secondary school did not have a strong academic record, so their daughter was entered for and passed the entry test to a selective girls' school fourteen miles away in North West London. She travelled to school by car in a parents' rota (with three white girls from the area) or by bus, tube and school bus (1 hr travelling distance).

> I let teachers know that I know the system and that I want the same for my child as they want for theirs. (Arran)

Arran's <u>2nd daughter and 1st son</u> are with a different partner whom he subsequently married, having moved from Hackney first to work for six years on contract in the Caribbean, then back to Bedford. Both his younger children attended local first and middle schools; and he anticipates no difficulty in them attending the local high school in due course. Throughout their primary schooling in Bedford, Arran has been Chair of Governors at his children's schools.

Errol: Errol's <u>son</u> was born in South London in 1985. Errol and his partner lived on the Lambeth/Croydon boundary and his son attended an independent fee-paying nursery school in Lambeth until the end of Year 2, when he was moved to a fee-paying, black-run independent school in Clapham.

> I chose a black independent school for very conscious black pride and positive esteem so that my son would be comfortable with himself. (Errol)

His son sat the Common Entrance exam at 10 and secured a scholarship place at a high performing independent boys' school in Croydon, but was subsequently removed from this school by Errol at end of Year 8, because both he and the school perceived his son to be coasting and not achieving.

> My son spent two years in an independent secondary school where he was popular but wouldn't push himself and underperformed. (Errol)

In the meantime Errol set up a community project school with other black parents and placed his son at the school.

> Negative notions of black culture abound in the majority of secondary schools. School is destroying our children – it is destructive to our spirits. (Errol)

Errol has been the main fundraiser and sponsor of the school, which has attracted a number of black Caribbean pupils who had been excluded from other schools. Errol's son now lives with his father, following the separation of his parents.

Devon: Devon has <u>three sons</u> who were born in Hackney where they attended a local community nursery. Devon and his partner bought a house in Hackney but rented it out once their children were about to start primary school and moved to rented accommodation in an outer London suburb achieving higher standards in its local schools. There Devon's sons made good progress. After a couple of years, the children's mother spent a year in St Lucia and her sons joined her to attend school in the Caribbean for six months since moving back to the Caribbean was in the couple's game-plan. On her return Devon and his partner separated and Devon's sons moved with their mother back to her family home in Canning Town to attend, against Devon's wishes, low performing schools, which were local and convenient to their mother's extended family.

> I cannot understand my former partner's choices about our sons' schooling but I am not in a strong position. (Devon)

Dennis: His <u>1st son</u> was born in Lambeth while both Dennis and his partner were relatively young and although the relationship did not last, he has remained very active in his son's upbringing. His son attended a fee-paying independent nursery and primary school until the end of Year 6. He then sat the selection test to gain a place at the newly opened City Technology College in a neighbouring borough, which he attended until Year 11. He is now in further education.

> My son went to private schools, not good ones, but chosen by his mother. I found them in flux, with poor headmasters and indifferent teachers. My son's mother did not have a very aggressive view of education, for some unknown reason, which I couldn't fathom. He then went to a new CTC which was just starting. His primary school had just left him because he was a big lad and quiet – they had just left him alone. (Dennis)

Dennis subsequently married and had a <u>daughter.</u> They lived in Lambeth and their daughter attended an independent, predominantly white fee-paying nursery and primary school in South London until Year 3 but Dennis and his wife moved her because of fears about negative self-image as their daughter approached puberty in advance of her white peers. She was then placed in a small black-run independent primary school for Years 4–6.

> My daughter is a different ballgame. She went to a black nursery, then we put her into a white private primary school but I pulled her out of that because she was too big (physically) for the school and I didn't want her to define herself amidst an all white school, because the reference group would be young white girls half her size. I spoke to a black psychologist friend in the US who confirmed my concerns and on my return I pulled my daughter out of that school and sent her to another black-run private school and then life was much better – everyone was the same size as her and colour. On reflection her closest friends at the other school were Greek, Asian, not white – issues of what they had in common. (Dennis)

Dennis did a lot of research about secondary school choices and his daughter sat a number of entrance tests to independent and selective grammar schools. Eventually she passed the entry test to a selective mixed grant-maintained school in South East

London. Dennis has since separated from his daughter's mother and has remarried. He maintains regular contact with his children.

Owen: Owen's <u>1st daughter</u> was born in South London. She attended a local fee-paying independent nursery until the end of Year 2. She won a supporting scholarship (assisted place) to a local independent girls' school which included its preparatory department from Year 3 to Year 11. She left school to go to local FE College but became pregnant with a daughter and both now live with Owen.

> As parents we have put emphasis on an early start education-ally and starting them early and working consistently with the same independent pre-school. (Owen)

His <u>1st son</u> was born in Lambeth and followed the same route as his sister but attended the local independent boys' school. His <u>2nd son</u> also followed the same route as his brother and sister until Year 2 when he went to the local primary school.

> Secondary schooling has been more problematic. My second son didn't follow the same route as my first [independent schooling]. We tried the local City Technology College [CTC], which was newly promoted by the Tories which stressed science, mathematics and computing, rather than the arts. I see schools as grading pupils for the labour force. I wanted my son to have managerial options rather than manual work inter-spersed with periods of unemployment. (Owen)

Owen's son sat a technology proficiency test to attend a CTC unusually set up by the LEA. The CTC was subsequently inspected by OFSTED and placed in special measures. By this time his son had only one more year at the school and left at the end of Year 11 to complete A levels at a local FE College. Owen's <u>2nd daughter and granddaughter</u> followed the same route of independent nursery education until the headteacher retired and the nursery school closed.

> There was a practical dimension to our choice. We were working parents and it meant children in nurseries as soon as possible. It became evident that nursery fees were the same as the local prep school so all our children have started their education there and were prepared for entrance exams to fee-paying schools. My first daughter was able to win an assisted place scholarship to a local independent girls' school, but it has not been that easy for my second son and granddaughter. (Owen)

His youngest child is currently in a local primary school where Owen is an active member of a black parents group, which is critical of how the school is run. Owen is separated amicably from his partner and all the children (and one grandchild) live with him.

Colin: Colin's <u>1st son</u> was born in Hackney while he and his girl-friend were both teenagers. His son attended a local community nursery and primary school; however his son's education was interrupted by a period of residence abroad when his mother emigrated to the US. This did not work out as planned. On their return Colin's son came to live with him at his family home. Colin was very keen that his son did not attend an all boys' school as he had done.

> I wanted my first son to go to the local Catholic secondary school, I didn't want him to go to Home Beech. I didn't want him to go to a boys' school. No chance of that because I thought he couldn't go through what I'd been through. No chance of that. I don't know what I thought mixed would be better, less aggression – Catholic school, more authority. (Colin)

His son's mother was Jewish and they agreed a compromise whereby Colin's son attended the local mixed Catholic secondary school. This worked well in the Lower School, which was on a separate site but proved less successful after the move to the Upper School. Thereafter during his GCSE years Colin's son was periodically involved in petty crime and in contact with the police. He left school (before he was excluded) to complete his studies at the local FE College. Colin's son is in regular contact with his father and Colin's new family. Colin's 2nd son was born in Hackney. He attends a Steiner nursery school and local primary school in accordance with his mother's philosophy. Colin is considering moving the family to an outer North West London suburb in search of better secondary education options. He has lived and worked in Hackney all his life.

Five years ago I would have said that I'm not moving, they're going to have to educate my son, but now ... (Colin)

Carl: Carl and his partner live in Lewisham and have a son and daughter both below compulsory school age.

I am looking for a strong academic focus and a good percentage of black children; I would prefer state education. (Carl)

The impact of the Conservative administration's reforms for parents and their children in some areas of London is evident in the schooling accounts above. The turbulent minefield of inner London education during the late 1980s and 1990s forms the terrain across which the research participants and their children are trying to traverse in exercising their right to choose.

Recent studies on parental choice

In his inaugural professorial lecture[5] at the London Institute of Education in March 2003 Professor Stephen Ball described the interlocking inequalities of policies, families and institutional ordering as the domain in which the middle class parent is able to exercise parental choice most successfully for the benefit of their children. He describes the different ways that middle class parents, predominantly mothers, consciously build the social capital of their children and add value to the educational process of schooling. He illustrates the values of such parents by recalling an interview with a Mrs McBain. She described the state school down the road as somewhere it would be lovely to send her child too, 'except that *nobody* sends their children there'. By implication Ball posits 'she means the school is full of "others", "nobodies", children not like ours'.

In earlier research conducted by Ball and his colleagues Gewirtz and Bowe over a three-year period from 1991–94, the team focussed on three competitive clusters of schools in three geographically contiguous LEAs in London. The time frame is of relevance to this study since the majority of the participants had at least one child in secondary school during that time. Data was collected from 137 interviews with parents, teachers and governors as well as with officers of the LEAs. The research defined three categories of parents exercising parental choice. The first group were defined as *disconnected choosers* (who are almost without exception working class); *privileged/skilled choosers* (almost exclusively professional middle class) and *semi-skilled choosers* (from a variety of class backgrounds). Their central tenet however is that choice is

> powerfully informed by the complex lives families lead and by their biographies – in short their position within a social network.
>
> (Gewirtz et al, 1995:93)

Privileged/skilled choosers are characterised by both an inclination and a capacity to engage with the opportunity of choice – to exercise what Bourdieu is quoted as signifying 'cultural competence to "read" schools' (quoted in Ball et al, 1996:100). *Semi-skilled choosers* have the same inclinations 'but limited capacity to engage with the market'. These parents are defined as wishing to 'render choice into a more certain and objective process but cannot do this on the basis of their own judgements' (Ball et al, 1996:102). *Disconnected choosers* are described 'as working on the surface structure of choice, constrained by programmes of perception which rest on a basic unfamiliarity with particular aspects of schools and schooling' (Ball et al, 1996:106).

The Organisation for Economic Co-operation and Development (OECD) produced a comparative report on international practice in parental choice policies – *School: A Matter of Choice* (1994) concluded:

> Nobody likes choosing a school that is considered by one's friends to be undesirable. Few privileged families wish their children to attend schools mainly with children from less privileged backgrounds. Many parents believe, despite mixed academic evidence on this point, that their children will learn better alongside other children who are clever, than in a mixed ability setting. Such considerations, and particularly those associated with race and class, do not tend to show up directly in surveys of reasons for choosing schools. Few people like to admit to social or racial prejudice. However they are prominent in assessments of why parents choose made by many headteachers and local officials interviewed for this study. (OECD, 1994:29)

The voice of the white middle class 'privileged-chooser' is evident in the tone of the OECD report but the seven men's accounts demonstrate the complexities and ambiguities of exercising parental choice, particularly in a London setting. None of the seven black men conform exclusively to any one of the typologies of choosers described earlier (Gewirtz et al, 1995), but they all to some extent consciously try to *emulate the behaviours* of privileged choosers. For example, the decisions of Owen and Dennis to send their children to fee-paying independent nurseries arises from a canny belief in the cost-effectiveness and added value of securing a solid foundation in basic skills for the same price as ordinary nursery fees. However it is initially a more effective strategy for Owen than Dennis. Carl affirms his commitment to state education but Devon and Arran's experiences demonstrate that this too is far from straightforward and may require sacrifices – in Arran's case involving an extended family of parents, friends and carers to accompany children to schools up to an hour's travel away due to perceptions about the quality of education available locally. In that regard the parents in this sample are seeking to overcome Tomlinson's view by making themselves as knowledgeable as possible about the 'intricacies' referred to below:

> Although most minority parents in Britain are, in crude socio-economic terms 'working class', their values and expectations have always approximated those of 'middle class' but without the detailed knowledge of the education system and its intricacies that middle class parents in Britain usually possess.' (Tomlinson, 1984:274).

Black Caribbean parental choice in education is often a complex, at times ambiguous, embodiment of a family's intergenerational educational values and aspirations. Despite espousing radical political views in some cases, the educational choices of most of the men are inherently conservative, as evident in the vignettes of black Caribbean choosing.

Studies on parental involvement at home

Many of the early references to black Caribbean parenting styles were derived from studies commissioned by the ILEA to investigate concerns about the educational performance of immigrant pupils in

London schools. In 1970 Michael Rutter and his team of educational psychologists conducted interviews with 58 children of Caribbean origin and 106 children from non-immigrant families from a random selection of all 10-year-olds in an inner London borough. The researchers considered background environmental factors such as housing and employment and concluded that their most striking finding was the similarity between West Indian and non-immigrant families. The only significant cultural differences were around parental discipline and on attitudes to play, signalling less interaction between parent and child in the early years of socialisation (Rutter et al, 1974). Taylor's research in 1981 confirmed Rutter's findings.

The failure of first-generation Caribbean families to understand the importance of 'play' in the early years of their children's development was an area of concern; but it could be argued that in common with their white peers, most immigrant children enjoyed their most creative play outside of the home, in the gardens, parks and streets of urban England and this would have been the case in the Caribbean, albeit in a different setting. The Rampton Inquiry noted that a disproportionate number of West Indian women are forced to go out to work because of their economic circumstances and quoted the 1971 census data which showed that 68% of West Indian married women went out to work compared with the national average of 42% (House of Commons, 1981:15). The committee concluded that this might have a detrimental impact on children in their pre-school formative years. Colin reflected on his own upbringing and his low tolerance of 'play' as a parent:

I am very proud of my younger son's IT capacity but that wouldn't have happened if I'd have got my way when he was breaking computer mouses when he was little. But now he can do everything with a computer, because his mum was willing to let him mash up the mouse, even the computer. (Colin)

Bagley, Bart and Wong (1979) investigated the factors involved in the academic success of 150 black 10-year-olds attending London schools. The authors concluded that the parents of high-achieving children were highly critical of English culture and institutions and imbued in their child positive 'ethnic self image'. These parents were characterised as non-authoritarian and their children viewed positively by teachers.

Channer, in her research on successful black Caribbean achievement concludes:

> the weight of responsibility [is] carried by black parents in a society which denies their children basic rights and interprets their behaviour in an unfavourable light. (Channer, 1995:19).

Black Caribbean parenting values, styles and behaviours of the seven men reveal some common approaches but also some important differences. Colin's experiences of fathering two sons could not be more different. His first son's secondary schooling began well but his parenting style left much to be desired by his own assessment and replicated many of the 'mistakes' he felt his parents made with him. His only defence was his youth; both he and D's mother were teenagers when he was born.

> It was a lovely school for the first two, three years of his life there. But then he went to the Upper School and I think I didn't do a lot with D. I used to send him to his room to read, like my parents used to send me to my room to read. I checked his work but I wouldn't really read through it too tuff again, I didn't read it with him. Because he lived in the family home, my sister took on a lot of the parenting role. I didn't have the time, I was on the street. I'd go home every night, spend some time with him, not get him ready for bed but be around when he was getting ready for bed.

Once he go to bed, I'd be out and not see him until the next afternoon. (Colin)

Colin admits he has had to re-construct his parenting style with his second son and has learned a lot from interacting with his partner's education and parenting expectations and reflecting on his past behaviours.

> With N it's a different thing and I'm quite strongly thinking about his schooling. N's education will be different. His mum has already put money by for school, his gran has done a PEP [savings plan] for when he goes to university. There's like the expectations are that he can do what he wants. If he says he wants to be a doctor, they buy him a toy skeleton. I wanted to save up my money to send D [first son] to private school, I was earning good money through all sorts of things. I found out what was the best one, one in a place called Marlborough but me and his mum split up and before I knew it he was leaving secondary school. (Colin)

Dennis believes that having high expectations of himself as well as his children and making those expectations explicit are at the heart of his parenting philosophy. He has been unashamed in his determination to model a different approach.

> Yes I consciously critiqued my parents' life. I did it to my father at seventeen, straight to his face and said I'm not going to live the life you lead, I'm very different. I asserted my independence as soon as I could, I was very clear it would be different. Although I had my son young, I was determined that he would do better and I've been there to guide him, not put inordinate pressure, but that he would do something he would be proud of. (Dennis)

Like some of the other fathers in this study Dennis takes the role of parent-educator very seriously.

> We travel a lot and I took my children to Holland which wasn't the usual sand and sea and I told my son 'You read the map, tell us what train or bus to take' and that was very affirming. He went back to Holland and led his friends; he had the wherewithal.
>
> (Dennis)

He does not believe in taking it for granted that this role should be left to the school and is prepared the play this role with his children's friends.

> I put my daughter onto work experience before the school did. We do that for our own kids as well as their friends. Because I know that life is about networks and so through one of my networks I got her into a music company – she was attracted to the glamour – and she was able to see how boring and mundane it was. It gave her great insight. She saw someone get sacked. (Dennis)

In the past, black researchers such as Stone (1981) have argued that Dennis's approach reflects a positive Afrocentric, pro-African view of the black community echoing African notions of the community as opposed to the individual. Malik argues persuasively that:

> the struggle for racial equality takes the form of a struggle for group identity. (Malik, 1996:1)

Dennis, Errol, Carl, Owen and Devon would share this Afrocentric communitarian approach. Errol has taken his philosophical beliefs about education sufficiently seriously to open his own alternative education centre with a group of like-minded black Caribbean parents. He has faced a difficult struggle with his son's education experiences and his own ambiguities about the 'cost' of an English education.

> I talk to my son about his dreams, but I am disappointed that he wants to be rich. (Errol)

Dennis is unashamedly 'pro-black' in his home environment, echoing the relatively separatist lifestyle his parents lived when he was younger but not their fear of 'white' society.

> My kids also know that I am in private aggressively pro-black and condemning of white racism and so debates around subjects become quite lively at home. Debate means more than engagement so there's a familiarity that the world isn't passive and without its difficulties. (Dennis)

He promotes himself as positive black achiever and a role model to his children but he deploys an authoritative role, which is not dissimilar to the role his father adopted with him, although Dennis would argue that the context is very different.

> I've got one, maybe several rules, but one cardinal rule, maybe two. I said I would beat them up if I found them following people. You've got a brain in your head, use it! The second cardinal rule is do your best, whatever they might be. If you say you tried and it didn't work out, then there's no conversation. The third thing is the value put on education, it's evident by the fact that both my children's mothers have academically achieved. My kids watched me as I did my MBA and my son, in particular who is good at maths, was roped in to help me with the mathematics in the MBA. They have a sense that there are benefits to be gained. So he knows that

it's to be strived for. I said to him don't be doing yours at my age, do bits of study but get the bulk of it out of your way while you're young. They've seen, watched, observed and assisted and therefore have a sense that there's value to it. (Dennis)

Owen also has sympathy with an Afrocentric philosophy but does not romanticise 'the community' recognising that there are also negative pressures at play. He adopts an unconditional approach to his parenting, which reflects the grounded down-to-earth, loving practical affirming approach which he feels his parents adopted with him.

When my son went to his local education authority's CTC it was in transition from the old to the new. We had to pay close attention to support my son in the face of the fashion-setting gangsta rap cool image where if you get good grades, it is considered counter-cultural! Just as I had in High Towers so I urged my son to make the most of it and he survived with sufficient interest in education to go on to college. I was disappointed with his GCSEs but I didn't put it on him. When I sat my maths exam at school, one look at the paper told me that I was not equipped to do it, to pass it so I left after a few minutes. I knew I was going to fail, so I take control. (Owen)

Devon has adopted a similar parent-educator strategy to Dennis but is less authoritative in his approach:

We go places and choose activities like tennis which broaden their horizons but also their discipline. (Devon)

As a young boy, Devon felt the lack of a clear steer from his own father very keenly and has been determined not to make a similar mistake, even though the same disruptive domestic circumstances which forced him to change schools regularly is replaying for his own sons.

> I make my guidance explicit and I insist on homework being done. I make my expectations and goals explicit and encourage my children to do the same. (Devon)

A consistent finding in the literature on black Caribbean achievement is a view held by teachers that black Caribbean parents, particularly fathers, are not perceived as 'active' parents, when it comes to their children's education, particularly in secondary education. The accounts of parenting styles provide examples to counter this view. Mirza noted in the course of her school-based research that:

> the issue of black parental 'fear' of the educational system was often brought up in staff meetings to account for the poor participation in all aspects of schooling; in contrast the matter of the school failing in its role to encourage parental attendance was not emphasised. (Mirza, 1992:74)

Tomlinson notes that the research literature of the 1990s still suggests that educational professionals regard ethnic minority parents as

> posing problems for schools, rather than as assets in the educational process. (Tomlinson, 1993:131)

Recent studies on parental involvement in school

Vincent's typology of parenting behaviours (1996) provides a helpful framework to interrogate the accounts of black Caribbean parental involvement in their children's schooling in this final section. Vincent defines *school-supportive parents* as those who accept the teachers' view of 'appropriate parental behaviour' and who tend to have the closest relationships with teachers. Of the sample approximately one quarter of parents could be characterised in this way. At both schools in her research, Vincent found that 'this group was mostly, but not exclusively, composed of white parents'. In this study, Arran's behaviour is probably the closest to this 'type' in his involvement in his younger children's schooling in Bedford, a shire county market town. He maintains a regular relationship with his first daughter whose schooling experience in London typifies the difficulties that many aspirant black Caribbean parents face, but he is not actively involved in those dilemmas on a day-to-day basis.

> I am less exercised as I have already beaten the system I know that teachers cannot cope with the idea of a bright black child. (Arran)

Arran's education options for his younger children are simpler in terms of choice and diversity and in any case he has chosen to be active as a parent-governor. Nevertheless their progress in school has not been completely straightforward.

> I am suspicious that my son gets the same report messages that I did – dissent not acknowledged by teachers hence the 'talks too much in class' remarks. (Arran)

In Vincent's study, the *detached parents* comprised working class adults from all ethnic groups, who assumed it was the exclusive responsibility of the school to instil their children with 'school knowledge'. Vincent quite rightly suggests that their apparent lack of interest stemmed from a lack of confidence and perceived capacity to influence their children's progress. Eight of the forty-five parents comprised this group. Colin's behaviours with his first son would conform to some extent to this 'type' and despite the new learning he has gained in the parenting of his second son, his instincts were for a partnership with teachers which is idealistic and equitable, but in the current climate, would be perceived as aggressive. Colin's behaviours cannot compensate for his lack of consistent support of his son at home and his son's disaffection.

> I think the process that I went through went by like flash, when my first son was in the latter stages of secondary school, he was in a lot of trouble and I'd be up there, saying I don't want to hear he's in trouble now when you've known for three weeks, you've got my number, you've got my address. I don't want to come to Parents' Evenings and hear that since February, he's been frigging about. I can't do anything with that. I will work with you around supporting my son but don't be calling me up to reprimand because I will tell you in front of him, that when you see him, you see me. Imagine my face next to his. I'm not sending him here to go on with no rubbish. You ought to feel by right able to say to D that I'm going to phone your dad and give me a chance to do something. Some responded but then the next year he would have a different tutor or year master and I had to start that process again. I see the same thing now in Hackney with my god daughter and I go up the school with her mum, and it's the same thing.
>
> (Colin)

By contrast the experience with his second son is significantly different.

> With my second son N [fifteen-year gap and with a different partner, a middle class woman] he is dark into concentration and even though I know he should be, I still find it difficult. In the

evenings his mum plays two or three games with him. He's got masses of games and she'll sit there for two hours every night on the computer with his CD. I mean N's been to the theatre more times than I have, to museums, goes to drama classes, goes to Circus School and he's 5! So N has had his horizons broadened and his confidence levels, which I didn't think about with D. Then, I thought we're from Hackney, we're hard, don't be scared of nothing and now, I look at N and think D couldn't handle that.

(Colin)

More than half the parents in Vincent's study were characterised as *independent parents* who were not seen at school very often and were labelled 'apathetic' by the teaching staff. Vincent found, however, that these parents had developed 'to varying degrees' an 'oppositional logic' which led them to reject the traditional school supportive roles. This group were clear that inequality was the defining feature of the power relationship between school and parent and showed no inclination to collude in their own 'colonisation'. This 'type' provides the most interesting mirror to the approaches developed by Dennis, Devon, Owen and Errol (before he took his son out of the formal school system).

The concept of 'an oppositional logic' is highly relevant, although the accompanying descriptor of 'apathetic' is less easy to confirm from the seven accounts. Few of the seven men define their engagement with their children's schooling as unequivocally as Dennis, but they aspire to a similar degree of involvement.

I'm there in full force, bald, black and in their face at every parents' evening. (Dennis)

Dennis would describe himself as a highly assertive parent *because* his 'oppositional logic' is very strong. He has recast the teacher–parent relationship in the purest of consumer terms, where his expectations and his aspirations converge and are given weight by the educational reforms introduced by the Conservatives and supported by the first Labour administration in 1997. A key element in his security and confidence is the experience of exercising the power to change the curriculum, which he enjoyed at secondary school, where black Caribbean pupils were instrumental in securing Black Studies in the school's curriculum. Central to Dennis's parenting is the belief that the school is *under contract* to deliver a relevant and high quality of education to both his children and he intends to hold them fully accountable.

> What my experience of school has taught is that this is an environment where I don't trust teachers, I don't hold them in much regard, particularly white ones because they don't have my children's interests at heart and they have to prove themselves otherwise. So I was talking to my daughter's history teacher in her school [mainstream selective secondary] and she scored brownie points because she was so absolutely clear by the way she talked about the curriculum. We're going to study the America Civil Rights movement and I said to her, OK we can talk. Why go and do something that's peripheral and marginal for you to understand the world? (Dennis)

For Dennis, it is extremely important that his children experience him as a strong and uncompromising advocate and supporter of their right to a high standard of education. This is in direct contrast to his experience as a child.

> I am now one of the most unfriendliest of parents to teachers, if I see one not coming up to scratch, I will kick them into orbit and get very heavy. If my daughter or son say that a teacher has

another agenda, I will be in there like a shot, speaking to everyone, letting them know that I will do damage. When my son's
secondary school was lax, not pushing him at all, I went in there
and spoke to everyone concerned and said to buck up, that I
expect, I know better or else I would find a school that could
educate my son. I paid for a tutor to add extra strength to that.

(Dennis)

Commentary

Research into how parents interact with schools is still relatively
small and the domain of a few researchers. Many of the books which
might have acted as guides for the seven black men treat parents as
a largely homogenous group (Taylor, 1986; Partington and Wragg,
1989; Wolfendale, 1992) and in most cases the 'parent' being
discussed is normally the mother (David, 1993). When some authors
do engage with issues of 'race', their guidance is often naïve:

Many parents of children from ethnic minorities are also
concerned that their own children should also have every chance
to progress to further and higher education. Evidence from recent
reports suggests that more black pupils than expected were put
into remedial classes and one suggested explanation is again that
teachers' expectations might have been too low. Parents who feel
concerned that their child is not being encouraged to develop his
or her talents fully should not hesitate to go to the school and
discuss in a positive manner how a proper level of achievement
can be secured. (Partington and Wragg, 1989:47)

Much of this discourse is also deracialised in its conclusions and
continues to suffer from what Atkins et al (1988) identified as one
particular weakness:

most of the work concerning relations between families and schools is viewed entirely from professional perspectives, through the eyes of schools and teachers and on their terms; rather than those of parents and children. (Atkins, Bastiani and Goode, 1988)

References to parents are typically mediated via teachers despite good intentions of committed researchers. David argues that

in most of the literature on the relations between families and education, little consideration is given to gendered notions of parents or children in a family context. (David, 1993:6)

Troyna (1987) argued strongly that ethnic minority and majority group experience are so different that direct comparison between them is invalid; the experiences of the seven men both support and refute that view. No significant differences between parents from different ethnic groups emerged from a survey of parents and pupils from Camden and Wandsworth LEAs by David et al, despite the sample including ethnic minority parents (David, West and Ribbens 1984). A similar picture emerged in an earlier DfES commissioned study of home–school links by Jowett, Baginsky et al (1991). More recently Crozier (2001) has been critical of the adoption of a 'one-size-fits-all' approach to parents.

The situation is improving as a consequence of the recent government focus on narrowing the achievement gap between different ethnic groups – the Aiming High strategy. Recent studies on the educational achievement of black pupils (ALG, Class Acts, 2003; LDA, Rampton Revisited, 2004) have stressed the need to work more equitably with black parents. Some schools are actively helping black parents to establish family learning environments which are more conducive to educational achievement and are developing meaningful home–school partnerships.

Black-family learning environments

> If educational policies are designed to reduce group differences in children's achievement, then conclusions from much previous research emphasise the necessity of incorporating in such policies considerations of family learning environments. (Marjoribanks, 1980:12)

The seven accounts support Marjoribank's contention about the importance of researching family learning environments. Furthermore, they raise issues about the extent to which black Caribbean families transmit their learning from their potentially devastating encounters with institutionalised racism into a developmental discourse within the family, in order to assist in building their children's self-esteem/self-worth: Gordon's journey from surviving to thriving (2001).

Bronfenbrenner's hypothesis is that if we had a deeper contextual understanding of the ecologies of human development, we might begin to adjust the settings to design and operate policies more effectively to benefit under-performing and excluded groups. The experiences of the seven black men provide an insight into how individual parents are seeking to address the systemic under-achievement of black Caribbean children within their families.

Conclusion

This chapter has drawn on the generational perspectives of the seven black men on the parental strategies and interventions they deploy as second-generation parents of black Caribbean heritage. The practice of black Caribbean choosing has been examined through the lived experiences of seven black Caribbean parents. In a recent OECD publication *Parents As Partners in Schooling* (1997) the 'business case' for the more active engagement of schools with ethnic minority parents is made:

For good economic and social reasons, the children of working class, ethnic minority and other excluded families now need to be drawn into the circle of education, which in the past tended to keep them out. If such excluded groups continue to underachieve educationally, OECD countries will not only find that their economies suffer from the wasted human potential, but that marginalised groups will become a serious problem to society as a whole. (OECD, 1997: 22)

Ball's recent definition of parental choice is of particular relevance to this study.

Parental choice is about getting from the present to a particular kind of class and social location in the future. It is about *prediction, imagination and assurance*. (Ball, 2003:163; emphasis added)

For the seven second-generation black Caribbean fathers, the dream is to produce children who achieve, but not at any price; and to produce a third generation of black Caribbean adults with the security of 'prediction, imagination and assurance' – a generation at ease with themselves and their blackness; proud and self-respecting with a belief in equality of educational opportunity. How black parents are constructing this parenting discourse is considered in the next chapter.

Chapter Four

Critical Reflections

Introduction

This chapter explores the reflexive accounts of the seven black men by considering the generational interplay between immigration, settlement, education and achievement. How this has impacted on the construction of a black Caribbean parenting discourse is located in Bronfenbrenner's 'micro-system – the pattern of activities, roles and interpersonal relations experienced by the developing person in a given setting' (Bronfenbrenner, 1979:22). The 'ecological transitions' – key shifts in the lives of the participants (Bronfenbrenner, 1979:36) were the focus of the concluding section of the life history interviews, which examined the degree to the inter-connections and continuities from their immigrant parents to themselves as well as the discontinuities. Set against a changing context of educational reform, which heralded new relationships between parents and schools, the personal biographies continue to bear testimony to the value of a 'good' education and the devastating effects of failing or underachieving.

Ecological transitions

The book began with the premise that not enough is known about how black Caribbean parents experience education in the UK. This chapter focuses on the lessons that the seven black men have drawn from their own schooling which impact on the choices they make for their children. In reflecting on their experiences – from the early days of settlement as children of first-generation immigrants through primary and secondary schooling; through the transition from school to further (or higher) education to employment and adulthood; becoming parents and their educational aspirations and school choices for their own children – they were asked to reflect on the extent to which the values of their parents had been transmitted to them as second-generation parents and to identify the key features of the strategies they adopt to overcome the institutional and emotional barriers they feel their children face. Elements of this discourse are summarised below:

Arran's mother emigrated to pay for an education for her five sons, while his father stayed behind in Trinidad to take care of the family. All five sons completed their schooling: four of the five are professionally qualified as barristers, solicitors or teachers; the fifth is a local calypsonian. **Purposeful ambition underpinned by hard work and personal sacrifice is a strong generational theme in Arran's family; Arran's mother delivered on her promises.** Arran recalls early Caribbean memories of the family budgeting so that his oldest brother could eat the special 'brain food', required in his parents' view for him to succeed in winning the all-island scholarship to study at a Canadian university. That he was successful was a tangible demonstration of that ambition and single-mindedness which characterises his generational experience of migration and education.

Once in London, a similar purposefulness drove Arran's mother to put her son's name down for the first purpose-built comprehensive school in Hackney. Arran was sent for from Trinidad to join the early cohorts. Together he and his mother planned his route to university and devised strategies to overcome the many institutional hurdles placed in his way as he journeyed from the remedial set, where he was placed on arrival (despite ability) to the Sixth Form, university, and an eventual post-graduate certificate of education.

> I wanted to live out my mother's dreams. (Arran)

Arran adopts a similar approach in his ambitions for his three children. He is Chair of Governors at his younger children's school; his oldest daughter has already achieved the family aim and is now the second generation in Arran's family to attend university.

Another connecting thread has been **the emphasis on hard work and self-advancement through part-time study**. Arran's mother took evening classes in catering and bookkeeping to transform herself from manual unskilled factory worker to be in a position to successfully apply for the position of resident housekeeper to a wealthy doctor in New York. She emigrated to the US once Arran had begun his university course. Arran too has retrained from teacher to psychologist through a mixture of part-time and sponsored in-service training. He has been trying to complete a PhD part-time.

Arran believes that by **being involved in his children's schools it will signal to teachers that he, like his mother, is a parent to be taken seriously with aspirations similar to theirs**. It is an approach that connects him to his past and is derived from a key moment in his schooling, when his resolve faltered and a quiet word from his Head of House brought him up short.

> He talked about my mother's sacrifice and that he thought I was letting her down. He made a direct link and that was a turning point – the intervention of a teacher, as a human being who knew about discrimination and education, was important. (Arran)

Arran's mother never returned to live in Trinidad but settled in the US and on her retirement until her death, spent each year visiting her sons and their families in England, Canada, Jamaica and Trinidad. Arran's father also emigrated to the US but retained the family home in Trinidad.

Errol sees little tangible connection between his parenting strategies and those deployed by his parents. His mother's **unconditional love is a strong theme** but her illiteracy meant that she was unable to intervene to support Errol's education and remained a passive supporter. Errol's father was similarly functionally illiterate and this did not change throughout their lives. Errol's parents adopted similar positions to Dennis's parents in taking succour from their religious beliefs, in this case Catholicism, which preached conformity and accommodation. Errol conformed to his parents' approach for most of his primary and early secondary education; he maintained a low profile, had only white friends and tried to fit into English society. However as the radicalism of the US Civil Rights Movements began to impact on the school and the wider black African and Caribbean Brixton community, Errol's neutral, deracialised position was unsustainable.

> I remember a white friend asking me how I felt about the death of Martin Luther King and I didn't know who Martin Luther King was. I was thirteen years old and I had no idea who the man was, but this boy was putting me into a racial group in a way that I hadn't thought of before. (Errol)

That incident began a journey of **involvement in radical politics, community action which runs parallel to his involvement in his son's schooling.** He was an active member of a group involved in designing a Black Studies course, which he helped to teach at High

Towers school. As a parent, 'radical' in the case of schooling meant educating his son where possible outside the state sector, which was seen as detrimental to black self-empowerment. Like others in this study he sent his son to an independent pre-school nursery before enrolling him a black-run independent primary school. It was only when it was clear that his son was underachieving at a prestigious boys' independent secondary school that his patience with the English education system was exhausted and Errol decided to set up an alternative school for pupils like his son. Errol displayed **active, principled and creative approaches in direct contrast to the passive style of his parents**, and yet their impact on his son's achievement has been questionable.

Devon's parenting style seeks to fill the gaps he felt so keenly in the fathering he received. Throughout the interview the absence of a guiding father whose aspirations were clear and purposeful was almost tangible. Divorce and domestic turmoil had serious implications on the continuity and stability of Devon's school life.

> School could have given me a firm grounding but it just added to the violence and turbulence of my life. (Devon)

Lack of expectation and guidance were the two key issues which he has sought to counteract in **his own parenting by providing a stable, aspirational and strategic overview of the journey to manhood that his sons will follow**. He and his partner, the mother of his sons, deliberately moved out of Hackney so that the children could start their primary education in a more affluent outer London suburb to be better positioned in their choice of secondary schools. He has sought to broaden their horizons as early as possible to mirror the positive formative experiences which his primary education gave him. **He has maintained strong Caribbean links.**

However for the second time in his family's history, unstable domestic circumstances have impacted on a child's schooling, since Devon and his sons' mother have now separated and his sons have moved back to join their mother's family in inner London. Despite his high aspirations for a stable family life, he has been unable to deliver and his sons' education has been disrupted. Devon has focussed on limiting its adverse impact and has been steadfast in the values he brings to what he sees as **his strategic role as their father**: guiding and steering his sons through their schooling.

> I make my values explicit. I insist on the importance of home-work. I try to instil a sense of discipline and application in all areas of work. (Devon)

Devon felt his own schooling was a disappointment. He was asked to leave the sixth form, despite beginning the course, and was forced to go to college.

> School gave me an experience of dubious value. (Devon)

After that Devon describes a period in the wilderness before quali-fying as a youth worker and eventually moving into management with a large not-for-profit leadership development organisation.

Dennis concluded his life-history interview by reflecting on the journey travelled in just two generations of settlement in England.

> My children can see that my parents were of a different time and mobility. My son drives, my parents never drove. (Dennis)

'Drive' has been one of the many powerful metaphors used by Dennis to describe his **determination to better himself and secure**

an even better life for his children. Dennis described his life as a battle, his schooling as a 'battlefield' and his parents' faith and churchgoing as a retreat and a betrayal.

> My father's interpretation of the scriptures was narrow. If they had a Saturday school, it was reading the Bible. It wasn't a catalyst, not an enabler, its narrow interpretation, an accommodation. Nobody white was ever in that church, yet there was a culture of complacency and deference. (Dennis)

Dennis is a harsh critic of his parents and their failure, in his eyes, to fight on his side to acquire a 'good' education. Dennis was denied access to the Sixth Form of his South London secondary school and eventually went to an FE College in North London on the recommendation of friends and former pupils who were active in the college's Afro-Caribbean society as they had been active in fighting for a Black Studies curriculum at school – an early example of **the networking that Dennis perceives as a vital resource for his children and their friends**. After an abortive attempt to get into higher education, Dennis is now an entrepreneur with an MBA and a portfolio of interests in the black cultural and arts sector in London. He owns property in South London.

All his significant relationships have been with professionally trained, highly qualified black Caribbean women. Dennis has recently remarried and does not live with the mother of either his son or daughter; however he retains a strong influential involvement in the parenting of his children and their education. Dennis's partners have all shared **his strong belief in black self-empowerment**. Both children went to black-run nurseries and independent primary schools. His son went to one of the first City Technology Colleges and his daughter went to a selective local grammar school.

Dennis has been mindful at all times of the need to offset any negative impact of schooling on the positive self image and self-esteem that he has been determined to secure for his children. He sees himself as their strongest supporter.

> At one point I put my daughter in an independent prep school [not black-run] but I pulled her out again because as she was maturing physically, I didn't want her to define herself in an all white school – her reference point would be young white girls half her size. I shared my concerns with a black US psychologist who confirmed my decision. (Dennis)

Dennis feels he has succeeded, not only in protecting his children from institutional racism and low teacher expectations, but also in **demonstrating to his children that he is a powerful advocate and able to make a difference on their behalf.** In this way he has broken the link between the parenting he received and the parenting he discharges.

> My daughter, now in terms of futures, she's got too many options. The school has been encouraged to take her seriously. (Dennis)

Dennis's parents have moved back to Jamaica despite being in poor health and against their son and his siblings' advice.

Owen sees a strong sense of connection between his parenting style and that of his parents. The values his parents brought from their rural Jamaican upbringing are transported to urban London largely unshaken and are re-affirmed in the **unconditional love which is at the core of Owen's parenting.** His parents emigrated first leaving Owen behind with an aunt but the connection was never lost because of the routine and regular contact by letters and parcels, which they maintained until the family was reunited. Owen went to school in Jamaica and remembers arriving 'literate and numerate' to attend primary school in London.

> I had to reckon with being called names and being teased which was a new experience. I remember thinking to myself 'they can do and say whatever they want, but I'm over that. I'm better than this.' (Owen)

Always a quiet member of any class and in danger of being over-looked, Owen never felt he was ever really noticed or consulted throughout his compulsory education. He felt he only found a voice once he left school and went to a further education college in North London, which a number of former schoolmates attended. He became a pioneering member of the first black poetry collective in South London, went on to higher education and trained as a librarian. It is this **strong sense of cultural self-worth that Owen feels characterises the intergenerational link in his parenting.**

Owen lives in an extended family and shares the parenting of four children and one grandchild with his partner. Their parenting in his view has been complementary with a **strong shared understanding of the education system and strategies to maximise its benefits for their children.**

> For us the school had a clear academic brief. As parents we were confident of our capacity to deliver their social and cultural skills.
>
> (Owen)

This was evident in their decision to send their children to an independent nursery because they felt that the curriculum offered there gave their children an educational advantage and provided access to the 'assisted places' scheme, which was a Conservative policy designed to provide financial support to low-income parents whose children were able to win a place at a fee-paying school. Their first daughter was able to attend a prestigious South London girls' school and a pattern was established for their other children until the scheme was phased out. Owen and his partner then turned to the new state-funded City Technology Colleges, which were also independent of the local education authority. The pattern has not been as effective for his sons as his daughters but the same philosophy of **supportive non-judgemental parenting** has been maintained throughout.

> My son survived with sufficient interest in education to go on to college to do his GCSEs. I was disappointed but I don't put it on him. (Owen)

Owen's parents returned to rural Jamaica to the house and land they saved to buy from the moment they arrived in London.

Colin has reflected on the very different contexts both personally and politically in which he has parented his two sons in the area of North London where his parents originally settled after migrating from Antigua. Colin had the educational opportunity to go to grammar school but persuaded his parents to back his desire to go to the local boys' comprehensive in common with the majority of his black and white primary school peers. Despite having a strong primary education and the ability to do well, the influences of this neighbourhood 'street' culture proved more attractive and he succumbed to the two prevailing sub-cultures of the school: one officially sanctioned – participating in school sports at the expense of more academic subjects – and the other unsanctioned – involvement in gambling, extortion and fighting. He was finally permanently excluded from school but was able to find work locally. He fathered his first son (D) as a teenager, while still living at home. His son's education was disrupted by periods abroad spent with his mother who tried unsuccessfully to settle in the USA. D followed a similar pattern of secondary schooling to his father, although he attended a mixed Catholic school. He too was excluded but has been unable to acquire any economic or employment stability, and is regularly involved in criminal activity, over which his father exerts little influence.

In the meantime, Colin has found both economic stability and regular employment. He has acquired professional, vocational qualifications and is now in a stable relationship with his second son's (N) mother and is very involved in her extended family. Confident and aspirational, Colin's parenting of his second son is in marked contrast to his early parenting of D and the parenting he himself received from his immigrant parents. The generational pattern of allocating insufficient time to parenting; **the tension between the energy required to sustain employment and the energy required to sustain one's child in education** was replayed for his first son, but finally broken by the engagement of a different intergenerational perspective modelled by his second son's mother and her family.

> I've been camping with N for the pleasure of putting him in a field and not having to say 'Stop' – that's the contrast between country and town. I know N is having a childhood and D didn't really have one. D knew how to play us [his mum and me] off against each other. (Colin)

A different set of strategies emerged which Colin acknowledges were personally challenging to his learned behaviours up to that point. His key standpoint on the values of a 'good' education, that **'a decent education is his right', were aggressively asserted but passively defended.** At the end of the interview he acknowledges

that his resolve has been shaken and that the pursuit of an acceptable education may require him to move from his birthplace to the
outer London suburbs.

> Five years ago I would have said that I'm not moving, they're
> going to have to educate my son, but now ... (Colin)

Both Colin's parents are alive and have returned to Antigua to settle
in the house Colin and his mother bought on his mother's retirement.

Carl feels his parents were very successful in **providing a strong
politically conscious family discourse on racism and its impact on
the experience of black people, not just in his family, but more
widely**. He recalls his parents as advocates, always present at
parents' evenings, always prepared to challenge inequalities in his
treatment and provide explanations for such events.

> There were no secrets. We watched television, we talked about
> what's happening for black people, how black kids were being
> treated. You've got to remember that this was the Sixties, black
> power, black pride coming forward. (Carl)

Carl's **parents showed they valued education by the priority they
gave it at home.** They celebrated their children's achievement,
published notices of their success in the *Jamaican Weekly Gleaner* (the
main island broadsheet published in Jamaica and in the UK) and
lived out the dream of their hard work being worthwhile because of
their children's success in gaining opportunities which were only
available to the privileged few in the Caribbean. All four children
have degrees and are professionally qualified.

Carl uses his experience of his parenting as a resource in his work as a social worker specialising in black fostering and adoption and in the weekend workshops he runs for black men on fathering. His children were under-five at the time of the research interview but both he and his partner share a strong desire for their children to be educated in the state sector.

Carl's parents are retired but have decided to remain in the UK to be near their children and grandchildren.

The relevance of an ecological approach

A key hypothesis of Bronfenbrenner's ecological theory of human development is that children who see their parents performing and exerting influence in the more power-rich settings in society, gain a stronger sense of identity and capacity to realise their potential. It is this belief that underpins Dennis's confidence that he can ensure his children's success in British society; his certainty is gained from the collective experience of his peers (who through their political activity were powerful for and to each other) and not from his parents.

> The thing that High Towers [secondary school] gave me ultimately was a group of peers who did well and we've had an amount of self-confidence and awareness. We're seen by the 'whiteworld' as engaging. I'm one of four black consultants in the arts promotion world and similarly in the voluntary sector. *The power of that peer group, at school and since, has helped me to organise and gain confidence, which I now try to project on to my children.* Although my son calls me 'Bighead' I prove to him that it can be done, I can organise a Jazz Festival, book out the Albert Hall for four nights. Black people can do it. He doesn't begin to imbibe a sense of 'can't do'. (Dennis; emphasis added)

Dennis tracks this back to 1968, when he saw Tommy Smith, US 400-metres Olympic gold medal winner, raise a defiant clenched Black

Power salute whilst on the rostrum, which was broadcast world-wide. Errol also talked about:

> The powerful impact of the 1960s Civil Rights movement on pupils and their teachers. (Errol)

For Arran the key shift was when his Head of House intervened after seeing him address all the black boys in the school at the head-teacher's behest. Arran describes this moment as a turning point, when a person in authority saw a similar potential in him as a human being, regardless of his 'race'. In his dealings with his children's schools as a school governor, he feels confident that teachers already see him as having the same aspirations for his children as they have for theirs. Errol does not share Arran's optimism about the payback for participating in the system.

> Becoming a school governor has a limited effect – better to be seen to do something different. (Errol).

Second-generation black Caribbean parenting discourses

The experience of the parent in a racialised society has been considered from the perspectives of seven black Caribbean men in this study and is unusual in providing a multi-faceted and generational picture of black parenting. A number of themes recur in the accounts:

Ambivalence
In some cases, the accounts reveal a generational ambivalence about the benefits of an English education derived initially as a result of the experience of secondary education and its disappointing conse-

quences, both as a child and as the parent of a child. For Errol this led him at one low point to consider moving his son to be educated in the Caribbean.

> I fear that life in England will break my son. I observe a more gentle process in St Lucia where at least the colour of your skin is not the factor. (Errol)

Errol's experiences have shaped his beliefs and values have led him ultimately to reject mainstream education for his son. He has tried to educate his son in the independent and state sector but has rejected them both. Eventually Errol resolved these tensions by establishing an alternative school in partnership with other black Caribbean parents. He fears that educational failure has become an intergenerational feature of his family.

> The history of education is a history of failure in my family. When I look round at all my brothers and their families, my cousins, my nephews and nieces, I am the only one who succeeded education-ally. (Errol)

Errol's fears that the education system will 'break' his child are echoed by African-American parents in an ethnographic study by Signithia Fordham, which resonates with the biographical accounts in this study.

> The school as an institution is both embraced and rejected by the members of the community. School officials and the larger society tend to see it as the institution that will transform the community residents from their marginal human status to almost full membership in Euro-american civilization. This ambivalence is everywhere apparent. It is most discernible in the almost univer-

sal command: 'Go to School' and in their simultaneous reluctance to become involved in school and school-related activities.

(Fordham, 1996:28)

Dennis recalls a similar set of ambivalent statements, used routinely by his immigrant parents:

> My parents would say things like: 'Don't let knowledge turn you fool.' There was a tension between wanting you to learn and recognising that education was having a disorienting effect for some children in trying to balance the Whiteworld and the Blackworld. (Dennis)

Tough love

Equally problematic is the sons' recall of such 'tough love' exhortations to be 'twice as good as the whites'; warnings about conforming with school discipline exemplified in the threat, 'Don't let me have to come up the school' with its implied violence, which might lead to the plea, 'Don't make me have to beat you'; a familiar picture for other second-generation black Caribbean adults, including Uvanney Maylor, a black academic.

> Struggling to survive was undoubtedly a feature of black immigrant life in Britain, but it did not warrant repression of feelings. It was not an equal exchange, I was a child who did not understand the intricacies of life as my father perceived them. I saw only two worlds – the loving and the unloved. (Maylor, 1995: 41)

This is in stark contrast to the experience cited earlier of Carl's parents whose shared critique of racism was such a potent force in Carl's upbringing; or Owen's with his commitment to unconditional love as a powerful ingredient in countering the negative impact of racism on his children's self-esteem.

Aspirational

The men also experienced the equally positive generational dreaming – aspirational parenting, to which enquiries into the achievement of black Caribbean pupils consistently refer (House of Commons Rampton, 1981; Swann, 1985) and which the quote from Lord Pitt embodies:

> It is a fact that immigrant families are very ambitious for their children, that is natural. If you grow up in a community in which you have got to struggle hard for everything you make, in which you are discriminated against right and left, what you really want is that your child will not suffer it and if you see in order not to have to suffer it the child needs to have a very high professional qualification, your ambition is that the child shall have a very high professional qualification ... it is a perfectly natural reaction.' (Extract from evidence submitted by Lord Pitt to the Select Committee on 4 February 1969:254).

Arran's account of his mother's illegitimacy as the motivation for her ambitions for her family and the importance of education as the route is also a good example.

> There was an unquestioned expectation that we would go to university and we did. (Arran)

Dennis has pinned his hopes on the deracialising effect of information and communication technology. This is evident in his choice of a City Technology College for his son.

I see technology as a great leverage. (Dennis)

Owen makes similar choices of schooling for his son but his aspirations are not simply educational; like Errol he is keen that his son's self esteem and love of learning will not be eroded by the negative impact of London secondary schooling.

Vigilance

Dennis's approach to parental involvement in his children's schooling can be characterised by its vigilance. He is monitoring, unashamedly, the education offered to his children and intervening if and when he finds it wanting. This is in marked contrast to his parents' approach to his schooling, which he describes as 'abandoning us to the wiles of the secondary school system'. Carl's parents demonstrated a similar vigilance to that deployed by Dennis in their regular attendance at parents' evenings at both his primary and secondary school; their interventions and explanations were always timely and helped to maintain his morale. This confident sense of parenting as advocacy was evident through Carl's life history interview.

Attritional

In echoes of the early experiences of the seven men, Fordham defines schools as battlefields in which pupils either conform to or avoid the acquisition of culturally appropriate skills – the latter in order to retain a sense of power and agency, which is seen by professionals as counter-intuitive but is seen by their pupils as appropriate behaviour (Fordham, 1996:39). While this is largely seen at the time as heroic resistance (see particularly the accounts of Dennis and Colin), or an example of pupils shielding themselves from learning (McKenley et al, 2003), for some of the participants, hindsight tends to place a different, hard-edged perspective.

Mixed emotions more and more as I've learned and become aware of what should have taken place at school. Home Beech taught me a kind of terrorism, that's what it taught us. I think the other people had a different experience, some of the older pupils but for us in our year, there was a lot about standing up for yourself.

(Colin)

Colin unconsciously reflects this in the way he interacts with secondary schools on behalf of his family. He craves a mutually respectful relationship with teachers, which cannot be sustained in the way schools are organised currently.

I will work with you around supporting my son but don't be calling me up to reprimand because I will tell you in front of him, that when you see him, you see me. Imagine my face next to his. I'm not sending him here to go on with no rubbish. You ought to feel by right able to say to D that I'm going to phone your dad and give me a chance to do something. Some responded but then the next year he would have a different tutor or year master and I had to start that process again. I see the same thing now in Hackney with my goddaughter and I go up the school with her mum, and it's the same thing. (Colin)

Colin is frustrated to find that his involvement is always at the point of no return, at which point his only recourse is to petition aggressively on his family's behalf.

Collective
The importance of the Civil Rights Movement and the energy of political activism, which it fuelled, were key influences touching the lives of the seven participants.

Our parents supported Martin Luther King, the children Malcolm X. (Arran)

1968 was a turning point – the clenched fists at the Olympics. (Dennis)

Their school days provided them with lifelong friendships and peer networks, which have been of critical significance. Examples include: the decision to use independent nursery schools rather than child-minders was shared among a network of aspirant black Caribbean families in South London; the choice of an FE College in central London with an established Afro-Caribbean Society built on the network of former High Towers pupils originally involved in designing the Black Studies curriculum at school. Ball's (2003) research on white middle class strategies to build social capital through the conscious building and use of networks provides an important analysis of how such groups exercise parental choice in education. To a certain extent each of the participants seeks to emulate what they see as successful white middle class strategies to secure educational advantage in education. This is evident in Devon's choice of tennis lessons for his sons; Errol's decision to choose the independent sector to educate his son from 3–15 (at which point he felt it was doing more harm than good); and Owen and Dennis's research of school choices and decisions to opt for selective grant-maintained schools or city technology colleges, which they perceive as a cut above the remaining state-funded comprehensives.

Commentary

To investigate the way the self-consciousness of others is utilised to produce self-formation lies at the heart of the biographical method ... there is no such thing as a notion of self-hood or self identity that is genetically transferred. We are joined to the past and to the future because it is a constituent feature of mind to have memory and to have projection. (Erben, 1996:160)

The parents in this book are seeking by their behaviours to dispute Erben's notion that 'genetic transfer' does not exist. Their accounts demonstrate the emotional need of many black parents to believe that the 'genetic transfer' in Erben's construction of identity can be achieved. I identify two second-generational strands:

Continuous intergenerational experiences
For Owen, an enduring theme was the quiet confidence his parents' sense of themselves and their Caribbean rural roots conveyed to him and which he in turn applies unconditionally to his own children.

> There were no great debates, just an underlying assumption that we mean each other well which runs deep in all their everyday practice – courtesy, cleanliness, love and self worth. (Owen)

> My parents made it a priority to live a humble life yet it was an enjoyable party life. They accomplished so much given their low salaries and minimal resources. My father went to the betting shop, but didn't leave his mortgage in there. I got a sense of gambling – not prepared to gamble what I'm not prepared to lose. I buy a lottery ticket but my life is not a lottery. (Owen)

This was characterised by a strong strategic view of family life as enduring and generational as well as generative of values, leading to a deep personal sense of self-worth, which he feels he has inherited from his parents and tries to build in his son.

I live up to my expectations of myself as opposed to living down to others' expectations. (Owen)

Another way of conceptualising the consistency of intergenerational values is an acceptance (or rejection) of a *parental inheritance*. Carl reflected on the importance of his family's debates about the impact of racism and their 'rational explanations for irrational behaviours'. He felt this consciousness has given him an understanding of the 'nuances of English life' from which he has drawn in his working life as a social worker and in his community activist work with black men's groups. Both Arran and Carl share the experience of their parents' high academic goals for them as children, which they now hold for their own children. Arran expressed this as:

an unquestioned expectation that I would go to university and I did. I try to convey this to my children. (Arran)

I stayed on to do A levels in the Sixth Form. I did feel I could have done better but it did not spoil my future plans and I went on to Higher Education. (Carl)

Discontinuous intergenerational experiences

For Dennis, Devon, Colin and Errol, there is a conscious critique of their parents' approach and a rejection of this aspect of their parental inheritance. Dennis, in particular, feels a need to draw a clear line between the first and second generation in his family, to break the link and establish a different generational inheritance for the generations to come. Dennis presented his parental values as constructed in direct opposition to the behaviours of his father and yet a clear theme which connects the father to the son is their distrust of white society. Devon attempts to set up the kind of stable family environment, the absence of which he felt had a detrimental impact on his education. But his own turbulent domestic circumstances in their turn run the risk of destabilising his sons' education.

Both Dennis and Devon believe the key role of a father is to present a strategic framework for their children's development and for both a successful education is critical. For Dennis this is characterised by an assertive, interventionist approach to parental involvement at home and at school, which borders on the aggressive, authoritarian parenting of his own father. In Dennis's case there is an intergenerational theme but it is not one that he acknowledges. Dennis aspires to the confrontational mode based on his strong critique of his parents' inability to intervene on his behalf. Dennis sees access to equality of educational opportunity as a war of attrition in which he is seeking to re-define the terms of engagement in which the education of his children will take place; his watchword is vigilance rather than resilience.

> What my experience of school has taught is that this is an environment where I don't trust teachers, I don't hold them in much regard, particularly white ones because they don't have my children's interests at heart and they have to prove themselves otherwise. (Dennis)

Colin veers between both modes. He aspires to the confrontational model and shares Dennis's experience of parents unable to intervene on his behalf. But Colin has yet to assess sufficiently accurately the depth of perseverance and resilience required to maintain the engagement with schools. He is still ambivalent about the kind of self-improvement momentum demonstrated by Dennis, despite his close observation of this intergenerational approach in the influence of his partner's white middle class upbringing on their dual heritage son. Errol has rejected the religious values of his parents and their naïve passivity in relation to their engagement with schooling. Errol has also rejected mainstream education entirely and has set up an alternative school with other black Caribbean parents.

Resilience+

Resilience and perseverance describe parenting behaviours and strategies which are having *some* success in ensuring that black Caribbean pupils develop sustained learning power (resilience+), which their parents hope will propel them along the path of lifelong learning. Owen, Dennis, Devon, Colin and Arran demonstrate this conviction, whilst adopting *very different strategies*.

Holberton's description in 1977 of black under-achievement and the qualities parents require to give their children a sporting chance of succeeding against all odds has been a strong influence on this study. His key word is *perseverance*. Owen and his partner's decision to send their children to independent prep schools from ages 3–7 because they had worked out that these were better value for money than placing their children with childminders is an interesting example of parents seeking to build learning power as early as possible.

Professor Guy Claxton of the University of Bristol describes *resilience* as one of the four components in the Building Learning Power framework[1] he has constructed in his work with the national literacy strategy; resourcefulness, reflectiveness and reciprocity are the other three. However on the basis of this study, applying the learning power principles in working with parents of under-performing groups, particularly black Caribbean parents, would be an important area for further research, particularly on the concept of resilience. Owen, Devon, Arran and Dennis demonstrate this *resilience* in their parenting styles, combining the vigilance and stamina required to maintain the level of parental engagement that participants in this study identify as critical in securing an education that does not destroy their children's self-esteem and appetite for learning. Colin has yet to fully embrace this approach, which is clearly modelled by his new partner in her parent-ing. Errol's beliefs and experiences lead him to develop an alternative Afrocentric approach to education in line with his political beliefs about self-determination.

In a chapter entitled: 'Roots and Wings: Conceptual underpin-nings for Research and Contributions Related to Diversity', Eugene E Garcia (1999) talks about his various personas – Eugene the academic, Gene the son, brother, husband and Gino the Hispanic – to discuss the schooling experiences of Hispanic families like his own. In so doing, he also is making an important point about roles and contexts. Not all black Caribbean parents are able to access the repertoire of behaviours and strategies displayed in this study to be powerful on behalf of their children: ambivalent, tough-loving, aspi-rational, vigilant, attritional and collective. Nevertheless, these provide a very different parenting curriculum to the citizenship, rights and responsibilities agenda as currently configured.

From surviving to thriving – towards a more public discourse involving black Caribbean parents

Of equal importance is the need for second-generation immigrant communities to have a stronger, *public* representation and dialogue about their journey from basic survival as children and young adults to their current (however tenuous) shift to developing thriv-ing strategies, which might act as a powerful counter-weight to the negative impact of racism on their families. Such discourse might help others to reject the pathology of racism and avoid the risk of turning all black Caribbean individuals into perennial victims. Entering into a public discourse on the positive aspects of combat-ting institutional racism is highly problematic and requires a degree of confidence and risk-taking, but it is a discourse some second-generation black Caribbean subjects are well placed to lead. Dennis has the most ambition for this role:

I want to share what I've learned, want to use the leverage that we've earned for the generation to follow. I know white people, I can read them. (Dennis)

Again Dennis illustrates this point when reflecting on his move from surviving to thriving in British society:

Our education was a painful grounding. We could have become accepting of the poverty, we came out with a sense of challenge.
(Dennis)

This study seeks to contribute to this public discourse about black Caribbean parenting and engage critcally with policy developments to promote the involvement of parents of under-performing groups.

Developing cultural intelligence (CQ) – new terms of engagement for educators with those they serve?

Garcia's work (1999) over the past decade has focussed on those programmes that positively identify with aspirations of diverse minority populations in the US. He pays homage to the teachers, classrooms, schools and communities that have recognised the *significance of who they serve* and are making educational success a reality thereby 'honouring their roots and providing the wings'. Garcia concludes that respect for the individual is not enough and says:

Instead, what must be added is respect for, and recognition of integrity of the culture in which the individual develops and resides. (Garcia, 1999:100)

This is a key finding of this study and an area for further research. The intergenerational experiences of racism in wider society but also in the workplace and at school are part of the identity construction and cultural discourse of the black Caribbean parents in this study. Is Garcia describing a body of knowledge, an emancipatory standpoint, a set of learned behaviours which might usefully be termed *cultural intelligence* and have resonance for other ethnic and social groups in the UK? It is clear from the importance that the participants in this study attribute to social justice and anti-racism that education professionals have to adopt new approaches to engage in meaningful dialogue with black Caribbean parents in order to overcome the low expectations that most black Caribbean parents have about the ability of schools to really address the negative impact of racism (immediate and remembered) on them and their children. The implications of this and other findings are considered in the final chapter.

Chapter Five

Conclusions

Introduction

> The geological layers of our lives rest so tightly one on top of the
> other that we always come up against earlier events in later ones,
> not as matter that has been fully formed and pushed aside, but
> absolutely present and alive. I understand this. Nevertheless, I
> sometimes find it hard to bear. (Bernard Schlink, 1997:215[1])

The desire to pay attention to the rarely heard voices and experiences of black Caribbean parents and their children (Gilroy, 2000) is
the justification for this book. Based on a study designed to apply
Bronfenbrenner's ecological approach to human development
(1979) to the generational experiences of seven black Caribbean men
and their families, I hoped that each layer of generational experience
– immigration, acculturation to English life, engagement with the
education system, the lived experience of secondary schooling, post-
compulsory education and un/employment – would contribute to a
more complex reading of black Caribbean parenting and educational achievement.

I was motivated by Schlink's reflections above on the experiences
of second-generation Germans coming to terms with the legacy of
Nazism. I wanted to explore the intergenerational discourses on
schooling within black Caribbean families to learn more about the
reasons why some families are able to triumph over the negative

effects of institutional racism on their own and their children's schooling. Finkelstein asks a number of critical questions about how the experience of education transforms relationships in immigrant families. Bernstein foreshadowed those contentions nearly a decade earlier, when considering whether schools make a difference in redressing inequality:

> It points to the question that although family and school are not themselves major levers of radical change – those lie in economic and political structures – family and education shape mental structures and so forms of feeling and thinking which they militate for or against changes in cultural reproduction. (Bernstein, 1975:30)

I wanted to consider these questions about the impact of family and education on black Caribbean pupils' 'mental structures' and how that might affect educational achievement and to look at the impact of schooling on black Caribbean people's lives using a combination of an ecological approach (Bronfenbrenner, 1979) and life-history methods (Denzin, 1989). The home as an ecology, in terms of interactive relationships and patterns, seemed a useful way of shedding light on the interconnections between experience and parenting, between values and behaviours.

Back to the future?
Much is made about the importance of knowing one's history as a key element in the construction of identity. The mobilising impact of the Black Power, civil rights and Women's Liberation movements which legitimised the struggle for equality, politicised key groups of teachers and pupils in the late 1960s and 70s, including the seven men. These movements provided the context for their formative years and produced networks which sustain them thirty years later.

Dennis, Owen and Errol define their turning point moments within this wider political context of South London. Their North London counterparts Arran, Devon, Carl and Colin share a similar experience of a collective sense of their blackness and their masculinity; but there is also the converse when the encounter between teacher and pupil is deracialised and humanising (Arran, Errol). But it is equally important to reconnect to that history in a personal intimate sense as opposed to a heroic one – to explore the reasons for the failures as well as the successes. The seven fathers see this as an important role for the black family – to provide, as Carl's parents did for him, a racialised discourse to help understand and overcome the institutional racism, which remains an important hurdle.

Interestingly, the seven men identify no similar social movements affecting the political consciousness of their children, currently engaged in secondary schooling in this country, despite hard-won initiatives such as the Race Relations Amendment Act (2001). Metaphors of schools as battlefields, in which there is a struggle to secure educational opportunity, continue to resonate across the generations. Errol's bitter recriminations, that education in this country has failed everyone in his extended family except him, is more the rule than the exception. Dennis's assessment that his brothers have made poor decisions about their own as well as their children's education is the kind of viewpoint which is absent from the research literature.

The background factors which contribute to the achievement of black Caribbean children are often generational and complex, and require sensitive engagement by education professionals. What is absent from those political narratives are the personal stories: the migration histories, the struggle to settle and prosper, and in some cases the triumphant return. The stories need to be reclaimed and affirmed as significant by black Caribbean families themselves. Reconnecting with powerful family narratives of economic migration and aspiration might be an important source of motivation for our children.

Black parenting

The book reminds us that black Caribbean parents are a group whose behaviours, attitudes and styles of engagement are under-researched and by implication, under-valued. The accounts of parenting styles generated in this book counter a consistent research finding that black Caribbean parents are not perceived as 'active' parents by teachers when it comes to their children's education. This is typically demonstrated in low turnout at parents' evenings and general interactions with school, but participation in these activities reveals little about parental involvement in the key setting – the home. A range of parenting styles emerged from the second-generation parents, which demonstrate continuities or discontinuities from the parenting styles of the first generation. However, what all seven fathers have in common is a desire to produce children who are at ease with themselves and their blackness. The book shows the struggle of black parents to minimise the negative impact and effects of under-achievement and institutional inequalities in schooling on their children's self-esteem.

Policy implications

European governments have also recognised that there are negative consequences if Britain and other countries fail to deliver equality of educational opportunity:

> For good economic and social reasons, the children of working class, ethnic minority and other excluded families now need to be drawn into the circle of education, which in the past tended to keep them out. If such excluded groups continue to underachieve

educationally OECD countries will not only find that their economies suffer from the wasted human potential, but that marginalised groups will become a serious problem to society as a whole. (OECD, 1997:22)

The OECD report also suggests that parents should be seen as 'partners in pedagogy' (op cit:25) in recognition of the major role parents play in the informal education of their offspring, but this takes on a different meaning for black Caribbean parents who include strategies to combat racism as key elements in the informal parenting curriculum; in such cases partners in pedagogy has very different connotations. Ball (2003) makes a similar point when he states that:

The individualism of the school consumer is, in particular locations, mediated and encouraged through collective and familial memories and expectations. (Ball, 2003:113)

Mac an Ghaill makes a critical point about the wider societal importance of this challenge, but from a different standpoint:

One of the main claims of postmodernists is that we are experiencing a fundamental shift, marked by a sense of discontinuity, fragmentation and uncertainty. Hence it might be assumed that, in engaging with such questions, ethnic minority communities, many of whom have a long history of social displacement, would be an essential reference point to draw upon. In most postmodern accounts, however, these groups are absent, resulting in a failure to address issues of migration, social marginality, cultural belonging and a sense of home. (Mac an Ghaill, 1999:5)

Implications for schools

Thus far, 'colour-blind' generic parenting approaches noted by Ball (2003), Crozier (2001) and Vincent (2002), evident in much of the research literature, have failed to promote greater parental engagement of black Caribbean parents with schools. Much of the literature on parental involvement makes reference to ethnic and cultural diversity but as additional elements, for example, parents with English as An Additional Language or those whose children have special educational needs, which have to be taken into account when engaging with parents. The ecological approach makes a strong case for more culturally-informed interventions to increase the participation of black Caribbean parents.

Taken as a small body of research the educational and parenting biographies in this book offer accounts of how black Caribbean parents articulate their roles of parent-educator and parent-advocate on behalf of their children. As stated earlier in Chapter 4, Dennis feels it is extremely important that his children experience him as a strong and uncompromising advocate in his support for their right to a high standard of education. Devon takes his role as parent-educator seriously. Both these parents have moved into the role of parent as commissioner of education services, of which secondary schooling is one important piece but not the whole picture.

The seven accounts remind us that the first generation of black Caribbean immigrants were economic migrants with aspirations for themselves and subsequent generations of their families.

There is a historic memory in minority ethnic communities of aspiration and struggle which I see as a positive gift – that feeling that I'm doing well as long as my child has done better which I hold on to and work with. (Primary headteacher, quoted in McKenley and Gordon, 2002:16)

Accessing this vein of generational aspiration, however residual, to engage with the educational values black Caribbean parents bring to the schooling of their children is essential as the above extract from a primary headteacher would attest. But not all primary and certainly few secondary headteachers and their staff feel confident or necessarily willing to engage with the life histories of their parent body.

Good practice exists among schools across the country (OFSTED, 2002; McKenley et al, 2003). Much is made of child-centred education and personalised learning, but secondary schools really engaging with parental aspirations in partnership are in a minority. However the majority of secondary schools as they are currently configured would find it hard to respond to the demands of parents like Colin for a more interactive and dynamic relationship. But the ramifications of not addressing such concerns are also apparent in this book and manifest in the loss of confidence and parental support.

The levels of disillusion and distrust revealed by black Caribbean parents in this book are not atypical, as evident in the submissions by individuals and community organisations to the various select committee enquiries referred to in earlier chapters. Poor levels of attainment have done little to dispel the lack of confidence many black Caribbean parents feel about their children's education. Jasbir Mann recalls her first actions as a newly promoted headteacher, to engage the minority ethnic parents in her school community:

I decided to work on the school's mission and to involve parents and the community as well as staff. I asked everyone, 'If I were a parent at this school what would I want?' And this was very powerful. Parents gave very different answers than anticipated by most of the staff, who felt the parents would be grateful for their contributions. Instead parents said involvement was on the teachers' terms. So I had to act quickly. I drew up a five-year plan with short, middle and immediate response, focused on values and valuing each other. Listening and acting was the right thing to do. (Quoted in McKenley and Gordon, 2002:15)

This has serious implications for the current dynamics of parent–school relationships. The challenge of leading diverse multi-ethnic schools is only just becoming part of the leadership discourse in the UK and with that a growing realisation that strategies for engaging black Caribbean pupils and their parents are not working. Gordon notes, in her recent review of the literature on the internal and external barriers to advancement for individuals of black and minority ethnic heritage, that the differences between the US and UK strategies are telling. Although the argument concerns black and minority ethnic (BME) adults, the parallels with pupils are very similar. The US strategies include: the development of conflict resolution competencies to enable individuals to handle the racism they will inevitably experience as they develop careers, and skill-building programmes which help individuals to manage their 'rage' over the experience of racism.

What Gordon describes as significant about the US strategies is that they are organisationally based, suggesting a shared responsibility between the organisation and the individuals of black and minority ethnic heritage. This contrasts markedly with the UK experience where their race experiences seem to be something ethnic minorities are expected to work on individually (see Gordon's articles in McKenley and Gordon, 2002:44). Currently the UK strategies do not produce systematic or organisational solutions, although the Race Relations Amendment Act (2001) is a serious attempt to redress the balance and promote race equality across a range of institutions including schools; assessing its impact on black Caribbean achievement is a key area for further research.

Dr Tony Sewell has been involved in project work with excluded young black Caribbean pupils in London schools in Lambeth (2002–3). In a chapter entitled: 'Black Boys and schooling: an intervention framework for understanding the dilemmas of masculinity, identity and underachievement' (Majors, 2001), Sewell and Majors develop the concept of 'ego recovery – a social and psychological position where African-Caribbean boys can achieve, driven by a reconstructed masculinity'. Sewell goes on to state that:

> It is more than giving African-Caribbean boys a new set of textbooks that contain black characters and pictures. It presupposes a commitment by staff to a form of emancipatory teaching. (Sewell and Majors, in Majors 2001: 200).

Clearly there is a case for further research into these initiatives as well as the opportunity to develop other culturally appropriate programmes of study, either consulting and/or involving black Caribbean parents in their design.

Implications for black Caribbean parents

> If these problems are to be addressed parents who themselves did not have an effective education must nevertheless learn how to support their own children's learning. (OECD, 1997:22)

The book also demonstrates the dangers of assuming that the onus for increasing the participation of parents in their children's education lies entirely with schools – black Caribbean parents have to begin to engage in dialogues about effective family learning environments. I would argue that there is a need for second- and third-generation immigrant communities to engage more publicly in debates about black Caribbean achievement. Dennis illustrates this point when reflecting on his move from 'surviving to thriving' in British society:

> We could have become accepting of the poverty, we came out with a sense of challenge. (Dennis)

Racism and the consequences of educational inequality have been devastating for members of some of the families. Errol concluded his life-history interview with a bitter critique of the differential impact of education on the rest of his family.

> The history of education is a history of failure in my family. When I look round at all my brothers and their families, my cousins, my nephews and nieces, I am the only one who succeeded educationally. (Errol)

King (1999) shared a similar experience to Errol:

> As the years passed, however, I watched as my family members and peers were utterly destroyed by the same alienating schooling that promoted and enabled my 'success'. (King, 1999:109)

But as the seven black men demonstrate, some black Caribbean parents have developed effective adaptive strategies to overcome the barriers to their children securing equality of educational opportunity. However, whilst these are under-researched and are not part of a wider discourse, the strategies remain individual or at best shared within extended family circles.

Areas for further research

New Government initiatives

The DfES has been funding a national study on raising the achievement of 'African Caribbean' pupils involving thirty secondary schools in the main urban conurbations including London; involving parents is a key dimension to this study which will run until 2005. In addition, there has been a DfES Key Stage 3 strategy pilot project on raising the achievement of black Caribbean boys sponsored by the London Challenge. A key feature of both programmes is the active engagement with black Caribbean parents in support groups. The projects are challenging schools to listen and learn from the voices of black parents, and build on the capacity and desire for a more equitable partnership in the education of their children. These are important developments, which arise from the Government's consultation on how it might raise the achievement of ethnic minority pupils (*Aiming High*, DfES, 2003), particularly those of Caribbean heritage. From October 2005, the lessons learned from both projects will be encompassed in the Black Pupil Achievement Project involving some eighty schools as part of the National Strategies. Evaluating the impact of black parental engagement should form a separate strand.

Black family learning environments

The book has revealed the importance of resolving the gap between the prevailing binary positions typically adopted by parents, schools and reflected by researchers in this field: 'teacher racism' versus 'unrealistic parental expectations'. Research has tended to be located in schools and about how schools interact with parents as opposed to how parents interact with schools, with research located in their community and homes. A number of schools are appointing home–school liaison workers who act as an independent bridge between home and school; some are based in schools and do not have an outreach function whilst others do home visits and in some cases, such functions are performed by learning mentors. Nevertheless, the impact of this work is under-researched.

The histories of urban schools serving those early multi-ethnic communities

One of the many personal challenges in conducting this research has been the powerful interplay between my biography and that of the seven men. As the daughter of one of the first group of black Caribbean families to settle in London (my parents came to Britain in 1953 and I was born in 1955), for much of my education, I was often one of few black pupils in primary, secondary and university. I was well placed to observe the impact of the transition from mono-cultural to multi-ethnic schools on white working class pupils – those whose families did not engage in the 'white flight' to the suburbs until much later, or remained in inner London. I believe this group of white adults has equally interesting insights into the impact of immigration and acculturation on the development of post-war London education.

I was in compulsory schooling during the time when grammar and secondary modern schools were turning into comprehensives against the backdrop of political ferment and structural change in education. Like my former school, this book refers to two schools, both since closed – their histories unrecorded but still accessible through the life histories of the teachers and pupils who attended them. These school histories, which I contend are largely unwritten and under-researched, are important records of the transformation of London society following the Second World War.

The case for ecological studies in education

Finally, there is more scope in applying an ecological approach to work in this field. Bronfenbrenner's theory of human development provides an opportunity for research that recognises the power inequalities that exist institutionally and how those inequalities are mediated through the different settings which are layered upon an individual's or group's construct of themselves as learner/s. Ball makes a valid point in his recent work on the class strategies of the middle classes in engaging in the education market:

> While I would not want to turn back the clock as far as under-playing the role of institutional differentiation and other social factors in producing educational inequalities, there has been a neglect of the actions of families, and particular family members, in recent times ... we now have the theoretical resources which enable attention to be paid to the differences within and between families without an immediate collapse into social pathology.
>
> (Ball, 2003: 5)

Like the middle class parents in Ball's sample the seven black Caribbean parents in this book are 'seeking to achieve some narrative coherence, linking and making consistent the lives of their children with their own' (Ball, 2003:165). The case for further research into the adaptive strategies used by black Caribbean parents is demonstrated clearly in the biographies of the seven black men; so too is the importance of using culturally-sensitive and appropriately multi-faceted methodologies to engage with the interplay between home, school and community in building culturally affirming parent–school relationships and effective family learning environments.

Notes

Introduction
1. Simon Clements HMI (retired) in a paper presented to Rotherham LEA in 1995.
2. As I write, a novel on the early settlement of a Jamaican couple in London has just won the Orange Prize for Fiction 2004 . *Small Island* is written by Andrea Levy, whose father was on the *Empire Windrush*.
3. In some education authorities the term 'dual heritage' is used to define this group.
4. I have recorded their ages at the time of writing in 2005.

Chapter One: Migration and Settlement
1. Extract from 'I is a long-memoried woman' by Grace Nichols (1980).
2. Extract from 'Colonization in Reverse' by Louise Bennett (1982).
3. See the novels by Sam Selvon, E R Braithwaite and the plays of Caryl Phillips.
4. Davison noted that the decision to migrate was essentially an impetus 'organised by private initiative with a minimal degree of governmental control or regulation with one notable exception, Barbados, which gave official encouragement and assistance to migration to Britain' (Davison, 1962:26).
5. Quoted in Cropley, A (1983) *The Education of Immigrant Children*.
6. Baroness Ashton, Parliamentary Under-Secretary for Education convened an Ethnic Minority Achievement Forum in Church House on 8 July 2002 to seek the views of a range of 'expert' practitioners to inform government strategy.
7. *Wondrous Obsession* (2003) provides a Hollywood fictional account of a West Indian family settling in London in the 1950s.

[8] The London Transport Executive entered into an agreement with the Barbadian Immigrants' Liaison Service and as a result several thousand Bajans were loaned their fare to London (Layton-Henry, 1992).

[9] 'Seamstress' in *Unfamiliar Harbours* by leslie goffe (1984).

[10] See Alan Little's conclusion that 'Just as the education system has failed to meet the needs of the children from working class background, so now, to an even greater extent it is failing to meet the needs of children from different cultural backgrounds' in a chapter entitled: 'Achievement of Ethnic Minority Children in London Schools' in G K Verma and C Bagley (1975). Alan Little was Director of Research & Statistics for the ILEA (1962–72).

[11] Professor A R Jensen's thesis that intelligence was largely determined by genetics and that US compensatory education programmes to raise the intelligence of groups who had low scores in IQ tests were bound to fail. This deterministic view was published in an article for the Harvard Educational Review in 1969.

[12] Gus John writes: 'I was a secret observer on the people of my race during the winter of 1969–70. It was not a role I relished but it was necessary if someone was to look deeply and objectively into the sudden decline in racial harmony in Handsworth, Birmingham to operate incognito in the immediate period after Powell's infamous anti-immigration speech in Wolverhampton in 1968' (Humphry and John, 1971:9).

Chapter Two: The Secondary Years

[1] Powell quoted in the memorandum submitted jointly from Brent CRC and Brent Teachers' Association to the Select Committee on Race Relations and Immigration in March 1973.

[2] In more recent years there has been some movement on the importance of collecting reliable data, if only on the nature and size of the non-English, Scottish and Welsh (ESW) community. The 1991 official census was the first to include racialised categories: white; black Caribbean; black-African; black-other (with description); Indian; Pakistani; Bangladeshi; Chinese and any other ethnic group (with description).

[3] Evidence to the Enquiry on the Problems of Coloured School Leavers (Para 3521:1144).

[4] The ILEA Language Survey showed that although immigrant pupils numbered 15% of the total numbers of pupils in ILEA schools, they comprised 28.4% of children in ESN schools; of those three-quarters were of West Indian origin.

5   Title of film directed by Spike Lee (1988); subsequently used as the title for Chapter 15 in *Windrush: The Irresistible Rise of Multi-Racial Britain* (1998) by Mike Phillips and Trevor Phillips (London: Harper Collins).
6   Reflected in the poetry of black Caribbean artists like Linton Kwesi Johnson and the Black Ink Collective featured in political journals such as *Race Today*; bewilderment and near despair in the plays by Caryl Phillips and Jacqueline Rudet; rebellion in the films by Horace Ove and Franco Rossi and confusion in novels such as *To Sir With Love*: many of which are now out of print or rarely cited (McKenley, 2001).

Chapter Three: Home–School Relations
1   Extract from evidence reported by a Chief Inspector from Her Majesty's Inspectorate to the Parliamentary Select Committee on Race Relations and Immigration, House of Commons, 1969:179.
2   See the poems in *Dread, Beat and Blood* by Linton Kwesi Johnson, 1975.
3   One consequence is that at the time of writing (summer 2004), there are 217 admissions authorities in London, although proposals to address the situation are being discussed by a pan-London body of education officers and civil servants.
4   Gewirtz, Ball and Bowe (1995) conclude that 'race'-informed choosing is a neglected aspect of much of the literature on parental choice.
5   Lecture entitled: 'The More Things Change … Education Research, Social Class and "Interlocking" Inequalities'.

Chapter Four: Critical Reflections
1   Launch of the Learning to Learn Online Discussion Board, June 2004.

Chapter Five: Conclusions
1   The extract is taken from a longer section in the acclaimed book *The Reader* by Bernard Schlink (1998): 'For the last few years I've left our story alone. I've made peace with it. And it came back, detail by detail and in such a fully rounded fashion with its own direction and its own sense of completion, that it no longer makes me sad. What a sad story, I thought for so long. Not that I now think it was happy. But I think it is true, and thus the question of whether it is sad or happy has no meaning whatever. At any rate, that's what I think when I just happen to think about it. But if something hurts me, the hurts I suffered back then come back to me, and when I feel guilty, the feelings of guilt return; if I yearn for something today, or feel homesick, I feel the yearn-

ings and homesickness from back then. The geological layers of our lives rest so tightly one on top of the other that we always come up against earlier events in later ones, not as matter that has been fully formed and pushed aside, but absolutely present and alive. I understand this. Nevertheless, I sometimes find it hard to bear. Maybe I did write our story to be free of it, even if I can never be.'

Bibliography

ACER Project, Racism and the Black Child – West Indian Children In Our Schools. Follow Up Groups Report (1982).

ALG (2003) 'Class Acts: Diversity and Opportunity in London Schools'. London: Association of London Government.

Amos Hatch A and Wisniewski R (eds) (1995) *Life History and Narrative*. London: Falmer Press.

Amos V and Parmar P (1981) 'Resistance and responses: the experiences of black girls in Britain' in A McRobbie and T McCabe (eds) *Feminism for Girls: An Adventure Story*. [Reprinted in Arnot M and Weiner G (1987) *Gender and the Politics of Schooling*. London: Unwin.]

Angelou M (1993) *The Inaugural Poem: On the Pulse of Morning*. London: Virago Press.

Atkin J, Bastiani J and Goode J (1988) *Listening to Parents: an approach to the improvement of home–school relations*. Beckenham: Croom Helm.

Back L (1996) *New ethnicities and urban culture: racisms and multiculture in young lives*. London: UCL Press Limited.

Bagley C (1975) 'The Background of Deviance in Black Children in London' in G K Verma and C Bagley *Race and Education Across Cultures*. London: Heinemann.

Bagley C (1977) 'A Comparative Perspective in the Education of Black Children in Britain'. Paper presented to a seminar at the Centre for Information and Advice on Educational Disadvantage, Manchester.

Bagley C, Bart M and Wong J (1979) 'Antecedents of Scholastic Success in West Indian ten-year-olds in London' in G K Verma and C Bagley (eds) *Race, Education and Identity*. London: Macmillan.

Ball S J (1981) *Beachside Comprehensive: A Case Study of Secondary Schooling*. Cambridge: Cambridge University Press.

Ball S J (1987) *The Micro-Politics of the School: Towards a Theory of School Organisation*. London: Methuen.

Ball S J, Bowe R and Gewirtz S (1996) 'School choice, social class and distinction – the realization of social advantage in education' *Journal of Education Policy* Vol 11, No 1, 89–112.

Ball S J 'The More Things Change … Education Research, Social Class and "Interlocking" Inequalities.' Inaugural Professorial Lecture, London Institute of Education March 2003.

Ball S J (2003) *Class Strategies and the Education Market: The middle classes and social advantage*. London: Routledge Falmer.

Banks J A and McGee Banks C A (eds) (1995) *Handbook of Research on Multicultural Education*. NY: Simon & Shuster Macmillan.

Barrow J (1987) *The Two Kingdoms: Standards and Concerns. Parents and Schools: Report of an Independent Investigation into Secondary Schools in Brent 1981–84*. London Borough of Brent.

Becker H S (1986) *Writing for Social Scientists*. Chicago: The University of Chicago Press.

Bennett L 'Colonization in Reverse' in M Morris (ed) (1982) *Selected Poems*. Jamaica: Sangsters.

Bernstein B (1975) *Class, Codes and Control Vol.3 Towards a Theory of Educational Transmissions* (2nd edition). London: Routledge & Kegan Paul.

Bhatnager J (1970) *Immigrants at School*. London: Cornmarket Press.

Black Peoples Progressive Association & Redbridge Community Relations Council (1978) *Cause for Concern West Indian Pupils in Redbridge*.

Blair M, Holland J and Sheldon S (1995) *Identity and Diversity: Gender and the Experience of Education*. Clevedon, England: Multilingual Matters.

Bourne J, Bridges L and Searle C (1994) *Outcast England*. London: Institute of Race Relations.

Bowker G and Carrier J (1976) *Race and Ethnic Relations: Sociological readings*. London: Hutchinson.

Brah A (1996) *Cartographies of diaspora: contesting identities*. London: Routledge.

Bravette G (1997) 'Towards Bicultural Competence: Researching for Personal and Professional Transformation'. Unpublished PhD Dissertation, School of Management, University of Bath, England.

Brighouse T (1994) 'Urban Deserts or Fine Cities? – Education: The Alchemist's Stone'. The TES Greenwich Education Lecture 21 April 1994.

Bronfenbrenner U (1979) *The Ecology of Human Development*. Massachusetts: Harvard University Press.

Brown Phillip (1994) 'Education and the Ideology of Parentocracy' in M J Halstead *Parental Choice in Education*. London: Kogan Page Ltd.

Bryan B, Dadzie S and Scafe S (1985) *The Heart of the Race: Black Women's Lives in Britain*. London: Virago

Burchill B (1984) 'West Indian Parents and Schools Working Paper 3, Race, Education and Research: Rampton, Swann and After'. University of London Institute of Education.

Burgess R G (1983) *Experiencing Comprehensive Education: A study of Bishop McGregor School.* London: Methuen.

Burgess R G (ed) (1984) *The Research Process in Educational Settings: Ten Case Studies.* Falmer: The Falmer Press.

Burgin T and Edson P (1987) *Spring Grove: The Education of Immigrant Children.* London: Institute of Race Relations and Oxford University Press.

Buzan T with Buzan B (1993) *The Mind Map Book.* London: BBC Books.

Campbell C (ed) (2002) *Developing Inclusive Schooling: Perspectives, policies and practices.* London: Institute of Education.

Carter T with J Coussins (1986) *Shattering Illusions: West Indians in British Politics.* London: Lawrence & Wishart Ltd.

Central Advisory Council for England (1967) *Children and their Primary Schools* (The Plowden Report). London: HMSO.

Centre for Contemporary Cultural Studies (1982) *The Empire Strikes Back.* CCCS University of Birmingham in association with Hutchinson.

Channer Y (1995) *I am a Promise – the School Achievement of British African Caribbeans.* Stoke-on-Trent: Trentham Books.

Chessum L (1997) '"Sit down, you haven't reached that stage yet": African Caribbean children in Leicester Schools 1960–1974' *History of Education,* 1997, Vol 26, No 4, 409–29.

Clark R M (1983) *Family Life and School Achievement: Why Poor Black Children Succeed or Fail.* Chicago: University of Chicago Press.

Coard B (1971) *How the West Indian Child is Made Educationally Subnormal In The British School System.* London: New Beacon Books.

Cohen L and Cohen A (1986) *Multi-Cultural Education: A Source Book for Teachers.* London: Harper & Row Limited.

Coleman J et al (1969) *Equality of Educational Opportunity.* Cambridge, Mass: Harvard University Press.

Collins Patricia Hill (1990) *Black Feminist Thought: Knowledge, Consciousness and the Politics of Empowerment.* New York: Routledge.

CRC (1974) The Educational Needs of Children from Minority Groups.

Cresswell John W (1994) *Research Design Qualitative & Quantitative Approaches.* California: Sage Publications.

Cropley A J (1983) *The Education of Immigrant Children: A Social-psychological introduction.* Kent: Croom Helm Ltd.

Cross M and Entzinger H (eds) (1988) *Lost Illusions: Caribbean minorities in Britain and the Netherlands.* London: Routledge.

Crozier G (2000) *Parents and Schools: Partners or Protagonists.* Stoke-on-Trent: Trentham Books.

Crozier G (2001) 'Excluded Parents: the deracialisation of parental involvement' in *Race Ethnicity and Education*, 4, 329–41.

Cullingford C (ed) (1996) *Parents, Education and the State*. Hampshire: Arena-Ashgate Publishing Ltd.

David M (1993) *Parents, Gender & Education Reform*. Cambridge: Polity Press.

David M, West A and Ribbens J (1984) *Mothers' Intuition: Choosing Secondary Schools*. London: Falmer Press.

Davison R B (1962) *West Indian Migrants: Social and Economic Facts of Migration from the West Indies*. London: Institute of Race Relations with Oxford University Press.

Deem R (1980) *Schooling for women's work*. London: Routledge.

Denzin N K (1989) *Interpretive Biography*. California: Sage Publications.

Denzin N and Lincoln Y (eds) (1994) *Handbook of Qualitative Research*. London: Sage Publications.

Department of Education & Science (DES) (1965) Circular No. 7/65 *The Education of Immigrants*. London: HMSO.

Department of Education & Science (DES) (1971a) *Potential and Progress in a Second Culture. A survey of the assessment of pupils from overseas; Education Survey 10*. London: HMSO.

Department of Education & Science (DES) (1971b) *The Education of Immigrants; Education Survey 13*. London: HMSO.

Department of Education & Science (DES) (1972) *The Continuing Needs of Immigrants; Education Survey 14*. London: HMSO.

Department of Education & Science (DES) (1981) Circular 1/81 *Education 1980: Admission to Schools*. London: HMSO.

Department of Education & Science (DES) (1991) *The Parents' Charter: You and Your Child's Education*. London: HMSO.

Department for Education (DFE) (1992) *Choice and Diversity – A New Framework for Schools*. London: HMSO.

Department for Education & Skills (DfES 0183/2003) *Aiming High: Raising the Achievement of Minority Ethnic Pupils*. London: HMSO.

Dhondy F, Beese B and Hassan L (1982) *The Black Explosion in British Schools*. London: Race Today Publications.

Dickinson P (1982) 'Facts and Figures: Some Myths' in J Tierney (ed) *Race, Migration & Schooling*. London: Holt, Rinehart & Winston.

Dodgson E (1984) *Motherland: West Indian women in Britain in the 1950s*. London: Heinemann.

Donald J and Rattansi A (eds) (1992) *'Race', Culture and Difference*. London: Sage.

Drew D (1995) *'Race' Education and Work: The Statistics of Inequality*. Hants: Avebury.

Driver G (1979) 'Classroom Stress and School Achievement' in V S Khan *Minority Families in Britain*. London: Macmillan.

Ely M (1991) *Doing Qualitiative Research: Circles Within Circles*. London: Falmer Press.

Erben M (1996) 'The Biographic and the Educative – auto-biographical method'. Seminar paper presented at Institute of Education Research Design Lecture series, Summer 1996.

Erben M (1996) 'The purposes and processes of biographical method' in D Scott and R Usher (eds) *Understanding Educational Research*. London: Routledge.

Evans P C C and Le Page R B (1967) *The Education of West Indian Children*. London: NCCI.

Eysenck H J (1971) *Race, Intelligence and Education*. London: Maurice Temple Smith.

File N and Power C (1981) *Black Settlers in Britain 1555–1958*. London: Heinemann Educational.

Finkelstein B (1983) 'Exploring Community in Urban Educational History' in Goodenow and Rantch (eds) *Schools in Cities*. New York: Holmes & Meier.

Fitzherbert K (1967) *West Indian Children in London*. Occasional Papers on Social Administration. London: Bell & Sons Ltd.

Fordham S (1996) *Blacked Out: Dilemmas of Race, Identity and Success at Capital High*. Chicago: University of Chicago Press.

Foster P (1990) *Policy and Practice in Multicultural and Antiracist Education*. London: Routledge.

Foucault M (1980) *Power/Knowledge*. Brighton: Harvester Press.

Fuller M (1980) 'Black girls in a London comprehensive school' in R Deem (ed) *Schooling for women's work*. London: Routledge.

Garcia E E (1999) 'Roots and Wings: Conceptual Underpinnings for Research and Contributions Related to Diversity' in C A Grant (ed) *Multicultural Research: A reflective engagement with race, class, gender and sexual orientation*. London: Falmer Press.

Gewirtz S, Ball S J and Bowe R (1995) *Markets, choice and equity in education*. Buckingham: Open University Press.

Gibbes N (1980) 'West Indian Teachers Speak Out' published by the Caribbean Teachers Association and Lewisham CCR.

Giles R H (1977) *The West Indian Experience in British Schools: Multi-Racial Education and Social Disadvantage in London*. London: Heinemann.

Gillborn D (1990) *'Race', Ethnicity and Education: Teaching and Learning in Multi-Ethnic Schools*. London: Unwin Hyman Ltd.

Gillborn D (1996) 'Sociology of "Race" and Education'. Institute of Education seminar, Spring 1996.

Gillborn D and Gipps C (1996) *Recent Research on the achievements of Ethnic Minority Pupils*. London: OFSTED Publications.

Gillborn D and Mirza H (2000) *Education Inequality: Mapping race, class and gender: a synthesis of research evidence.* London: OFSTED Publications.

Gillborn D and Youdell D (2000) *Rationing Education: Policy, Practice, Reform and Equity.* Buckingham: Open University Press.

Gillborn D (2002) *Education and Institutional Racism.* London: Institute of Education.

Gilroy P (1987) *There Aint No Black In The Union Jack: The cultural politics of race and nation.* London: Hutchinson.

Gilroy P (1993) *The Black Atlantic Modernity and Double Consciousness.* London: Verso.

Gilroy P (2000) *Between Camps: nations, cultures and the allure of race.* London: Allen Lane.

Gipps C and Murphy P (1994) *A Fair Test? Assessment, achievement and equity.* Bucks: Open University Press.

Glaser B and Strauss A (1967) *The Discovery of Grounded Theory: Strategies for qualitative research.* New York: Aldine Publishing Company.

Glazer N and Young K (1983) *Ethnic Pluralism and Public Policy.* London: Heinemann.

Goffe L A (1984) *Unfamiliar Harbours.* London: Black Ink Publications.

Goldman R J and Taylor F M (1966) *Coloured Immigrant Children: A Survey of research, studies and literature on their educational problems and potential in Britain.* Educational Research 8 (3), 163–83.

Goodenow K and Ravitch D (eds) (1983) *Schools in Cities.* New York: Holmes & Meier.

Gordon Gloria Bravette (2001) 'Transforming Lives: Towards Bicultural Competence' in P Reason and H Bradbury (eds) *Handbook of Action Research: Participative Inquiry of Practice.* London: Sage Publications.

Grant B (1993) 'Reparation nor repatriation'. Article in New Statesman & Society 15.10.93.

Grant Carl A (ed) (1999) *Multicultural Research: A reflective engagement with race, class, gender and sexual orientation.* London: Falmer Press.

Green J (1990) *Them: voices from the immigrant community in contemporary Britain.* London: Secker & Warburg.

Griffiths M and Troyna B (1995) *Anti-racism, Culture and Social Justice in Education.* Stoke-on-Trent: Trentham Books.

Grosvenor I (1987) 'A Different Reality: Education and the racialization of the black child' *History of Education,* 4, 299–308.

Guba E G and Lincoln Y (1994) 'Competing Paradigms in Qualitative Research' in N Denzin and Y Lincoln (eds) *Handbook of Qualitative Research.* London: Sage Publications.

Gundara J (1982) 'Lessons from History for Black Resistance in Britain' in J Tierney (ed) *Race, Migration and Schooling.* London: Holt, Rinehart & Winston.

Gurnah A (1987) 'Gatekeepers and Caretakers: Swann, Scarman and the social policy of containment' in B Troyna (ed) *Racial Inequality in Education.* London: Tavistock Publications.

Hall S (1967) *The Young Englanders.* London: Community Relations Commission.

Hall S (1992) 'New Ethnicities' in J Donald and A Rattansi (eds) *'Race', Culture and Difference.* London: Sage.

Hall S (1998) 'Postscript' *Soundings*, 10, Autumn 1998, 188–92.

Halsall E (ed) (1970) *Becoming Comprehensive: Case Histories.* Oxford: Pergamon Press Ltd.

Halsted Mark J (ed) (1994) *Parental Choice and Education: Principles, Policy and Practice.* London: Kogan Page Ltd.

Hammersley M and Woods P (eds) (1984) *Life in School: The Sociology of Pupil Culture.* Milton Keynes: Open University Press.

Hawkes N (1966) *Immigrant Children In British Schools.* London: Institute of Race Relations and Pall Mall Press.

Hernstein R J and Murray C (1994) *The Bell Curve.* London: Macmillan.

Hidalgo N M, Bright J A, Sui San-Fong, Swap S M and Epstein J (1995) 'Research on Families, Schools and Communities: A multi-cultural perspective' in J A Banks and C A McGee Banks (eds) *Handbook of Research on Multicultural Education.* NY: Simon & Shuster Macmillan.

Hill Collins P (1990) *Black Feminist Thought: Knowledge, Consciousness, and the Politics of Empowerment.* London: Routledge.

Holberton R in ILEA *Contact* December, 1977.

Holstein J A and Gubrium J F (1995) *The Active Interview.* London: Sage Publications.

House of Commons (1969) *Select Committee on Race Relations & Immigration The Problems of Coloured School Leavers Vols 1–2 Report, Proceedings and Minutes of Evidence Session 1968–9.* London: HMSO.

House of Commons (1972) *First Special Report from the Select Committee on Race Relations & Immigration Statistics of Immigrant School Pupils Session 1971–2.* London: HMSO.

House of Commons (1973) *Select Committee on Race Relations & Immigration Fifth Enquiry on Education Session 1972–3 Vols 1–3 Report, Evidence and Appendices.* London: HMSO.

House of Commons (1981) *Interim Report of the Committee of Inquiry into the Education of Children from Ethnic Minority Groups: West Indian Children In Our Schools.* Chairman: Mr Anthony Rampton; London: Cmnd 8273 HMSO.

House of Commons (1985) *The Report of the Committee of Inquiry into the Education of Children from Ethnic Minority Groups: Education For All.* Chairman: Lord Swann; London: HMSO Cmnd 9453.

Hoyles E M (1970) 'The Two-Site School: The London Plan and Vauxhall Manor School' in E Halsall (ed) (1970) *Becoming*

Comprehensive: Case Histories. Oxford: Pergamon Press Ltd.

Humphry D and John G (1971) *Because They're Black*. London: Penguin.

Hyder K (1994) 'Home, Background and Ethnic Minority Achievement – Pupils of Caribbean Background'. Paper presented at conference on underachievement of ethnic minorities in Education in Britain and Europe.

Jensen A R (1969) 'How much can we boost IQ and scholastic achievement?' *Harvard Educational Review* 39, 1.

John G (1981) *In the Service of Black Youth: A study of the Political Culture of Youth and Community Work with Black Youth in English Cities*. Leicester: National Association of Youth Clubs.

Jonathan R (1993) 'Parental Rights in Schooling' in P Munn (ed) *Parents and Schools – Customers, Managers or Partners* . London: Routledge.

Jowett S and Baginsky M with Macdonald McNeil M (1991) *Building Bridges – parental involvement in schools*. Berkshire: NFER-Nelson.

Khan V S (ed) (1979) *Minority Families in Britain*. London: Macmillan.

King J E (1999) 'In Search of a Method for Liberating Education and Research: The Half (That) Has not Been Told' in C A Grant (ed) *Multicultural Research: A reflective engagement with race, class, gender and sexual orientation*. London: Falmer Press.

Klein G (1993) *Education Towards Race Equality*. London: Cassells.

Kleinmann S and Copp Martha A (1993) *Emotions and Fieldwork*. London: Sage Publications.

Kuhn T (1970) *The Structure of Scientific Revolutions*. Chicago: University of Chicago Press.

Kwesi Johnson, L (1975) *Dread, Beat and Blood*. London: Bogle L'Ouverture.

Lawrence D (1974) *Black migrants, White natives: A study of race relations in Nottingham*. Cambridge: Cambridge University Press.

Lawrence E (1982) 'In the abundance of water, the fool is thirsty: Sociology and black pathology' in *The Empire Strikes Back*. London: CCCS University of Birmingham in association with Hutchinson.

Lawrence J and Tucker M with Scott M and Varnava G (1988) *Norwood Was A Difficult School: A case study of educational change*. London: Macmillan Education Ltd.

Layton-Henry Z (1992) *The Politics of Immigration: Immigration, 'Race' and 'Race' Relations in Post-war Britain*. Oxford: Blackwell Publishers.

Little A (1975) 'Achievement of Ethnic Minority Children in London Schools' in G K Verma and C Bagley (eds) *Race and Education Across Cultures*. London: Heinemann.

London Council of Social Service (1967) *Commonwealth Children in Britain*.

LDA (2004) 'Rampton Revisited: The Educational Experiences of Black Boys in London Schools'. London: the Education Commission of the

London Development Agency.

Mabey C (1986) 'Black Pupils' achievement in inner London' *Educational Research* Vol 28, No 3, Nov 1986.

Mac an Ghaill M (1988) *Young Gifted and Black*. Milton Keynes: Open University Press.

Mac an Ghaill M (1999) *Contemporary Racisms and Ethnicities: Social and cultural transformations*. Buckingham: Open University Press.

Macbeth A (1989) *Involving Parents – Effective Parent-Teacher Relations*. Oxford: Heinemann.

Macdonald I, Bhavnani R, Khan L and John G (1989) *Murder in the Playground:The Burnage Report*. London: Longsight Press.

Maclure S (1970) *One Hundred Years of London education 1870–1970*. London: Allen Lane Penguin Books.

Macpherson W (1999) *The Stephen Lawrence Inquiry: Report of an Inquiry*. London: Stationery Office.

Majors R and Mancini-Billson J (1992) *Cool Pose: The Dilemmas of Black Manhood in America*. New York: Lexington Books.

Majors R (ed) (2001) *Educating Our Black Children: New Directions and radical approaches*. London: Routledge.

Malik K (1996) 'Universalism and difference: race and the postmodernists' in *Race and Class*. London: Institute of Race Relations.

Mangan J A (1993) *The Imperial Curriculum*. London: Routledge.

Mann J (1994) *Highbury Fields 'The most interesting' school in London*. Winchester: Edgeley Publications.

Manzoor S (2004) 'A cross to bear'. Article in *Guardian*, 10 June 2004.

Marjoribanks K (1980) *Ethnic Families and Children's Achievements*. Australia: Allen & Unwin.

Mason J (1996) *Qualitative Researching*. London: Sage Publications.

Maylor U (1995) 'Identity, Migration and Education' in M Blair, J Holland and S Sheldon *Identity and Diversity: Gender and the Experience of Education*. Clevedon: Multilingual Matters.

McCracken G D (1988) *The Long Interview*. London: Sage Publications.

McHardy A 'White Flight, black heat'. Article in *New Statesman & Society*. 9 Feb 1996.

McKenley J (2001) 'The Way We Were: conspiracies of silence in the wake of the Empire Windrush', *Race Ethnicity and Education* 4, 309–28.

McKenley J and Gordon G (2002) *Challenge Plus*. Nottingham: National College for School Leadership.

McKenley J, Power C, Demie F and Ishani L (2003) *Raising the Achievement of Black Caribbean Pupils: Good Practice in Lambeth Schools*. Lambeth LEA.

McNeal J and Rogers M (1971) *The Multi-Racial School: A Professional Perspective*. Middx: Penguin Books.

McRobbie A and McCabe T (eds) (1981) *Feminism for Girls: An Adventure*

Story. London: Routledge.

Meredith G (1971) 'The Changing Response of a Secondary Modern School in Handsworth, 1958–70' in J McNeal and M Rogers *The Multi-Racial School: A Professional Perspective*. Middx: Penguin Books.

Michaels A (1996) *Fugitive Pieces*. London: Bloomsbury Publishing.

Mirza H (1992) *Young, Female and Black*. London: Routledge.

Morris M (1982) *Selected Poems*. Jamaica: Sangsters.

Morrish I (1971) *The Background of Immigrant Children*. London: Allen & Unwin.

Morse J M (1991) 'Approaches to qualitative-quantitative methodological triangulation', *Nursing Research* 40 (1) 120–3.

Mullard C (1973) *Black Briton*. London: Allen & Unwin.

Munn P (ed) (1993) *Parents and Schools – Customers, Managers or Partners*. London: Routledge.

Murray R (2002) *How to Write a Thesis*. Maidenhead: Open University Press.

Nandy D (1971) 'Foreword' in J McNeal and M Rogers *The Multi-Racial School: A Professional Perspective*. Middx: Penguin Books.

Nehaul K (formerly Hyder) (1996) *The Schooling of Children of Caribbean Heritage*. Stoke-on-Trent: Trentham Books.

Nichols G (1980) *I is a long-memoried woman*. London: Karnak House.

Norquay N (1990) 'Life History Research: memory, schooling and social difference', *Cambridge Journal of Education* 20, 291–9.

OECD (1994) *School: A Matter of Choice*. Paris: Organisation for Economic and Co-operation and Development.

OECD (1997) *Parents As Partners In Schooling*. Paris: Organisation for Economic Co-operation and Development.

OFSTED (2002) *Achievement of Black Caribbean Pupils: Good Practice in Secondary Schools*. OFSTED Publications HMI 448.

Ogbu J (1974) *The Next Generation: An Ethnography of Education in an Urban Neighbourhood*. New York: Academic Press.

Ogbu J (1981) 'Origins of human competence: A cultural-ecological perspective', *Child Development* 52, 413–29.

Olowe S (1990) *Against the Tide: Black Experience in the ILEA*. London: ILEA.

Parekh B (1983) 'Educational Opportunity in Multi-Ethnic Britain' in N Glazer and K Young *Ethnic Pluralism and Public Policy*. London: Heinemann.

Parry O (1995) 'What's sex got to do with it?' Article in *Guardian*, 5 Sept 1995.

Parsons C et al (2005) *Minority Ethnic Exclusions and the Race Relations (Amendment) Act 2000*. DfES Research Brief No: RB616.

Partington J and Wragg T (1989) *Schools and Parents*. London: Cassell.

Patterson S (1963) *Dark Strangers: A study of West Indians in London.* London: Penguin.

Phillips M and Phillips T (1998) *Windrush: the irresistible rise of multiracial Britain.* London: Harper Collins.

Philpott S B (1977) 'The Montserrations: Migration Dependency and the Maintenance of Island ties in England' in J L Watson (ed) *Between Two Cultures.* Oxford: Blackwell.

Pitkanen P, Kalekin-Fishman D and Verma G (eds) (2002) *Education and Immigration: Settlement policies and current challenges.* London: Routledge Falmer.

Polkinghorne D E (1995) 'Narrative configuration in qualitative analysis' in A Amos Hatch and R Wisniewski (eds) *Life History and Narrative.* London: Falmer Press.

Power S, Edwards T, Whitty G and Wigfall V (2003) *Education and the Middle Class.* Buckingham: Open University Press.

Popkewitz T S (1984) *Paradigm and Ideology in Educational Research – The Social Functions of the Intellectual.* Lewes: The Falmer Press.

Pumfrey P D and Verma G K (eds) (1990) *Race Relations and Urban Education Practices: Contexts and Promises.* London: Falmer Press.

Radnor H (1994) *Collecting and Analysing Interview Data.* Educational Monegraph Series No 3: University of Exeter.

Rasekoala E (1997) 'The Fog Clears: Ethnic Minorities and Achievement', *Multicultural Teaching* Vol 15 No 2, Spring 1997.

Reason P and Bradbury H (eds) *Handbook of Action Research: Participative Inquiry of Practice.* London: Sage Publications.

Reay D and Mirza H (1997) 'Uncovering genealogies of the margins', *British Journal of Sociology of Education,* 18, 477–99.

Reeves F (1983) *British racial discourse.* Cambridge: Cambridge University Press.

Rex J (1973) *Race, Colonialism and the City.* London: Routledge & Kegan Paul.

Rex J (1986) *Race and ethnicity.* Milton Keynes: Open University Press.

Reynolds D, Hopkins D and Stoll L (1993) 'Linking school effectiveness knowledge and school improvement practice: towards a synergy', *School Effectiveness and Improvement* 4, 1 37–58.

Riceour P (1991) 'Life in Quest of a Narrative' in D Wood (ed) *On Paul Riceour Narrative and Interpretation.* London: Routledge.

Richards G (1995) 'Supplementary Schools – their service to education', *Multi-cultural Teaching* 14.1.

Rosen H (1998) *Speaking from Memory: the study of autobiographical discourse.* Stoke-on-Trent: Trentham Books.

Rubinstein D and Simon B (1969) *The Evolution of the Comprehensive School 1926–1966.* London: Routledge Kegan Paul.

Rudestam K E and Newton R R (1992) *Surviving Your Dissertation.* London: Sage.

Rutter M, Yule B, Morton J and Bagley C (1975) 'Children of West Indian Immigrants, I: Rates of behavioural deviance and psychiatric disorder'. *Journal of Child Development.*

Rutter M, Maugham B, Mortimore P and Ouston J (1979) *Fifteen Thousand Hours: Secondary Schools and their effects on children.* London: Open Books.

Schlink B (1998) *The Reader.* Phoenix Press.

Scott D (1996) 'Methods and data in educational research' in D Scott and R Usher (eds) *Understanding Educational Research.* London: Routledge.

Sewell S (1993) *Black Tribunes: Black Political Participation in Britain.* London: Lawrence & Wishart.

Sewell T (1994) 'Black British Youth Culture and Its Relationship To Schooling'. Paper presented at BERA Conference, Oxford 1994.

Sewell T (1995) 'A Phallic Response to schooling – black masculinity and race in an inner city compehensive' in M Griffiths and B Troyna *Anti-racism, Culture and Social Justice in Education.* Stoke-on-Trent: Trentham Books.

Sewell T (1997) *Black Masculinities and Schooling: How Black boys survive modern schooling.* Stoke-on-Trent: Trentham Books.

Sewell T (2002) 'The Race Challenge'. Article in *Sunday Times* 15 Dec 2002.

Showunmi V and Constance-Simms D (eds) (1995) *Teachers for the Future.* Stoke-on-Trent: Trentham Books.

Smith D J (1977) *Racial Disadvantage in Britain – The PEP Report.* Middx: Penguin.

Smith D J and Tomlinson S (1989) *The School Effect: A Study of Multi-Racial Comprehensives.* London: Policy Studies Institute.

Stansfield II J H (1994) 'Ethnic Modeling in Qualitative Research' in N Denzin and Y Lincoln (eds) *Handbook of Qualitative Research.* London: Sage Publications.

Steier F (ed) (1991) *Research and Reflexivity.* London: Sage Publications.

Stone M (1981) *The Education of the Black Child in Britain: The Myth of Multiracial Education.* London: Fontana.

Strauss A (1987) *Qualitative Analysis for Social Scientists.* Cambridge: Cambridge University Press.

Taylor F (1988) *Parents' Rights in Education.* Essex: Longman.

Taylor M (1981) *Caught Between: A Review of Research into the Education of Pupils of West Indian Origin.* Windsor: NFER-Nelson.

Thomas G (1992) 'Ecological Interventions' in S Wolfendale (ed) *The Profession and Practice of Educational Psychology.* London: Cassell Educational Limited.

Thompson P (2000) *The Voice of the Past* (3rd edn). Oxford: Oxford University Press.

Tierney J (ed) (1982) *Race, Migration and Schooling.* London: Holt, Rinehart & Winston.

Tomlinson S (1983) *Ethnic Minorities in British Schools.* London: Heinemann.

Tomlinson S (1984) *Home and School in Multicultural Britain.* London: Batsford Academic and Educational Ltd.

Tomlinson S (1986) 'Minority Parents' Views of Education' in L Cohen and A Cohen, *Multi-Cultural Education: A Source Book for Teachers.* London: Harper & Row Limited.

Tomlinson S (1993) 'Ethnic Minorities – Involved Partners or Problem Parents?' in P Munn (ed) *Parents and Schools – Customers, Managers or Parners.* London: Routledge.

Townsend H E R (1971) *Immigrant Pupils in England:The LEA Response.* Windsor: NFER.

Troyna B (ed) (1987) *Racial Inequality in Education.* London: Tavistock Publications.

Usher R (1996a) 'A critique of the neglected epistemological assumptions of educational research' in D Scott and R Usher (eds) *Understanding Educational Research.* London: Routledge.

Usher R (1996b) 'Textuality and Reflexivity in Educational Research' in D Scott and R Usher (eds) *Understanding Educational Research.* London: Routledge.

Van Manen M (1990) *Researching Lived Experience.* Ontario: The Althouse Press.

Verma G K and Bagley C (1975) *Race and Education Across Cultures.* London: Heinemann.

Verma G K and C Bagley (1979) (eds) *Race, Education and Identity.* London: Macmillan.

Verma G K (1985) 'The Role of the Media'. Background paper prepared for the House of Commons Inquiry into the Education of Children from Ethnic Minority Groups. London: HMSO.

Verma G K and Neasham A R (1990) 'Urban Education in Crisis: The Voice of The Parents of Brent' in P D Pumfrey and G K Verma (eds) *Race Relations and Urban Education Practices: Contexts and Promises.* London: Falmer Press.

Verma G K and Darby D (2002) 'Immigrant policies and the education of immigrants in Britain' in P Pitkanen, D Kalekin-Fishman and G Verma (eds) *Education and Immigration: Settlement policies and current challenges.* London: Routledge Falmer.

Vincent C (1996) *Parents and Teachers: Power and Participation.* London: Falmer Press.

Vincent C (2000) *Including Parents? Education, Citizenship and Parental Agency*. Buckingham: Open University Press.

Vincent C (2002) 'Parental involvement and voice in inclusive schooling' in C Campbell (ed) *Developing Inclusive Schooling: Perspectives, policies and practices*. London: Institute of Education.

Watson J L (ed) (1977) *Between Two Cultures*. Oxford: Blackwell.

Weinrich P (1979) 'Ethnicity and Adolescent Identity Conflicts' in V S Khan, *Minority Families in Britain*. London: Macmillan.

Williams C (1995) 'How Black children might survive education' in M Griffiths and B Troyna (eds) *Anti Racism, Culture and Social Justice in Education*. Stoke-on-Trent: Trentham Books.

Williams J (1987) 'The construction of women and black students as educational problems: re-evaluating policy on gender and "race"' in M Arnot and G Weiner (eds) *Gender and the Politics of Schooling*. London: Unwin.

Williams L (1988) *Partial Surrender: Race and Resistance in the Youth Service*. Lewes: Falmer Press.

Williams L (1990) in S Olowe (ed) *Against the Tide: Black Experience in the ILEA*. London: ILEA Publications.

Willis P (1977) *Learning to Labour: How Working Class Kids Get Working Class Jobs*. Farnborough: Saxon House.

Winkley D (2002) *Handsworth Revolution: The Odyssey of a School*. London: Giles de la Mare Publishers Limited.

Wolfendale S (1992) *Empowering Parents and Teachers Working for Children*. London: Cassell.

Wood D (1991) *On Paul Riceour Narrative and Interpretation*. London: Routledge.

Young M and Stours K (1997) Article in *New Times*, March 1997.

Index

Printed in the United Kingdom
by Lightning Source UK Ltd.
109207UKS00001B/61-267